Issues in English Creoles

Papers from
the 1975 Hawaii Conference

edited by

Richard R. Day

JULIUS GROOS VERLAG HEIDELBERG

CIP-Kurztitelaufnahme der Deutschen Bibliothek

Issues in English creoles : papers from the 1975
Hawaii conference / Richard R. Day, ed. - Heidelberg : Groos, 1980.

    (Varieties of English around the world :
    General ser. ; 2)
    ISBN 3-87276-245-1
NE: Day, Richard R. [Hrsg.] ; Varieties of English
around the world / General series

ISBN 3-87276-245-1   ISSN 0172-7362

© 1980 Julius Groos Verlag, Heidelberg

Druck und buchbinderische Verarbeitung
difo druck schmacht, Bamberg

ACKNOWLEDGMENTS

The papers in this volume were among those presented at the International Conference on Pidgins and Creoles, held in Honolulu, Hawaii, January 5-10, 1975, under the auspices of the University of Hawaii. The conference was made possible by funds allocated by the University of Hawaii and by a grant from the American Council of Learned Societies, which allowed scholars from outside the United States to attend.

As the organizer of the Hawaii Conference, I wish to thank the Social Science Research Institute of the University of Hawaii and, in particular, its Director, Donald M. Topping, for his generous and expeditious support. I should also like to thank the President of the University of Hawaii, Fujio Matsuda, for his opening remarks at the conference. It was particularly appropriate that President Matsuda address the conference, since he grew up speaking a variety of Hawaii Creole English.

I also wish to thank the members of the Steering Committee of the Hawaii Conference, without whose help the conference would not have been possible: Derek Bickerton, Michael Forman, Carol Odo, Andrew Pawley, William Peet, John Reinecke, and Stanley Tsuzaki.

Finally, I wish to thank the general editor of the series in which this volume appears, Manfred Görlach, for the encouragement he gave me. Without his constant help, this work would not have been published. I should also like to extend my sincere thanks and appreciation to Freda Hellinger who, despite last-minute changes, illegible handwriting, and other burdens too numerous to list here, did the final typing.

Richard R. Day
Honolulu, Hawaii

TABLE OF CONTENTS

INTRODUCTION

Richard R. Day
University of Hawaii

The 1975 International Conference on Pidgins and Creoles, Honolulu, Hawaii, was the third in a series of international conferences dealing with pidgin and creole languages. The two earlier conferences were both held at the University of the West Indies, Mona, Jamaica, in 1960, and 1968. By the time this volume appears, a fourth conference was held at St. Thomas, U.S. Virgin Islands, a return to the Caribbean (1979).

The Hawaii Conference was significant in at least two respects. First, since it was held outside the Caribbean, it perhaps marks the truly international interest in pidgin and creole linguistics. A look at the geographical classification reveals that the sixty-nine papers dealt with pidgins and creoles spoken in Africa (21), Austronesia (7), North America (9), South America (2), Caribbean (16), Hawaiian Islands (4), Asia (7), and Europe (8). (Since some papers deal with data from more than one geographic area, the total is more than sixty-nine.)

The Hawaii Conference is also significant in that it solidifies the movement, begun in 1960, of pidgin and creole studies from marginal to full status in linguistics. Most of the papers presented at the conference go beyond descriptions of linguistic systems to substantial contributions to current issues in linguistic theory.

The aim of the conference was to solicit papers and initiate discussion in three areas: (1) Universals in pidgins and creoles; (2) challenges of pidgins and creoles to linguistic theory; and (3) uniqueness and specificity in individual pidgins and creoles. The latter two categories attracted a large number of papers, while the first did not.

It was the intention of the planners of the conference to have the proceedings published in a single volume. However, the large number of papers, sixty-nine, precluded this arrangement. A number of the papers have been published in various places; the Appendix lists the participants and where their papers were published.

The purpose of the present volume is to make more accessible, for the use of researchers and students in the field of pidgins and creoles, some of the papers not yet published which deal with English-based creoles. It should be noted that eight of the ten papers were revised for publication in this volume. Only the papers by Bickerton and Cooper are published as originally presented at the conference.

Aside from their documentary value, these papers may be of interest for several reasons. First, they contain interesting data and observations on the languages themselves (especially Trinidadian Creole, Guyanese Creole, St. Kitts Creole, and Bahamian English).

The papers may also be of interest to scholars in pidgin and creole studies because of their relationship to the then-current theoretical models in linguistics. They reflect the concern which many of us had over the inadequacies of the transformational-generative model. As Rickford, for example, demonstrates in his paper on *doz*, the Chomskyan division between syntax and phonology cannot be maintained when trying to account for the reduction process of *doz*.

In addition, as is noted further in this introduction, the papers are important for the insights many of them have into the importance of variation. By the mid-1970s, variation had ceased to be the primary concern of a few scholars studying pidgins and creoles and sociolinguists, and became the proper concern of an increasing number of linguistic investigations. As we see in several of the papers in this volume, variation is a topic which must be confronted by those who investigate pidgins and creoles.

These papers are presented according to the geographic area where the linguistic systems are used. The one exception to this is the paper by Bickerton, since his data come from a number of areas. The range of the data presented by Bickerton is appropriate, since he is dealing with universals.

Bickerton takes issues with the widespread proposal that natural universals (i.e., those which correspond in some sense with the basic neurological equipment of the species and the innate linguistic knowledge of the child) are likeliest to surface during the development of pidgin languages. He proposes, instead, that such natural universals occur in the first generation of creole speakers, who can only call on innate knowledge to help them enrich the grammar of the previous pidgin-speaking generation. Bickerton claims that 'innovations' in the tense-aspect system of the speech of first-generation creole speakers in Hawaii cannot have been derived from pidgin speakers, from the first language of pidgin speakers, or from English. He compares these innovations with similar features in Caribbean creoles to show that they are non-arbitrary, and concludes that they can only derive from the direct realization of natural universals. They could not have come about through diffusion, he claims, because these innovations were seldom or never found among surviving speakers of Hawaiian Pidgin.

It is interesting to compare Bickerton's paper in this volume with his later thinking, as represented by Bickerton (1977). In this later work, one can see a refinement in his ideas as he adds additional data to bolster his claim.

I should also point out that, although it has been some years since the Hawaii Conference, relatively little has been done in the way of universals in pidgins and creoles. This is definitely an area which deserves more interest by scholars.

The next seven papers deal with creoles from the Caribbean area (including Guyana) and the challenge they present to linguistic theory. Many of the issues which these papers raise have yet to be clearly answered and they show the limitations of "traditional" transformational-generative grammar.

Roberts, for example, examines particular structures in Jamaican Creole within the framework of three different theories: standard transformational grammar; Bickerton's panlectal theory; and Ross's non-discrete theory. The object was to see which one most adequately accounted for the data. Roberts details the obvious problems which each theory has in accounting for the data. Apparently, what Roberts calls the 'non-discreteness in Jamaican speech' presents difficulties for these theories, although Ross's may be better suited than the others to handle this phenomenon.

Perhaps the main reason why studies of pidgins and creoles dealing with the theoretical issues in linguistics call for changes in theory is that they deal with variation. A great deal of linguistic theory has been based on the concept of a single speaker-hearer with little or no variation in his speech. This, of course, is an idealization, since variation is present in all languages.

Cooper, for example, uses data which exhibit variation from a Caribbean creole, St. Kitts, in his paper on decreolization and personal pronouns. He takes issue with an argument advanced by Bickerton dealing with three first person subject pronouns in Guyanese Creole. Cooper tries to make explicit the variation in the pronouns by more precisely defining the feature stress and by writing a more general rule than Bickerton did.

Sociolinguistics is one field of study which has benefited from the interest in variation and creoles. Many scholars have attempted to relate the variation found in their data from creoles to social factors. In the present volume, Winford discusses the results of a sociolinguistic investigation of a Trinidadian speech community where varieties of English range from a creole to a local standard English. Using a number of phonological and grammatical variables, he shows that these linguistic features exhibit a regular distribution over socio-economic groups. Winford also claims that each social group shows systematic style shifting in the same direction. This, he feels, indicates that the values which the speakers associate with the linguistic variables are rather uniform in the speech community. Winford's final conclusion--that the varieties of English used in the Trinidadian speech community are differentiated from each other by differences in the combinations of features and how often they are used in speech --raises one of the most fundamental problems in creole studies, *viz*, the nature of the creole speech model. That is, should such a community best be characterized as discrete, co-existent layers or as intrinsic variables as in a continuum? Winford does not offer any answers, but does try to clarify the issues which this question encompasses.

Another important insight which the study of linguistic variation in creoles has yielded is that its synchronic variability could represent what might have been diachronic change, under different conditions. Bickerton (1976) notes that Labov came to a similar conclusion in his work on English sound changes (cf. Labov 1966), which has aided present

understanding of historical change in phonology. Bickerton writes, "It
seems reasonable to suppose that present and future studies of synchronic variation in creole syntax may help to improve our knowledge
of a still-less-understood area, that of syntactic change" (1976:19).

The papers by Rickford and Washabaugh deal with this topic to some
extent. Rickford examines the reduction of *doz*, a marker of iterative
aspect in several English-based creoles in the Caribbean and in Sea
Island Creole (Gullah). He details the interaction of phonological
and syntactic considerations in the reduction process in an attempt
to understand why *doz* sometimes "disappears altogether."

Washabaugh examines three major, and conflicting, analyses in generative syntax of the *for...to* complementizer. He claims that evidence
from Caribbean English Creole offers a fourth alternative, a dynamic
analysis which purports to explain why the three major analyses are at
least possible within a synchronic view. Washabaugh suggests that *doz*
is an underlying proposition in the guise of a complementizer.

The concept of a creole continuum receives attention from the papers
by Craig and Shilling. Craig, in a study of Jamaican and Guyanese
creoles, suggests a grammar in which the forms of base sentences and the
lexis that could be manifested at the level of such sentences constitute very restricted sets, of a kind not so far suggested in current
linguistic theory. Craig claims that his proposed grammar would have
three advantages: (1) It would explain certain universal abilities of
speakers so far inadequately explained; (2) it would account for deep
level similarities as well as differences between English-based creoles
and English; and (3) it would permit variation within the continuum to
be handled by rules of an essentially morphophonemic kind, whether or
not the determinants of variable choices are known.

Shilling, on the other hand, reports difficulty in trying to place
Bahamian English, as used by both black and white Bahamians, on what
she calls a single continuum. But she sees a close relationship between
Bahamian Black English and other Afro-American dialects which suggests
that Bahamian Black English is undergoing a decreolization process
similar to that of the other English-based creoles. This seems to
support the hypothesis that general processes of decreolization can
be established as a framework within which individual creoles may be
described more economically.

The final two papers in the volume, by Berdan and Pfaff, treat
Black English in America. Berdan, looking for the origins of Black
English, investigates the process by which it generalized syntactic
rules and simplified constraints on their application. Berdan feels
that the differences in the rules between Black English and standard
English do not constitute proof of prior creolization, but are totally
consistent with such an origin.

Pfaff's concern is with the process of decreolization and their
effects on the linguistic and social correlates of dialect variants

found in post-creole speech communities. She finds that apparent inherent variability may be exaggerated by lumping together results of
individuals who share membership in socially defined subgroups. It
does not appear to be true, generally, that an individual's ranking
within the continuum of lects is constant across all linguistic features, although implicational relationships do appear to hold within
limited subsets of linguistic features. Pfaff further suggests that
differences in underlying lexical representations may be responsible
for a great deal of the variation that takes place in decreolization.

This brings to a close our brief introduction to the papers in this
volume. The field of pidgins and creoles in particular and linguistics
in general has benefited by the information presented in these papers.
The Hawaii Conference, as represented by the papers in this volume and
those published elsewhere (see Appendix) continue the legacy established
by the Mona conference and its proceedings. The issues discussed and
the questions raised at the conference demonstrate again that the study
of pidgin and creole languages may make sig..ificant contributions to the
integration of linguistics and society, and to the foundations of linguistic theory.

REFERENCES

Bickerton, D. 1976. Pidgin and creole studies. In: Annual Review of
    Anthropology, pp. 169-193. Palo Alto, Calif., Annual Review, Inc.

_____. 1977. Pidginization and creolization. Language ac-
    quisition and language universals. In: Pidgin and creole
    linguistics, ed. by A. Valdman, pp. 49-69. Bloomington, Indiana
    University Press.

Labov, W. 1966. The social stratification of English in New York City.
    Washington, D.C., Center for Applied Linguistics.

CREOLIZATION, LINGUISTIC UNIVERSALS,
NATURAL SEMANTAX AND THE BRAIN·

Derek Bickerton
University of Hawaii

*The following paper remains as it was written originally in
1974. Unfortunately, the pressure of other commitments has
precluded the author from revising it. It is reprinted here,
with all its defects, since the hypothesis it presented was
an original as well as a controversial one, and since its
only previous appearance, in the University of Hawaii Working
Papers in Linguistics, may have made it difficult of access
to some of its potential readers.*

This paper will call for a Copernican revolution in the study of
pidgins and creoles.

According to the conventional wisdom of the day, each individual
pidgin or creole constitutes 'a language' in much the same sense as Cree
or Hungarian or Nupe constitute languages--except of course that 'a pidgin is a contact vernacular, normally not the native language of any of
its speakers' (DeCamp 1971:15). Creoles, on the other hand, are 'pidgins
become primary languages' (Hymes 1971:16). Curiously enough, with only
one exception known to me (Sankoff and Laberge 1973), there is no work
which actually documents the creolization process, and for reasons which
I shall make clear, this in itself insightful and revealing paper can
only mislead us about the evolution of the majority of extant creoles.

It follows that if languages are entities, and if pidgins and
creoles are languages, then they will behave in many respects as other
language-entities behave, e.g., the elements which compose them will
have all 'come from' some other nameable language or languages, in just
the same way as the elements that compose English can be shown to have
come from Germanic, from Latin either direct or via Norman French, and
ultimately nearly all from Indo-European. In consequence, much of the
literature (e.g., Hall 1958, Weinreich 1958, Taylor 1959, Thompson 1961,
Whinnom 1965, etc.) has devoted itself to the genetic affiliations of
pidgins and creoles; and, from the viewpoint of the present paper, the
widely-touted differences between 'polygeneticists' and 'monogeneticists'
are trivial alongside of the mass of common presuppositions which they
share.

Now, if the conventional wisdom is wrong, some trace of its wrong-
ness should show up in terms of problems which it cannot solve and must
therefore ignore or minimize (Kuhn 1962, C.-J. Bailey 1971). Outstanding
among these problems in the pidgin-creole field is the high degree of
similarity to be found in the grammars of creole languages which should
have, on the face of things, quite different genetic affiliations. 'Polygeneticists' account for this by appealing to putative 'universals of
pidginization' (cf., in their very different ways, Ferguson 1971, Kay and
Sankoff 1974) although what these universals are and how they work is left
disarmingly vague. 'Monogeneticists' account for it by postulating a

1

common ancestor--blithely skipping over problems of transmission and the as-yet unanswered (and hardly even asked) question of where the grammar of that ancestor came from.

This was the state of play until the inception, in 1973, of the Non-Standard Hawaiian English Project, the first large-scale study of a plantation community in which 'a pidgin' and 'a creole' existed synchronically. Although this project is not yet completed, it has already accumulated a mass of evidence which shows, in a variety of ways, that the generally-accepted picture of pidgins and creoles described in the foregoing paragraphs cannot be corrected, and that a radically different account must be substituted.

Briefly summarized, this account would go as follows: we err if we think of 'pidgins' and 'creoles' as reifications; they can best be considered as dynamic processes, or rather stages in a single overall process. Nobody sets out to make a pidgin language. In its earliest stages, a pidgin is communication by any means and at any cost; at a rather later stage, it becomes an exercise in second-language learning under extremely adverse conditions. In neither of these stages is a pidgin stabilized or consistent; it is, indeed, something akin to the 'macaronic blends or interlingual corruptions' which DeCamp (1971:15) denied that pidgins were, and it is almost certainly the case that (as suggested by Silverstein (1972) for Chinook) speakers retain the basics of their native grammars and from these generate superficially similar (often, not all that similar) surface structures.

A pidgin can, of course, enter a further stage, in which it becomes stabilized over many years of use as a contact vernacular. It seems a reasonable assumption (though one it would take far too long to defend in detail) that this case, which is the case of Tokpisin, is a very rare one, and that most pidgins either die out (like Tay Boi) or creolize while still in an unstable condition. The most apparent counterexamples to this assumption--the forms of Pidgin English found in West Africa--may best be accounted for by the 'family genesis' theory of Valkoff (1966), Tonkin (1971) and Hancock (1972): an unstable, early-stage pidgin used in the coastal forts and their adjoining townships was creolised in mixed families and subsequently 'repidginized' by being used as a contact vernacular. Some typical paths of development for different languages and language-groups are shown in Figure 1.

Figure 1 suggests a critical circumstance which is probably true for a majority of pidgin/creole situations, and certainly true for Hawaii (as I shall show) and for Sranan and Saramaccan, which must have formed within the seventeen years between the English occupation of Surinam and its cession to the Dutch. This is, that they must have creolized while still in one or other of the first two process-stages described in the last paragraph but one--i.e., while they were still highly unstable, very poorly developed, and still without any true underlying structure of their own. In the case of Hawaii, we have empirical evidence for this, but it should be pretty obviously true for any plantation creole; I know of no case where people have practised birth-control while awaiting the development and stabilization of a vernacular. Hardly have the first slaves, indentured laborers, hired hands or whatever got off the boat than

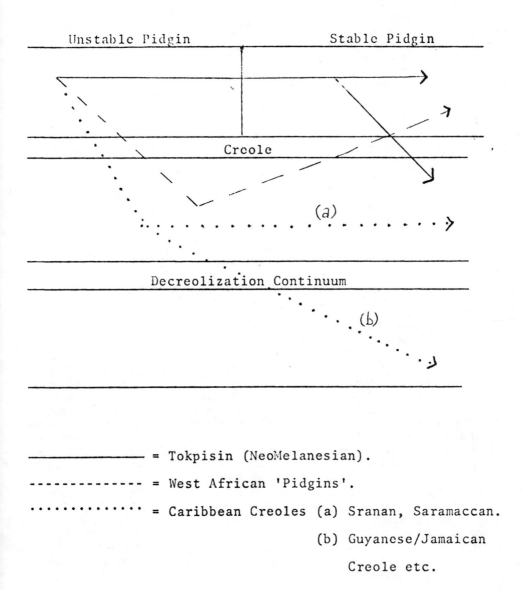

FIG. 1

Differential paths of pidgin/creole development.

they start to conceive offspring (as who wouldn't?), and within three
years there are people running around needing a native language to talk
to one another in.

In other words, *creolization must take place before a pidgin has
had time to stabilize.*

The only possible counter-argument to this contention is that of the
monogeneticists--that a single invariant pidgin was diffused around the
globe. I shall ignore this argument for the present, since I am shortly
going to disprove it for Hawaii, and, by implication, for other places
with a similar history.

We have, therefore, to consider the case of the child growing up
on a plantation five years or less from the time that that plantation was
started. The problem that confronts this child has, interestingly enough,
been best stated by a writer who has, in his sole reference to the field
(Chomsky 1966:87, discussed Bickerton 1971), dismissed its subject-matter
as 'invented parasitic systems', whatever that may mean. However, in a
quite different context, he insightfully observes that

> A theory of linguistic structure that aims for explanatory
> adequacy incorporates an account of linguistic universals, and
> it attributes tacit knowledge of these universals to the child.
> It proposes, then, that the child approaches the data with the
> presumption that they are drawn from a language of a certain
> antecedently well-defined type, his problem being to determine
> which of the (humanly) possible languages is that of the com-
> munity in which he is placed. (Chomsky 1965:27)

Now, what, precisely, is the data which the plantation child approaches?
Potentially it is threefold: (a) the ancestral languages of his parents
and the parents of his playfellows, (b) the pidgin, (c) the superordinate
language. However, under plantation conditions, (c) is virtually inac-
cessible, while (a) is unsatisfactory both linguistically (short of becoming
an infant polyglot, he could not communicate with *all* his peers this way)
and psychologically (the ancestral languages are 'old country talk', the
pidgin is the tongue of the land where his future lies). Thus the child
will largely discard (a) and (c) except for some lexical influence, and
concentrate on (b). But if he approaches (b) under the impression that
it represents 'a language of a certain antecedently well-defined type',
he is in for a disappointment; pidgin speakers in Hawaii aren't even
agreed on whether their language has SVO or SOV surface ordering. When
he finds out which of the possible languages his community speaks, he can
only conclude that it is an *im*possible one--too slow in tempo, too sparse
in vocabulary, too inconsistent phonologically, but above all deficient
in the distinctions it is capable of drawing between different types of
state, event or action, or between assertions and presuppositions, or
between definite and nondefinite referents, etc. How can he make good
these deficiencies? Clearly, only by reverting to the 'tacit knowledge
of linguistic universals' which he, along with every other child, possesses.

I am therefore claiming that what distinguishes a creole language
from a pidgin on the one hand and a developed standard language on the

other is simply that *a creole is much closer than either to linguistic
universals, in particular to natural semantax.*

Hitherto, the suggestion that universals of language are somehow involved in the pidgin/creole process has focussed entirely on the pidgin
stage (cf. Mühlhäusler 1972, Givón 1979, Kay and Sankoff 1974, etc.).[1]
But the implied assumption--that adults have readier access than children
to linguistic universals--is both inherently unlikely and contradicted by
what we have observed of pidgin speakers in Hawaii. It seems much more
plausible to suppose that, instead of a creole 'developing out of' a
pidgin, in more or less the same way as, say, Modern English developed
out of Middle English, creoles are quite literally invented, or re-
invented, each time they appear; that lexical items from the antecedent
pidgin serve simply as building-blocks out of which a quite distinct
type of edifice is erected; and that the similarities that exist between
creoles show that this process of invention is far from an arbitrary or
idiosyncratic one, but is based on innate knowledge common to all members
of the species.

In order to prove that the foregoing view of creole development is
the correct one, it will be necessary to show that:

(a) the similarities between creoles of distinct genetic history are
too great to be attributable to anything but some kind of genetic link, and

(b) there can be no genetic link.

I shall demonstrate these two points in that order.

In a conference paper, it would be absurd to attempt to cover all
the areas of similarity that exist between creole languages. Such a study
would involve examination of tense-aspect systems, types of determiner,
modes of conjoining and embedding, the relativization process, mechanisms
of assertion and presupposition, and focussing, to name only some of the
more central areas. In the present paper, I shall concentrate on the
first of these, and the reader will, for the time being, simply have to
take it on trust that the study of the other areas yields similar results;
future publications will deal individually with those areas. Fortunately,
similarities within tense-aspect, on both the syntactic and semantic
levels, are so striking that the case for creole naturalness can be pro-
visionally based upon these alone.

I propose to examine four creole tense-aspect systems, two of which
I am personally well acquainted with, while the other two are well documented, i.e., the Sranan, Guyanese, Haitian and Hawaiian systems. All of
these share the following characteristics:

(a) the zero form marks simple past for action verbs and nonpast
for state verbs.

(b) a marker of anterior aspect indicates past-before-past for
action verbs and simple past for state verbs.

(c) a marker of irrealis aspect indicates 'unreal time' (= futures, conditionals, subjunctives, etc.) for all verbs.

(d) a marker of nonpunctual aspect indicates durative or iterative aspect for action verbs, and is indifferent to the nonpast/past distinction; this marker cannot normally co-occur with state verbs.

(e) all markers are in preverbal position.

(f) all markers can combine, but in an invariant ordering, which is: 1. anterior. 2. irrealis. 3. nonpunctual.

(g) the meaning of anterior + irrealis is 'an unrealised condition in the past'.

(h) the meaning of anterior + irrealis + nonponctual is 'an unrealised condition in the past, of a nonpunctual nature', something like *if only X would have gone on doing Y ...*

(i) the meaning of anterior + nonpunctual is 'a durative action or series of nondurative actions taking place either before some other event under discussion, or during a period of time regarded as definitively closed.'

(j) the meaning of irrealis + nonpunctual is 'a nonpunctual action occurring in unreal time' e.g., a future progressive.

In Sranan, the nonpunctual marker is *e*, the irrealis marker *sa*, and the anterior marker *ben*. Voorhoeve (1957, 1962) treats *ben* as a simple past marker, but, as pointed out in Bickerton (1975, Ch. 2), this treatment is quite inconsistent with the data which he himself presents. Apart from this point of divergence, Voorhoeve's account of the Sranan system accords with our definition of the basic creole system with respect to both the syntactic rules and the meanings of the particles both individually and in combination. Thus the permitted combinations are *ben-sa* V, *ben-sa-e* V, *ben-e* V and *sa-e* V. Voorhoeve notes that the second and fourth of these are comparatively rare; however, combinations such as **e-sa* V, **sa-e-ben* V etc. are not only nonoccurring but would be judged ungrammatical by any informant.

In Guyana, the nonpunctual marker is *a*, the irrealis marker *sa* or *go*, the anterior marker *bin*. As described in detail in Bickerton (1975, Ch. 2), the semantics and syntax of the Guyanese basilectal system accord in every respect with the ideal system defined in (a)-(j), except for the apparent absence of the two combined forms *?bin sa a V* and *?sa a V*; this can be accounted for by an independently-motivated phonological rule that assimilates consecutive low vowels across morpheme boundaries, which preceded the shift from *sa* (now rare) to *go* and thus removed evidence for **bin go a V* and **go a V*.

Now, in itself, this similarity between Guyanese Creole and Sranan cannot be very persuasive, since the two languages are obviously fairly closely related. However, there can be no possible relationship between these two and Haitian Creole except through some proto-pidgin or proto-creole originating in West Africa at the very inception of European expansion. Yet the similarity falls little short of identity. In Haiti, the nonpunctual marker is *apre*, the irrealis *ava*, the anterior *te*. Again, the syntactic ordering is invariant and identical with that of Sranan and Guyanese Creole--*te* must precede *ava*, *ava* must precede *apre*. As for the precise semantic ranges of the markers, so many different and conflicting accounts of the language have been given that the linguist without firsthand experience is at a disadvantage; however, one of the fullest and most recent accounts (d'Ans 1968) agrees with that of our ideal system on almost all points (for instance, while Taylor (1971:294-295) claims that in Haitian Creole 'the iterative (habitual) function is merged with the completive', d'Ans (1968:126) states that, 'en emploi isolé', *apre* 'sera traduit par un futur proche, un progressif ou *une tournure marquant l'habitude ou la repetition*' (italics added)--clear indication that *apre* is a true nonpunctual rather than merely a progressive as in some accounts).

We must now turn to the situation in Hawaii.

Hawaii differs from the three areas so far discussed in that decreolisation has progressed much further there. In Sranan and Haiti, the systems I have described are used by the vast majority, if not the entire population; in Guyana, the system in its pure form is limited to a minority; in Hawaii, it is extremely hard to discover nowadays. Indeed, while Reinecke and Tokimasa (1934) and Tsuzaki (1971) cite, anecdotally, such forms as *us been go stay go* and *I no been go stay eat*, one recent investigator (Perlman 1973, Ch. VII, p. 24) came to the conclusion that 'such exotic concatenations ... are trotted out mainly to mystify *haoles*, who, if only short-term residents, are apt to find pidgin mysterious enough anyway.'

However, these 'exotic concatenations' still form part of the vernacular of a number of more conservative Hawaiian speakers. In order to prove that the 'ideal system' *is* still a system for such speakers, and not merely some ingenious 'polylectal' artefact, I shall take all my examples from the natural speech of a single informant (Joe A., 45, a Filipino construction worker born and raised in Kona, currently resident in Hilo) during a single hour of interaction with a close friend.[2]

In Hawaii, the nonpunctual marker is *stay*, the irrealis marker *go*, and the anterior marker *bin* (which through lowering of the nucleus and progressive weakening of the initial obstruent converts to *wen*). Just as in Guyana, the decreolisation process eventually turns the anterior marker into one of simple pastness, but, just as in Guyana, this process cannot take place until the first-phase marker (*bin*) has been entirely replaced by the second-phase marker (*did* in Guyana, cf. Bickerton (1975, Ch. 3), *wen* in Hawaii). If a Hawaiian native-born speakers retains *bin*, it has a mainly or exclusively anterior function. Thus, for Joe A., *bin* represents past-before-past where an action verb is involved:

(1) He never even tell--he bin tell him before, but the guy tell the Mexican guy, go ask the guy for downpayment.

With state verbs, however, it is equivalent to a simple past:

(2) So the guy bin like downpayment because he don't know me.

Irrealis *go*, alone, can have either a future meaning:

(3) When he come up, I go bring him down.

or a conditional one:

(4) So far as fire--slim chance, no?--not less somebody go fuck
    around.

Nonpunctual *stay* perhaps oftenest occurs as a progressive:

(5) You no stay work ('aren't working') 'cause you get sore
    back, huh, already?

However, it is also found as a clear iterative:

(6) One year I stay come up every day.

In this case, the reference is clearly past (but not anterior--there is
no suggestion that he *no longer* comes up), for, like Guyanese *a*, *stay* is
indifferent to the past/nonpast distinction, even where it has a clear
progressive meaning:

(7) One time I listen to husband and wife, eh?
    They stay fight ('were fighting'), eh?

For the complex structures, Tsuzaki (1971:332) has already claimed
that *been* will precede *go*, and that *go* will precede *stay*, as predicted in
our ideal system. Tsuzaki's claims are fully borne out by Joe A.'s output, except that in the complex forms--probably due to rapid speech
phenomena[3]--*bin* more frequently takes the surface form *wen*. Thus for
unrealised conditions of a durative nature we find *wen go stay* + V:

(8) No, shit, *I wen go stay figure* ('would have been figuring on')
    only about twenty-five thousand. (Joe has just found out that
    a house he is building for himself is going to cost him in the
    region of forty thousand dollars.)

For unrealised nondurative conditions we have *wen go* + V only:

(9) I *wen go order* ('would have ordered'), see? I was gon'
    order, I mean, from da-kine, Honolulu Roofing. (The re-
    formulation here is highly interesting, and will be dis-
    cussed below.)

For future progressives we find *go stay* + V:

(10) Whatever I save from the house rent *I go stay pay pay*
     ('I'll keep on paying').

For nonpunctuals located in a closed-off period of the past, we have *wen
stei* + V:

(11) You know where *we wen stay go* ('used to go') before?

Thus Joe has all the combinations permitted in our ideal schema, with meanings identical to those which the same combinations have in the three Caribbean creoles already discussed.

Indeed, between his system (still shared in whole or in part by numerous speakers on the 'Big Island' of Hawaii and in part by numerous speakers on the island of Kauai) and the three Caribbean ones, there is only a single difference, and that of no very great significance, although at first it might seem to be a counterexample to invariance of syntactic ordering. This is the occurrence of compound forms in which *go* follows, rather than precedes, *stay*:

(12) Kanaka guys--all us guys *wen stay go drink* ('used to go and drink') just like lolo ('crazy').

(13) But if you get loose money you *stay go fuck around* ('keep going and fucking around') over here.

Clearly this is not irrealis *go*, but something related to either (or both) (i) English *go and V* constructions (ii) Caribbean Creole English 'directional' *go*:

(14) You can see how the cow and the cart *walk go* and *walk come* ('travelled away and back again'), 186/240/20.[4]

(15) You get truck for come and *carry am go* a ricemill ('take it to the ricemill'), 171/220/21.

The preverbal position of Hawaiian go_2 creates the following ambiguity: there is no way of knowing (out of context) whether

(16) I go sell am.

means

(16a) 'I shall sell it'

or

(16b) 'I went and sold it'.

This ambiguity has driven a wedge into the Hawaiian version of the 'ideal system', in that go_2 is treated like a stative and marked with *bin/wen* for simple past, giving the opposition

(16c) I go sell am, 'I shall sell it'.
(16d) I bin/wen go sell am, 'I went and sold it'.

But this change simply moves the ambiguity elsewhere:

(17) I wen go sell am

now means either

(17a) 'I would have sold it'

or

(17b) 'I went and sold it'.

This is why Joe reformulates in (9). The context is that he had been going to buy vinyl flooring from his regular suppliers when Sid, the 'Mexican guy', offered him what sounded like a better deal. However, he remembers he is talking to his friend N., who is more decreolised than he, and he knows, therefore, that *wen go order* will be ambiguous between 'would have ordered' and 'went and ordered'. Since the whole point of the anecdote is that Joe didn't order from Honolulu Roofing, and *did* order from Sid, with unfortunate results, Joe has to reformulate so as not to spoil it.

However, apart from this minor restructuring around *go*, the basilectal Hawaiian system corresponds point by point with that of the French and English Caribbean Creoles. We must therefore ask how this can have come about.

Direct transmission can be ruled out straight away: there has been negligible historic contact between Hawaii and the Caribbean. Substratal influence can likewise be ruled out: none of the contributory languages (Hawaiian, Chinese, Japanese, Portuguese, Tagalog, Ilocano) has a verbal system remotely like the one we have sketched here. On the face of things, the only possible explanation must be a monogenetic one: that the original part of Haitian, Sranan and Guyanese Creole circumnavigated the globe on sailing ships, relexifying as it went, and finally took root in Hawaii. However, there are two arguments which indicate that this explanation is not a possible one.

The first concerns the verbal system of Tokpisin. According to Laycock, 'Beach-la-Mer ... is the direct ancestor of Melanesian Pidgin (1970:ix), and Beach-la-Mer is in turn descended from Chinese Pidgin English, which in turn, according to the monogeneticists, is a relexification of a Portuguese pidgin brought to the China coast in the sixteenth and seventeenth centuries. In any case, any world-circling pidgin would have had to pass through the Western Pacific in order to reach Hawaii.

However, if the similarities between Hawaiian and Caribbean systems are due to a common ancestor, and if this ancestor was also the ancestor of Tokpisin, then we would expect that Tokpisin would have an identical, or at least similar, verbal system. But it does not. To give only a few critical differences: stem form means, not 'past action, present state', but 'continuing actions near their end' (Wurm 1971:38); the future marker *bai* precedes the subject in older speakers and with simplex subject NPs (Sankoff and Laberge 1973); the continuous marker *stap* usually follows the main verb (Laycock 1970:xxii), as does *pinis* for completed actions; the nonpunctual category is split between continuous *stap* and habitual *save* (Wurm 1971:39, 43); nowhere in the literature is there any mention of anterior aspect, or of a combination of anterior and irrealis having a conditional meaning; complex combinations of tense and aspect markers do exist, but they bear no relation in syntax or semantics to those discussed in the present paper.[5]

Now it could be argued that Tokpisin once had a system like the others, but that it changed, probably under the influence of substratal languages. However, there is no evidence known to me which would support such an argument, and what little evidence we have about earlier stages of Tokpisin suggests that they were less, rather than more, like our 'ideal system', e.g., the former obligatory presubject positioning of *bai(mbai)*. Moreover, no such possibility could be raised against the second argument.

This concerns the relationship between pidgin and creole speakers in Hawaii. There are, in modern Hawaii, still many non-native-born survivors of the period 1900-1930, when the non-native population of the islands was at its highest, and when, therefore, pidgin speakers greatly outnumbered creole speakers. If there had been, in Hawaii, any kind of stable pidgin descendant from the common ancestor of Caribbean Creoles, then these speakers would most certainly still speak it.

However, what a pidgin, as distinct from a creole, speaker uses is something totally different from the basilectal creole system described here. For this fact, we can adduce the evidence of the pidgin speakers described by Nagara (1972), by Perlman (1973)--the ones who led him to deny even the existence of things like *bin go stay*!--plus the thirty or more non-native speakers recorded by the Nonstandard Hawaiian English Project. The differences between their speech and basilectal creole may be summarized as follows:

(a) None of the combined forms *bin go stay V*, *bin stay V*, *go stei V* or *bin go V* never occur in pidgin speakers, except (and even then only for a very few individuals) one may occasionally find the *bin/wen go V* of the *go and ...* construction type, i.e., for them, *bin/wan go V* never has its truly basilectal, conditional sense.

(b) *bin V* may occur, but it does so very rarely, and seldom if ever in its basilectal, anterior sense; what seems to happen for most pidgin speakers is that out of every few dozen past-reference verbs, one or two may be marked, quite unpredictably, with *bin*.

(c) *stay V* is also of very rare occurrence, and may be completely absent for most pidgin speakers. Locative *stay*--as in

(18) The book stay ('is') on the table

--is shared by all of them, however.

(d) *go* is commoner than the other two markers, and closer to its creole function, but its occurrences are still sporadic and unpredictable.

The most the pidgin can have done, then, is provide the lexical building blocks out of which the creole was constructed. The semantactic blueprint for the finished article, however, can have come from nowhere but the human mind.

At this stage in the argument, an apparent paradox emerges. We have argued that the creole tense-aspect system comes from innate knowledge, and it has always been assumed, I think without questioning, that innate knowledge equals linguistic universals. However, although, as we have seen, this system is shared by four creoles (and probably is or was shared by many more, e.g., Goodman (1964) shows that the Haitian system is almost identical with that of all other French creoles save the Indian Ocean ones), there is not, to the best of my knowledge, any non-creole language that shares it. How, the skeptic may well ask, can there be linguistic universals which hardly any language has?

Let us therefore examine more closely the proposition that innate knowledge equals linguistic universals.

The problem only arises through what one might call the Greenbergian view of universals. Greenberg (1963) established a tradition of searching for universals in the surface structures of differing 'natural languages'. Howard (1971), however, gives us good reasons for supposing that the only universals likely to be of more than trivial interest are those which reflect specific properties of the human brain. Now, there is no a priori reason why specific properties of the brain should be represented in all human languages--they may be, or they may not be, and there are good reasons for supposing that some of the more interesting ones may not be. For example, specific properties of the neural mechanisms that control speech are obviously involved in Stampian 'naturalness', yet as Stampe (1969, 1972) has convincingly shown, these 'natural' laws are things that so-called 'natural' languages systematically suppress. If we were to search for 'natural phonology' in the surface structures of the world's languages, we would be doomed to perpetual disappointment.

Now, if there is a natural phonology, neurally based, whose rules are differentially suppressed in different languages, why should there not be a natural semantax, neurally based, which, in all but the earliest stages of creolization, suffers a similar fate? Traugott (1973) has already suggested a natural syntax, akin to natural phonology, may exist, and speculated on possible connections between natural syntactic processes and the development of creoles.[6] I can see nothing obnoxious, and much that may be of use and interest, in the hypothesis that there is a natural tense-aspect system, rooted in specific neural properties of the human brain. For example, Whittaker (1971:213) has very pertinently observed that

> Someday man's understanding of the brain and its behavioral mechanisms will progress far beyond the contemporary awareness of a few biochemical properties of neurons, a rough approximation of electrical events and partially specified functions for some of the neuroanatomic structures. And when that day arrives, the biochemist, physiologist, anatomist, neurologist and all others concerned with brain function will suddenly be in need of a specification of behavioral units that can be correlated with their information.

I would like to propose the creole tense-aspect system as just such a unit. In order to operate it, a speaker needs to be able (a) to know the order in which past events occurred, (b) to distinguish between sensory input and the product of his imagination, (c) to tell whether something happened once only, or was either repeated or protracted in some way,

(d) to distinguish states from actions. The first three capacities underlie the anterior, irrealis and nonpunctual categories respectively. All
these capacities can be seen to be based on pre-existing features of perception, cognition and memory. (a) is a built-in feature of human memory
--we may have trouble remembering the exact date of an event, but not the
order in which events occurred. (b) is implicit in the difference between
memory and imagination--we can distinguish between what has happened and
what might have happened or might be going to happen (or at least, in-
ability to make this distinction has been regarded as grounds for forcible
separation from 'normal' members of the species). (c) is implicit in our
perceptive mechanisms, which can measure comparative durations and match
similar events to see whether they are 'the same' or 'different'; presumably differences in the frequency and duration of events have some
physical correlates in the biochemical nature of memory traces. (d) is
founded on our ability to perceive whether anything is happening or not
--state verbs, although (as Sag (1973) ingeniously shows) a fuzzy semantic
category, have in common the fact that they involve no optically visible
behavior. In other words, just as our articulatory mechanism is secondary
(i.e., based on adaptations designed for more efficient breathing, eating,
etc.), so our semantactic mechanism is secondary, being based on perceptual and cognitive processes which are probably common to other higher
mammals.

In contrast, it is difficult to see what would be the neurological
infrastructure of the 'past - present - future' analysis beloved of
traditional grammarians. Bull's 'point present (1960:17), which he takes
as a *sine qua non* of tense assignment, is in fact a highly abstract concept, and a consistent past-nonpast distinction may well be impossible
for cultures which do not possess sophisticated time-measuring instru-
ments.[7] Moreover, distinctions such as that between *I have visited
Chicago* and *I visited Chicago in 1970* (so natural to native speakers of
English, so abominable to put across to foreign learners!), which to a
greater or lesser extent are characteristic of most 'natural languages',
yet which could not possibly have any foundation in universal human capacities, look remarkably like the conventionalized suppressions of natural
rules that are demonstrated in Stampian phonology.

A further argument in favor of the naturalness of the creole system
is its symmetry, its economy and its exhaustiveness: with three basic
distinctions and invariant ordering, only eight options are open, and
all these are filled. How (very crudely and simplistically) the mind
might process data in terms of these distinctions is shown in Figure 2.
What remains unclear is why anterior should precede irrealis; on surface
logic, one might suppose that the action of deciding if an event was in
the memory or not would precede that of searching the memory for information on sequencing. However, anterior-first surface ordering seems never
to be violated, and some day we may know enough about the workings of the
brain to be able to say why.

This and one or two other details apart, we may conclude not merely
that early creoles express a natural, universal tense-aspect system, but
also that, given our knowledge of general human intellectual capacities,
this system seems a highly plausible one.

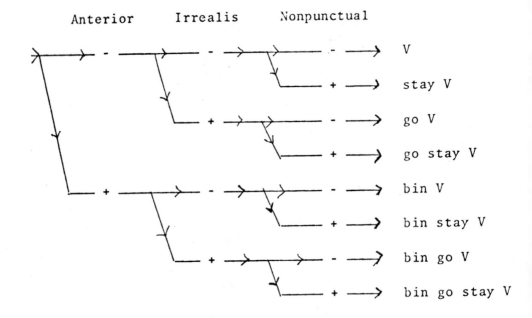

Anterior   Irrealis   Nonpunctual

V

stay V

go V

go stay V

bin V

bin stay V

bin go V

bin go stay V

FIG. 2

Hypothetical model for processing of Hawaiian

basilectal creole tense-aspect system.

The consequences of the present findings should be considerable.
For the general linguist, they will suggest a precise locus of information about 'the elusive beast we have all been questing with only scant
measure of success thus far--Universal Grammar' (Givón 1979:24). For
the pidgin/creole specialist, they will demand a radical rethinking of
the 'monogenesis versus polygenesis' and 'substrate versus superstrate'
debates, both of which have generated more heat than light in the course
of their existence, and which now prove, like most long-standing arguments, to have been unresolvable, depending as they did on unfounded
premises.

NOTES

[1]Givón's very perceptive paper comes quite close to the present
writer's position in some respects. However, he fails to distinguish
between pidgins and creoles in any very satisfactory manner, and seems
largely to share the common assumption (suggested also by C.-J Bailey in
much of his work) that pidgins, being 'maximally unmarked', are somehow

closer than creoles to a Universal Base. This view arises, I think, from a Greenbergian position on universals (discussed below): the Universal Base is simply a kind of lowest common denominator, what is left when everything that is marked in 'natural languages' has been stripped off. A totally different position on universal grammar will be taken in the present paper.

[2]Joe was recorded by one of my assistants, Nancy Nakamatsu, using 'reduced awareness' techniques (see the Appendix on Methodology in Bickerton 1975). The recording, on sides 1 and 2 of Cassette B152, is available in the offices of the Nonstandard Hawaiian English Project. Slowed-down versions of some of the more rapidly-spoken and complex verbal constructions are also available.

[3]Creole tense-aspect markers, being unstressed, are subject to extreme morphophonemic reduction in rapid speech; sometimes, as in the case of Guyanese *sa a* forms, the grammar itself may be affected. Compare the reduction of Haitian Creole *te*, *ava*, *apre* to *t*, *a*, *ap* respectively; of Sranan and Jamaican Creole *ben* to *b* and *ɔn* respectively; of Eastern Caribbean and Gullah *doz* to *z* and eventually Ø (for analysis of some of the processes involved, see Rickford 1974, and this volume 77-96).

[4]Citations of Guyanese data re identified by: speaker/number/ transcription page number/line number (see Bickerton 1975 for further details).

[5]For example, Wurm (1971:49) cites *bai tispela man klosap i kisim sik pinis nau*, 'At some indefinite point of time in the future this man will be just about to face the situation in which he will have just started to complete contracting an illness' [*sic!*].

[6]Traugott's paper, like Givón's, comes quite close to the real relationships between pidgins, creoles and naturalness, erring mainly through her belief (a widely shared one, incidentally) that creolization is a gradual process, spread over a couple of generations or so, rather than the virtually instantaneous one of the present account.

[7]In fairness to Bull, he does point out that, should there exist cultures without a Western time-sense, they would not necessarily treat tense in the way he describes it. However, he deliberately limits himself to the languages of 'dominant world cultures' (1960:20)--a phrase which nowadays, and rightly, has a much more sinister sound than it did in 1960.

REFERENCES

Bailey, C-J. N. 1971. Trying to talk in the new paradigm. Papers in Linguistics 4(2):312-339.

Bailey, C-J. N. and R. W. Shuy (eds.). 1973. New Ways of Analyzing Variation in English. Washington, D.C., Georgetown University Press.

Bickerton, D. 1971. Creole evidence for a causal operator. Working
    Papers in Linguistics (University of Hawaii) 3(2):31-34.

Bickerton, D. 1975. Dynamics of a Creole system. Cambridge, Cambridge
    University Press.

Bull, W. E. 1960. Time, Tense and the Verb. Berkeley, University of
    California Press.

Chomsky, N. 1965. Aspects of the Theory of Syntax. Cambridge, Mass.,
    M.I.T. Press.

Chomsky, N. 1966. Cartesian linguistics. New York, Harper and Row.

d'Ans, A. M. 1968. Le Creole Francais d'Haiti. The Hague, Mouton.

DeCamp, D. 1971. The study of pidgin and creole languages. In:
    Pidginization and creolization of languages, ed. by D. Hymes,
    pp. 13-39. Cambridge, Cambridge University Press.

DeCamp, D. and I. A. Hancock (eds.) 1974. Pidgins and Creoles:
    Current trends and prospects. Washington, D.C., Georgetown
    University Press.

Ferguson, C. A. 1971. Absence of copula and the notion of simplicity;
    a study of normal speech, baby talk, foreigner talk and pidgins.
    In: Pidginization and creolization of languages, ed. by D.
    Hymes, pp. 141-150. Cambridge, Cambridge University Press.

Givón, Talmy. 1979. Prolegomena to any sane creology. In: Readings
    in creole studies, ed. by I. F. Hancock, pp. 3-35. Ghent, E. Story-
    Scientia.

Greenberg, J. H. 1963. Some universals of grammar with particular
    reference to the order of meaningful elements. In: Universals of
    language, ed. by J. H. Greenberg, pp. 58-90. Cambridge, Mass.,
    M.I.T. Press.

Goodman, M. 1964. A comparative study of French Creole dialects.
    The Hague, Mouton.

Hall, R. A. 1958. Creolized languages and genetic relationship.
    Word 14:367-373.

Hancock, I. A. 1972. A domestic origin for the English-derived
    Atlantic creoles. Florida F. L. Reporter X.1/2.

Howard, I. 1971. On several conceptions of universals. Working
    Papers in Linguistics (University of Hawaii) 3(4):243-248.

Hymes, D. 1971. Preface. In: Pidginization and creolization of
    languages, ed. by D. Hymes, pp. 3-12. Cambridge, Cambridge
    University Press.

Hymes, D. (ed.). 1971. Pidginization and creolization of languages.
    Cambridge, Cambridge University Press.

Kay, P. and G. Sankoff. 1974. A language-universals approach to pidgins and creoles . In: Pidgins and Creoles: Current Trends and Prospects, D. DeCamp and I. A. Hancock (eds.), pp. 73-84.

Kuhn, T. S. 1962. The Structure of Scientific Revolutions. Chicago, University of Chicago Press.

Laycock, D. 1970. Materials in New Guinea Pidgin. Canberra, Australian National University Press.

Mühlhäusler, P. 1972. Pidginization and Simplification of Language. M.Phil. thesis, Univ. of Reading (Pacific Linguistics, B-26, 1974).

Nagara, S. 1972. Japanese Pidgin English in Hawaii: A Bilingual Description. Honolulu, University of Hawaii Press.

Perlman, A. 1973. Grammatical Structure and Style Shift in Hawaiian Pidgin and Creole. Unpublished Ph.D. dissertation, University of Chicago.

Reinecke, J. E., and A. Tokimasa. 1934. The English dialect of Hawaii . American Speech 9:48-58, 122-131.

Rickford, J. 1974. The insights of the mesolect . In: Pidgins and Creoles: Current Trends and Prospects, D. DeCamp and I.A. Hancock (eds.), pp. 92-117.

Rickford, J. n.d. Phonological reduction of *doz* and some other creole tense and aspect markers . MS.

Sag, I. 1973. On the state of progress in progressives and statives . In: New Ways of Analyzing Variation in English, C-J. N. Bailey and R. W. Shuy (eds.), pp. 83-95.

Sankoff, G. and S. Laberge. 1973. On the acquisition of native speakers by a language . Kivung 6(1):32-47.

Silverstein, M. 1972. Chinook Jargon: language contact and the problem of multilevel generative systems . Language 48:378-406, 596-625.

Stampe, D. 1969. The acquisition of phonetic representation . Papers from the 5th Regional Meeting, Chicago Linguistic Society. Chicago, University of Chicago Press.

Stampe, D. 1972. A Dissertation on Natural Phonology. Unpublished Ph.D. dissertation, University of Chicago.

Taylor, D. 1959. On function versus form in "non-traditional"languages . Word 15:485-489.

Taylor, D. 1971. Grammatical and lexical affinities of creoles . In: Pidginization and Creolization of Languages, D. Hymes (ed.), pp. 293-296.

Thompson, R. W. 1961.   A note on some possible affinities between
    creole dialects of the Old World and those of the New . R. B.
    Lepage (ed.), Proceedings of the 1959 Conference on Creole Language
    Studies. London, Macmillan, pp. 107-113.

Tonkin, E. 1971.   Some coastal pidgins in West Africa . E. Ardener
    (ed.), Social Anthropology and Linguistics. London, Tavistock,
    pp. 129-155.

Traugott, E. C. 1973.   Some thoughts on natural syntactic processes .
    In: New Ways of Analyzing Variation in English, C-J. N. Bailey
    and R. W. Shuy (eds.), pp. 313-322.

Tsuzaki, S. 1971.   Co-existent systems in language variation . In:
    Pidginization and Creolization of Languages, D. Hymes (ed.),
    pp. 327-340.

Valkoff, M. 1966. Studies in Portuguese and Creole. Johannesburg,
    Witwatersrand University Press.

Voorhoeve, J. 1957.   The verbal system of Sranan . Lingua 6:374-396.

Voorhoeve, J. 1962. Sranan Syntax. Amsterdam, North Holland Publishing
    Co.

Weinreich, U. 1958.   On the compatibility of genetic relationship and
    convergent development . Word 14:374-379.

Whinnom, K. 1965. The origin of the European-based creoles and pidgins .
    Orbis 14:509-527.

Whitaker, H. A. 1971. On the representation of Language in the Human
    Mind. Edmonton, Linguistic Research Inc.

Wurm, S. A. 1971. New Guinea Highlands Pidgin. Canberra, Australian
    National University Press.

THE ADEQUACY OF CERTAIN THEORIES IN ACCOUNTING FOR
IMPORTANT GRAMMATICAL RELATIONSHIPS IN A CREOLE LANGUAGE[1]

Peter A. Roberts
UWI, Cave Hill, Barbados

Whether one uses a theory of grammar that is based on SE or one that
is based on Creole or one that is based on neither specifically, one has
problems in showing clearly certain relationships in Jamaican speech. The
main reason for this seems to be that grammars put much more emphasis on
showing differences than on establishing relationships.

In Chomsky (1965:64-74) there is a sharp distinction made between
grammatical category and grammatical function, and Chomsky's grammar is
partially based on the notion of clear-cut grammatical categories represented by such symbols as (S, NP, V, etc.). In addition to the distinction made between category and function, subdivisions of grammatical
categories are given and these are lexical categories' and 'major categories'. Chomsky also mentions in passing the idea of 'higher-level' more
abstract grammatical categories.

Most of the people dealing with generative/transformational grammar
have adopted the notion of category and subdivision of category as set
out (not necessarily the details) by Chomsky. A few of them however have
tried to show that categories are not in all cases distinct from each other.
For example, there has been much written about nominalisation (Lees 1960,
Chomsky 1970, 1972), the result of which is that there is a general recog-
nition that categories are not simple in their internal structure. Note
for example Chomsky's own remark "... there is reason to believe that each
of these lexical categories (N,V,A) is to be taken as a bundle of syntactic
features ... It seems plausible that such abstract conditions form part of
a universal grammar, and that they determine the range of potential variation in the base structure" (Chomsky 1972:160-161).

Also in connection with the problem of the internal structure of categories there has been the argument put forward by Lakoff (1966) that verb
and adjective are subcategories of a category 'predicator', and there has
been the argument put forward by Ross (1969) that auxiliaries and verbs are
really members of the same lexical category *verb* and that there are "two
arguments which indicate that they must be main verbs."

Further to this argument about auxiliaries as main verbs, Ross has
put forward a more general theory of non-discrete grammar which he explains
thus:

> In (15) I give evidence that suggests that rather than discrete
> entities, such categories as N, A and V are to be arranged in an
> implicational hierarchy, or cline, or gradient, or, to use a term
> I favour, a squish, as in the case in (32) V - Present participle -
> Perfect participle - Passive participle -Adjectival noun - N.

Ross goes on to say:

The evidence on which this claim is based is largely of the
following form: some syntactic process applies more to V
than to A, and more to A than to N.

Ross bases this point on the conviction that there is a

need for changing the theory of grammar from a discrete theory
to a non-discrete one ... the law of the Excluded Middle has,
within the broad framework of generative grammar, always assumed
to hold.

Ross explains further

... I would argue that instead of being viewed as a device for par-
titioning the set of all strings, a grammar should merely impose a
partial ordering upon this set, for example, with respect to
grammaticality, the grammar should merely assert that string A is
better than string B. Similarly, constituent C is more NP-like than
constituent D; string M is better on reading Q than string N is,
etc., etc., etc.

... rather than being assigned to one of some number of discrete
categories, words should be given some value ... of the feature
[∝Nouny] (equivalently [∝Verby]) ... (Ross 1972)

There is another theory of grammar that has been put forward by
Bickerton (1971a, 1972), and although it is not directly related to the
foregoing, even though it has the idea of non-discreteness in it, it is
relevant to the problems of category in Jamaican speech from another point
of view. Bickerton's theory, in part, proposes to deal with 'synchronic'
and 'diachronic' factors at one and the same time and it tries to show that
the two views of grammar are in no real way separable. Bickerton's theory
is not primarily concerned with the internal analysis of grammatical structures (that is, the kind of analysis that generative/transformational
grammar deals with), but with relationships between different 'lects'.
However, the kind of grid that illustrates relationships between 'systems'
or 'lects' presumably will show relationships between the items in successive lects even if there is change in category of the item from one lect
to another. For example, if one lect was a nominal structure and another
a verbal structure, the grid should show, indicate or explain the movement
from one to the other.

The object of the present paper is to look at certain items or structures occurring in Jamaican speech in the light of generative/transforma-
tional theory of 'category' and 'function', in the light of Ross' non-
discrete theory, and also in the light of Bickerton's panlectal theory
(e.g., 1971a, 1971b, 1972). The intention is to find out whether any or
all adequately account for relationships in the Jamaican speech. The
specific items or structures in Jamaican speech that will be dealt with
are: (a) ∅, go and an in linked verb structures; (b) mus and se in indirect statements; (c) mek linking two clauses and (d) a/iz in topicalized structures.

(a)   In Jamaican speech one gets the following four structures:-

1. *go tek it up*	"go take it up"	(verb + ∅ + verb)
2. *go in go tek it up*⎫		(verb +...+ go + verb)
3. *go in an tek it up*⎭	"go in and take it up"	(verb +...+ an + verb)
4. *go an tek it up*	"go and take it up"	(verb + an + verb)

The following structures are highly unlikely if not impossible--at least none has been attested (to my knowledge):

> **go in tek it up*
> **go in an go tek it up*
> **go in go an tek it up*

In the first four sentences the two verbs *go* and *tek* are linked by ∅ in one case, by *go* in one case and by *an* in two cases.

An unsystematic test done with adults shows that only sentence 8 in the following seems logical:

> 5. *im gaan go bied, but im duon bied*
> 6. *im gaan an bied, but im duon bied*
> 7. *im gaan bied, but im duon bied*
> 8. *im gaan fi bied, but im duon bied*
>
> "he has gone to bathe, but he did not"

This suggests that structures with ∅, *go* and *an* are not distinct in meaning and can be taken as variants of each other.

The main problem presented by the forms ∅, *go* and *an* in sentences 1-7 is to determine the grammatical category to which they belong seeing that they all perform the same function and also to specify or name the function they perform.

To see first how transformational/generative theory solves this problem one can look at analyses of the linked verb construction done by Bailey (1966) and Williams (1971). The first remarkable fact one notices is that the two make different and contrastive analyses. Bailey regards the linked verb construction as "the reduced co-ordinate with verbs of motion" (133), whereas Williams not only regards the linked verb construction as a "direct generation," but also claims to disprove the connective-deletion hypothesis. It must be pointed out, however, that Bailey and Williams are not both dealing with the same language--Bailey deals with Jamaican Creole and Williams deals with Krio.

Bailey's analysis is as follows. "Given a sentence of form X - Vmo - an - Vb - Y, in which the action in Vb follows upon that in the verb of motion (mo), it is possible to delete *an*. Thus *im go*, 'she went', and *im tel Mis Jien*, 'she told Miss Jane', which when conjoined would yield *im go an tel Mis Jien*, 'she went and told Miss Jane', may be reduced to give *im go tel Mis Jien*." (133-4).

Bailey does not deal with _go_ linking two verbs in this section, but she later gives the sentence _mi a go bak a di plies go si ef_ ... the structure S + S$_1$ S$_2$ S$_3$. This means that the first _go_ and _si_ have the same status as the second _go_ and that they all three perform the same function. Such an analysis is clearly unacceptable when one bears in mind that _go_ and _an_ are mutually exclusive in that position, that the second _go_ does not add any meaning that was not previously expressed, and that sentences with _an_ in the middle do not seem to be distinctively contrastive in meaning with sentences with _go_ in the middle.

Even the analysis of _an_ and ∅ in terms of deletion can be disputed if one disregards _go_ for the moment. One can claim that the deletion hypothesis is contrary to historical development and that _Vmo - an - Vb_ has developed from the more African-type structure _Vmo - Vb_ under the influence of standard English (SE). For although deletion and addition are transformational operations in a synchronic grammar, they ought to reflect historical processes as far as possible, especially in this case where the polar influences are still in evidence.

In the analysis given by Williams the first point that one notices is that there is no distinction made between linked verb motion struc-tures and instrumental structures. He treats them all as "serial verbs". Williams uses the interpretive thoery of Jackendoff and proposes the following rules for the "direct generation of the serial verb":

$$S \rightarrow NP \quad Aux \quad VP$$
$$VP \rightarrow V \ (NP) \quad (PP) \quad (VP)$$
$$NP \rightarrow \quad (Det) \ N \qquad\qquad (1971:11)$$

He then puts the emphasis on the "lexical entries of verbs which can par-take in serial constructions" (12) thus giving a greater role to the lexicon.

It seems as if the case against 'connective-deletion' is stronger in Krio, for as Williams says: "Should it be necessary to posit an underlying connective which requires a rule to delete it, but which never occurs in the surface representation?" (8) He goes on to say: "the apparent corresponding _en_ and _fo_ forms are more paraphrases and not reflections of the underlying structure." (8)

Williams' rules will not work for the Jamaican sentences given, be-cause unlike Krio there are connectives (_an_, _go_) in the surface represen-tation. In addition, it does not seem logical to have _go_ in a higher VP than _tel_ in the sentence _im go an tel Mis Jien_.

Transformational/generative grammar clearly only provides two al-ternatives for the solution of the problem--co-ordination or subordin-ation--and neither of these works satisfactorily in the case of ∅, _go_ and _an_ in Jamaican speech.

The only solution that Ross' theory can provide in this case is to regard the linked verb construction as an instance of part co-ordination and part subordination. The detailed formulation of such a solution, however, is not easy, for it is not lexical categories that are primarily

involved but grammatical function. And even if the solution could be
restricted to grammatical category, one would still have difficulty
in finding criteria to set up a squish between ø, *an* (which is elsewhere
a coordinating conjunction) and *go* (which is elsewhere a verb). The
kind of squish that is possible and generally applicable in the case of
V - A - N is certainly not generally applicable in this case.

Bickerton's theory would not provide any solution to the problem of
co-ordination versus subordination, but as far as the interrelationship
of the forms ø, *an*, *go* is concerned, it would make a statement about the
order or pattern of evolution. However, there is another major problem
involved here and it is that one has to decide first whether there are
triggering/conditioning factors involved in the choice of any one form
in relation to the other two, and if there is evidence on both sides.
For example the two sentences

*truu mi neva di waan fiil fi go upa yaad *go* tek im auta im yaad
*"because I did not feel to go up to his yard to take him out of
  his yard"

*truu mi neva fiil fi go ina ya yaad *an* tek ya aut
*"because I did not feel to go into your yard to take you out"

were spoken almost consecutively, by the same speaker, in the same context, and this alternation between two forms would seem to parallel *fu/
tu* given by Bickerton for Guyanese speech. On the other hand one cannot
disregard the possibility that some other type of difference may be involved (for example, a difference in focus). A good supporting reason
for this is that in most cases evolutionary steps are reflected in
social use, that is, the form used in the most formal situation would
be the form latest in evolution or closest to the standard language, but
in this case the *an* form, which is closest to SE, is used when the
speaker is talking to a peer and the *go* form is used when the speaker
is talking to the interviewer. In other examples in a corpus of speech
of urban lower working-class children in Jamaica, there is no pattern
which shows *go* typical of formal or informal situation. This would suggest that for these children the difference between *go* and *an* is in some
way semantic rather than revolutionary or social. Notice also that
Bailey, who deals specifically with polar Jamaican Creole (JC), regards
the sentence with *an* (see above) as a JC sentence and does not exclude
it as she does other forms which she feels are influenced by SE.

The problem of the relationship between ø, *an* and *go* therefore remains and the different grammatical theories seem not to be able to
account for it completely or successfully in one way or another.

It was said that to generate the linked verb construction with
rules such as: *S → NP   AUX   VP*
                   VP → V   (NP)   (PP)   (VP)
                   NP → (Det)   N

        or   *S → S_1 S_2 S_3*

is to lose part of the essential relationship between the elements in
the structure. It seems that in order to account for structures with

go, *∅__* and *an* in a transformational/generative way one would have to propose a new kind of deep structure. This would be of the order:

$$S \rightarrow NP \quad VP$$
$$VP \rightarrow Vmo \quad (PP) \quad L \quad V$$
$$Vmo \rightarrow \underline{go}, \ \underline{gaan}, \quad \underline{an}$$
$$L \rightarrow \underline{\emptyset}, \ \underline{go}, \ \underline{gaan}, \ \underline{an}$$

The following transformations take place (where identical elements follow each other):

Tob: <u>go</u> <u>go</u> - <u>go</u>   *Topt:* <u>gaan</u> <u>gaan</u> - <u>gaan</u>

There is a certain semantic restriction: *gaan* (L) is used only after *gaan*.

One of the outstanding points in the above proposal is that the verb phrase has more than one verbal element. This analysis avoids the falseness of the deep structure of Williams (fig. 1) which puts *keri* in a higher cycle than *go* and both *keri* and *go* in a higher cycle than *gi*. It also avoids the falseness of the deep structure of Bailey which makes

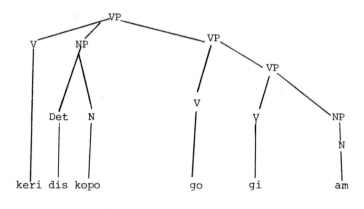

(Fig. 1)

a clearly repeated semantic element like the second *go* (fig. 2) the main feature of an independent S.

It also shows the closeness of the sentences-

9.   *(truu mi neva di waan fiil fi)*   *go upa im yaad <u>go</u> tek im auta*
                                                              im yaad

10.   *(truu mi neva fiil fi)*   *go ina ya yaad an tek ya aut*

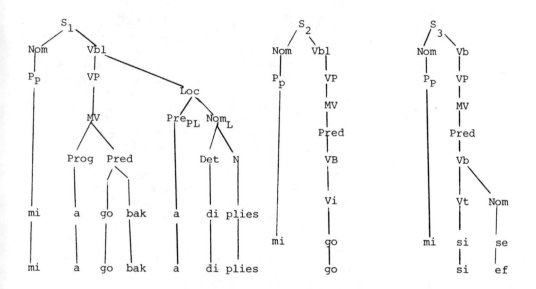

(Fig. 2)
(Some of the details which are not relevant are omitted)

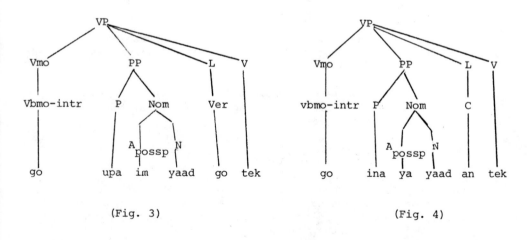

(Fig. 3)   (Fig. 4)

It is especially in dealing with the element L that Ross' theory
of nondiscreteness discussed above is very important. Although in figs.
4 and 5 L is rewritten as *ver* (Verbal) or C (conjunctive), this does
not mean that the one *ver* excludes the other *C*, or vice versa. What
it means is that in the case of *go* the outstanding feature of L is its
verbal nature. The main point is that L itself can be made up of a

combination of several features such as verbal, conjunctive, glide, focal and final and the feature _ver_ can be perfective.

If one is interested in putting creole languages in a transforma-tional/generative framework, it seems that to account for the relation-ship between ∅, _go_ and _an_ in the linked verb construction, one can only do it by using some new phrase structure rules, like the ones just given. The introduction of the obligatory element L into the verb phrase shows a meaningful relationship between items which can fall under this head-ing and the theory of non-discreteness explains the composition of L. The newness of such a proposal obviously opens it to severe questioning, but justification for this stems from the belief that the old proposals are limited. Such a proposal would also mean that the three forms (∅, _go_ and _gaan_) would not be set out hierarchically in lects, in the Bickerton manner, because they are not necessarily a reflection of an evolutionary pattern.

(b) The second of the problems has to do with the status of _se_ and _mus_ in indirect statements. Here there is a strong argument for fused elements, especially in the case of _se_. In addition, just as there was in the case of linked verbs variation between a verb form and a con-junction form, there is in this case the same kind of variation, which suggests that it is not such a restricted phenomenon.

_se_ is used most often to introduce an indirect statement or ques-tion, paralleling the use of _that_ in SE when it introduces noun clauses. Examples of the use of _se_ in the children's speech are:

11. _a truu se aal di taim mi get biitin?_ (46.B) [see note 1]
     "is it true that I get beaten all the time?"

12. _da taim Brada Shaak fain aut se a wan eg up de_ (65.A)
     "by that time Brother Shark found out that it was one
     egg that was up there"

13. _a di nuo se as ya kom ya sie taim fi guo in_ (46.A)
     "I knew that as soon as you came you would say that
     it was time to go in"

14. _im nuo se a duon laas_ (68.A)
     "he knows that I'm not lost"

Although _se_ may be regarded as equivalent to SE _that_, in cases where social variation (change in form to suit formality or informality of context) is involved, the two forms are not necessarily mutually exclusive, as is seen in the sentence

15. _Big Boi fada tel im se dat im waan somting_ (71.A)
     "Big Boy's father told him that he wanted something"

The problem arising from the co-occurrence of _se_ and _dat_ is that one cannot regard the two forms as merely social variants or that if they are indeed social variants in polar lects, in the middle levels the one or the other form changes in meaning or status. The best solution to the problem seems to be that *se* cannot be completely isolated from the verb *se*/*sie*. This connection is seen more clearly in sentences in which the main verb is one that involves the action of speaking. For when *se* is used after these verbs, it seems to take on some of the meaning of the verb, in addition to its function of introducing a noun clause. In some cases the latter function seems to have almost disappeared, e.g.,

> 16. *wa im tel yuu se?*
>   "what did he tell you?"

> 17. *mi tel im se mi wi kyach im bak a skuul (52.A)*
>   "I told him that I would catch him back at school"

In these two sentences, it is possible to treat *se* as roughly the equivalent of SE *that* and regard the semantic connection with *se*/*sie* as non-existent or negligible. It is not possible to do this in the case of the following sentence, however.

> 18. *no, ya kyan taak to im and se 'ai laik telivishun', ya sii (5.B)*
>   "no, you can talk to him and say 'I like television', you see"

For the last sentence is immediately followed in the corpus (the same speaker) by

> 19. *ya kyaan taak to im se 'ai laik telivijun'*

which has to be regarded as a variant of the preceding sentence. In the latter sentence *se* performs its normal function--introducing a clause after a certain type of verb--but there is no denying that it has some of the semantic content of the verb *se*/ *sie*.

> 20. *di man goin aks ya se if ya av eni boifren (90.B)*
>   "the man is going to ask you if you have any boyfriends"

In (20) *se* is used in a way in which it is not used in SE. In spite of this, it can still be regarded as introducing a subordinate clause. A comparison of the last example with the following:

> 21. *run go if ya sii it up de so fi mii (68.B)*
>   "run go and see if you see it up there for me"

shows that such subordinate clauses are not always signalled and introduced by *se*. It suggests that the presence of *se* has to do with the semantics of the preceding verb.

Another reason for relating *se* to *se*/ *sie* is that *se* does not immediately follow the main verb *se*/ *sie* to introduce a clause, e.g.,

> 22. *an so di man se im mus kom in de nau (46.A)*
>   "and so the man said that he should come in there now"

> 23. *ya ier di man sie ya musn get auta chier (46.B)*
>   "didn't you hear the man say that you shouldn't get out
>   of the chair"

However, when it is not immediately following, _se_ may be used:

> 24.   *an Brada Tukuman se tu ar se shii mus tek aaf ar kluoz (70.A)*
>   "and Brother Tucumah said to her that she was to take off
>   her clothes"

In the previous case the main verb _se/sie_ can be regarded as doing both
the work of the main verb and the work of _se_.

The semantic relationship between structural _se_ and verbal _se/sie_ is
hard to deny. Moreover, it seems that as the respective areas get closer
the interaction increases. _se_ cannot then be analyzed and segmented in
terms of the structures in which it occurs and cannot be separated from
se/sie, since there are no discrete divisions in its semantic field. This
means that it is not a matter of _se_ - _se/sie_ changing its category in
relation to the use or absence of another structural element (e.g., _an_,
dat), because it is the non-discrete semantic field that makes use or
absence of the structural feature possible and not the opposite process.

There are also problems of linking involved in the verbal _se/sie_.
In the sentences

> 25.   *an di masta put im up in di trii se im gain biit im (90.B)*
>   "and the master put him up in the tree saying that he was
>   going to beat him"

> 26.   *den Brada Anansi go ina di waata se im a fish (65.A)*
>   "then Brother Anancy went into the water saying that
>   he was a fish"

there is little doubt that _se_ is related to "speak" or "talk", that is,
the idea of "saying". There is little doubt either that the subject of
_se_ is the subject of the preceding verb. The problem is determining the
reason for the unusual construction.

It cannot be claimed that a coordinating conjunction has been deleted in the sentences, because to posit such a conjunction would mean
that the action "say" followed in time the action of the preceding verb,
and this is not so. The fact that the actions of the two verbs can be
regarded as simultaneous suggests that _se_ is in its structure like the SE
gerundive. However, even if _se_ in these sentences were regarded as a
kind of gerundive, there are two factors which still make it unusual.
The first is that in the children's speech there is the _a + verb/ verb-in_
form which more closely parallels the SE form. The second is that it is
only in the case of the verb _se_ that the simple verb form is used as a
gerundive. One therefore not only has to account for the different structural possibilities of _se/sie_, but also has to explain why this is possible
only in the case of _se/sie_ and no other verb. It is clear that the uni-
fying factor in the different structures of _se_ and _se/sie_ is semantic.
In the sentences given _se_ and _se/sie_ occur in the following structures:

> (a)   *se (main verb)*
> (b)   *tel se (introducing clause)*
> (c)   *tel se dat/aks se if*

(d) *taak an se*
(e) *go se (like the SE gerundive)*

It is safe to say that none of the current transformational/generative grammars can account for the grammatical status of *se* without at the same time destroying the link between the five structures. Ross' theory of non-discreteness is applicable here, but even this has its short-comings, because one cannot specify any squish for *se*. That is, one can-not say that *se* ranges from a verb to an 'introducer' or from a verb to an adjective (gerundive). Also, there is no observable scale for *se*, not even one between 'ideal" JC and SE, that would fit in with Bickerton's panlectal evolutionary theory.

It is quite possible that *se* had in the past two or three distinct structures and that historical and semantic factors have caused the present non-discreteness. However, it is difficult to include these factors in a theory of grammar. Modern semantic theories of grammar recognize the fact that deep structure does not have any grammatical categories, but the case of *se* shows that even at a level near to the surface grammatical categories are indistinct and not binding. It seems as if the semantic element is stronger than the grammatical category or that the grammatical category is not a function of competence, but super-posed on it.

No attempt is being made here to give a grammatical description which can predict the possible occurrences of *se*. The reason for this is that no precise way can be found to show how the semantic element works in this case.

mus in indirect statements is not as problematic as *se*. The problem in the case of *mus* is that it can occur with or without an overt subject:

27. *mi gi wan gyul an di gyul se mus gi ar a fuk (71.A)*
     "I gave a girl and the girl said to give her a fuck"

28. *wan man se wii mus stie de (91.B)*
     "a man told us to stay here"

In the first sentence *mus* is like SE *to* and in the second *mus* is like a modal in SE. The dual nature clearly arises out of the fact that *mus* is a higher social variant of *fi* and that *fi* is a type of infinitive marker and at the same time is verbal.

It is difficult to explain the development of *mus* in this context, seeing that a change from JC *fi* to SE *to* is the shortest and most obvious one. In this use there is no semantic difference between *mus* and *fi*, and the two are mutually exclusive in this context. Consider also the follow-ing pairs:

29. *im tel mii se mii fi dringk muo waata (52.B)*
     "he told me to drink more water"

30. *an Brada Tukuma se to ar se shii mus tek aaf ar kluoz (70.A.)*
     "and Brother Tucumah told her to take off her clothes"

31. *an mii tel im fi stop (52.A)*
     "and I told him to stop"

32. *im tel ar se mus go ina di fiil (70.A)*
     "he told her to go into the field"

As far as transformational/generative theory is concerned, the problem here is not really one of deep structure, because there is no basic conflict if one regards *mus* as a modal with an optional overt subject. This is the same status that *fi*, its lower social variant, has. The question of infinitive marker is therefore eliminated from this type of analysis. This is justified by the fact that *fi* does not occur as a pure infinitive marker as SE *to* does in the type of SE sentences like *To err is human* - *fi* always has an element of modality in that it occurs after another verb. That *to* directly replaces *mus* in the SE equivalent of the first sentence above and that *to* is an infinitive marker in SE do not affect the status of *mus* given here.

One of the early examples which Bickerton uses to illustrate his panlectal theory is the *tu/fu* contrast in Guyanese speech. However, Bickerton does not deal in detail *tu/fu* as modals or in indirect statements and he does not mention any variant like *mus*, so that we do not know how *mus* would fit into his grammar. Bickerton is interested only in those cases where no triggering factors other than evolutionary factors can be given as reasons for the variation between *fu* and *tu*, but one should, at the same time, look at the wider area of variation between *tu* and *fu* and whatever else these may vary with, whatever the reason, in order to make a more general statement about the variation. It should be safer to extrapolate from the more general area than from the restricted area.

To set up the three forms *fi*, *mus*, *tu* as lectal equivalents means that the category in which they are is very broad, that is, it has features of an infinitive marker and features of a modal auxiliary. To restrict the lectal equivalents to *tu* and *fu* means that the relationship between *mus* and the other two is not very close. The first alternative seems better, but it must be borne in mind that the kind of "free" (non-social, non-semantic) variation that operates between *tu* and *fu* can hardly operate between *mus* and the others because of the difference in category (when they are used in other structures) between *mus* on the one hand and *tu* and *fu* on the other. Therefore in this case it is Bickerton's theory that has difficulty in accounting for the relationship between the different items.

(c) The third person is included here because it presents a feature of linking which does not occur in SE and also because it is connected to the two previous cases--it shows the phenomenon of an apparently finite verb linking two clauses, as a conjunction would. The problem is the status of *mek* between two clauses.

The difficulty of analyzing the status of _mek_ is recognized by Bailey (1966). She says: "In place of the subject nominal, _mek_ may have a statement of fact as its subject. That is, both the subject and the object of _mek_ may be facts, the object being the result or effect of the subject fact." (Bailey 1966:117) She also gives the following footnote: "These sentences may be alternately analysed as the conjoining of the two core sentences by the causal conjunction _mek_. In this case the choice of analysis has been arbitrary, although not entirely unmotivated. It was influenced by such sentences as

a bikaaz mi en sik mek mi kudn kom

in which _mek_ seems to be rather a verb than a conjunction." (Bailey 1966: 117)

mek therefore has evidence to support it both as a verb and as a conjunction.

There is no basic difference between Bailey's examples and the examples in the speech of the children. Examples of the children's use of _mek_ are as follows:

33. _just gi mai mada mek shii kyan bai fi mi (3.B)_
    "just give my mother so that she can buy for me"

34. _im an duon av on no wach mek im duon nuo di taim (46A)_
    "his hand doesn't have on a watch and this brings it about that he doesn't know the time".

35. _di bwoi dem, ya nuo, musa shiek aaf dis ting mek it drop daun pon wii (59.B)_
    "the boys, you know, probably shook off this thing and made it drop on us"

36. _an bata ya up mek ya ded (23.B)_
    "and batter you up and cause you to die"

37. _turn it on mek a hier, sir (73.A)_
    "turn it on and let me hear / so that I can hear"

It is interesting to note that example 22 is an instance of "early lexicalisation" (_mek ded_ - "kill"). This is an additional possibility of _mek_ and not a completely different structure. This suggests that all four sentences can be thought of as having a deleted co-ordinate conjunction before _mek_. In fact, in the children's speech _mek_ does occur preceded by _an_, so that one can set up a relationship between _mek_ and _an mek_. This relationship, however, is not a social or evolutionary relationship. (Both structures, _mek_ and _an mek_, are used in the peer-group situation and the interview situation, and there is no difference that can be observed between the two age groups in their use or non-use of the two structures.) However, as in other structures, _an_ separates the two verbs and puts equal focus on both of them. When _an_ is not used there seems to be more focus on the second verb than there is on the first, but if there is a significant pause after the first verb, the same effect is created as if *an* were used.

In the children's speech there are no examples of *so dat from which one can set up a causative variable (in the same way that there is an instrumental variable). In any case *so dat would not always neatly re- place *mek* in all structures e.g.,

> 38. *am im daiv an kyach di baal an mek di man aut (76.B)*
>   "and he dived and caught the ball and caused the man to be out"

> 39. *a gain lik ya mek ya buk flai wie (11.B)*
>   "I'm going to hit you and make your book fly away"

> 40. *waan mi fi shuut an mek ya ded? (12.B)*
>   "do you want me to shoot and kill you?"

There are therefore three possibilities for the status of *mek*. The first is that *mek* can be regarded as a verb; the second is that it can be regarded as a causal conjunction; the third is that *mek* can be thought of as having the same subject as the clause that precedes it and being joined to the preceding clause by a co-ordinate conjunction which is sometimes deleted in the surface structure.

If one regards *mek* as a conjunction (second possibility) or as being preceded by a conjunction (third possibility), it is difficult to account for topicalized sentences like the one given by Bailey. However, it cannot be denied that *mek* has features of a conjunction and it must be borne in mind that one of the guiding reasons for regarding *mek* as a causal conjunction is that in many cases it can be glossed directly by SE *so that* and it is indeed replaced by *so that* on levels of the Jamaican continuum which are near to SE.

As far as the first possibility is concerned, to regard a statement of fact (a clause with a finite verb) as the subject of a sentence (in the surface structure) is quite unusual for any theory of grammar. In most grammars the subject of the kernel sentence is an NP. However, it cannot be denied that *mek* has features of a verb, seeing that it is used as a verb elsewhere. Again as far as the first possibility is concerned, in sentences in which a clause precedes *mek* in many cases it is not the total clause that is the subject of *mek*, but only the subject of the clause.

As far as the third possibility is concerned, it is only in cases where only the subject of the first clause is the subject of *mek* that *mek* can be said to be preceded by a co-ordinating conjunction which is de- leted in the surface structure. Where the whole clause is subject (e.g. 34, 35, 36, 37) one cannot posit a coordinating conjunction.

It should be quite clear that to regard *mek* as any single one of the three possibilities as is suggested by Bailey's 'alternately' is inadequate for all the occurrences of *mek*. It is not simply that either one can suffice and that it is just an arbitrary choice. To account for

all the occurrences of *mek* all three possibilities have to be included in
a description of its grammatical status. The major problem is that there
is no specific grammatical category in any theory of grammar that can accommodate all these possibilities at one and the same time. Like *se* the
possibilities of *mek* do not fit into a squish or scale. They are held
together by the causative element and the constant form. Here again it
seems as if semantics is stronger than grammatical cateogry, or that
grammatical category is much more fluid in this system than in SE. As
such it seems a contradiction to try to propose a specific grammatical
structure for *mek*.

A panlectal analysis of *mek* would most likely give the other lectal
equivalents of *mek*. For instance, in one case it may show *mek* related to
so that; in another case to *and made*; in another case to *and let*; and
there may be other equivalents. Such an analysis will cause one to look
at *mek* as several different items with a common sound rather than as a
single item at a certain level which has several equivalents in others.
The grammatical function of *mek* in the children's speech can be clearly
specified in terms of a single operation. It is only when one thinks of
the relationship with SE that the idea of several operations comes into
being. It is true that panlectal grammar takes a broad view of language
--it unites synchronic and diachronic, it looks at the whole speech community and not sections of it--but in this case it runs the risk of losing
sight of important factors which can be seen from a narrower point of
view.

(d) The fourth problem is to try to determine what kind of grammatical
category the topicalizer belongs to. For although the topicalizer itself occurs at the beginning of the sentence and as such is different
from the other links dealt with, the whole topicalization construction
is not different, because if one looks at the SE construction(*it is* ...
that) one can see that it has *that* connecting the two parts of the sentence, which suggests that a similar link should be operating in the
children's topicalization construction. To try to determine the nature
of grammatical category of the topicalizer is therefore the same as to
try to determine the nature of the link between the two parts of the
sentence. Here again there is conflict.

The connection between *iz* topicalizer and *iz* copula seems to be
quite clear. The connection between *a* topicalizer, *a* copula and *a* particle does not seem so clear.[2] The point here is that in many instances *a*
topicalizer does not seem to fit into the traditional category verb. For
example in the sentences:

41. *a das wai im kaal trii a wii (79.B)*
     "that is why he called three of us"

42. *a musii Maaliin yuuz to larn ar fi dans (79.B)*
     "it is probably Marlene that used to teach her to dance"

43. *a fling stuon dem fling stuon an bus it (2.B)*
     "they threw stones and burst it"

44. *a musii im kom from Yuu Sii tuu (87.B)*
    "it is probably him that came from UC too"

45. *a dis ya chier ya no set gud, ya nuo (88.B)*
    "this chair is not well set, you know"

it is difficult to show that *a* is a verb. In addition, there is no
difference in intonation between

a tuu baiskl wuda beta and *tuu baiskl wuda beta*

to suggest that there is a structural difference between the two.
Furthermore, *a* is optional.

When *a* is replaced by *iz* in the children's speech, the topicalizer
grows closer to the verbal structure of SE and no longer occurs in sentences like the ones given above (except for the third one). However,
it never becomes identical with the SE structure, that is, there is no
appearance of *that* or an equivalent.

46. *iz dat taim mii baan (46.A)*
    "it is that time that I was born"

47. *iz shii di tel mi dat not tuu long ago (91.A)*
    "it is she that told me that not too long ago"

48. *nuo, iz not tuelv skuul let uova (69.A)*
    "no, it is not at twelve that school finishes"

49. *ov kuors iz mii rait dis (14.B)*
    "of course it is me that wrote this"

In fact, it now can be regarded as being restricted rather than changed
basically: As such it has features of an "introducer" and features of
a verb.

In the case of *a/iz*, therefore, one can set up a scale or squish,
as Ross suggests, between the two structures. The major problem no doubt
is saying exactly what category is at one end of the scale and what is at
the other. One, however, cannot refuse to recognize the fact that just
as there is identity or connection between the topicalizer verb and the
copula in SE and other languages, there is also this connection in the
children's speech. It cannot, in the face of such strong evidence, be
regarded as a mere coincidence. This makes the problem of the grammatical status of *a* itself even more complicated, because by a general
occurrence in several languages the topicalization is the copula and so
is a verb, whilst on the other hand in the specific structures in which
it occurs there is great difficulty in showing that it is a verb, unless
one makes this category even more vague than it is.

The importance of establishing the status of the topicalizer in the
children's speech is that it is necessary to establish the basic structure of the whole sentence. To regard the topicalizer as a verb would

mean that in example 43 *a fling stuon* is the main clause. If the topic-alizer is regarded as a kind of preposition or "introducer" *dem fling stuon* is the main clause with a fronted element in focus.

There is no final solution to the problem of focus as it affects deep structure neither in the present case nor more generally in the theory of grammar. It is not the intention here to propose a solution to this problem, because it is felt that no helpful working solution is possible. The intention here is not only to point out the problem of focus in general, but also and more specifically, to show the special nature of the topicalizer in the children's speech. As far as a working analysis of the surface structure of topicalized sentences is concerned, it seems better to regard these sentences (especially those with *a*) as having one verb with an element fronted for focus. To try to analyze these sentences in terms of two verbs poses far too many problems.

Note that Bailey (1966) regards topicalization, which she calls 'in-version', as a transformation. She says: "Any of the following con-stituents of an utterance: nominal (Nom), predicator (Pred), locative (Loc), time (Tm), or manner (Man), may be given prominence by inverting the sentence, and bringing this constituent into a fronted position." (85). Bailey, however, is not so clear in her own mind about the status of *a*. She says: "Inversion is accomplished by an introductory *a* (equivalent to English 'it is' or French 'c'est' and possibly identical with the equating verb) which is immediately followed by the prominent item." (85). It is evident from these comments about *a* that Bailey has not worked out a grammatical status for this form—it is not specifically mentioned in her summary of the "Distributional subclassification of the word classes." (60-62). Allsopp (1962), dealing with Guyanese Creole, regards *iz* as an alerting signal, but he identifies it with SE *it is* and tries to link it to Gaelic *is*.

A panlectal grammar would obviously link *a* to *it is* in several stages. This in itself provides no solution to the composition of the category of *a* as it is used in the speech of a group (the children) who do not have the SE structure in their speech. Thus, there is no clear reason for regarding *a* as a verb phrase as there is for regarding *it is*. The theory, therefore, is not helpful in this case.

Concluding Remarks

The most important fact that arises out of this analysis of certain links in Jamaican speech is the different grammatical categories that are involved, and the influence of semantic elements in this regard. One has cogent reasons for claiming that even in its deep structure the children's language is a mixed system and this means a system that has evolved beyond the point of simple borrowing or mixing on the surface.

The kind of ambivalence or duality that Reisman (1970) points out in more cultural and lexical items in Antigua is clearly not a unique or isolated situation. Ambivalence, duality or, in more grammatical terms, non-discreteness is very evident in the linguistic system of these Jamaican children. One of the main causes of this kind of non-discreteness is that since, in comparison with SE, there are fewer lexical items in the children's system, the semantic and functional load of each item is greater if one thinks that the amount of meaning to be expressed is the same in both cases.

The main area in which there is semantic and functional load is in the verb. It is unquestionable that the verb is a primary grammatical category and that such categories as adverbs and prepositions do not have the same status as the verb. It should be quite clear also that the logical relationship between kernel sentences (at a conceptual level) which is expressed on the surface in SE, for example, by conjunctions, may be expressed elsewhere by verbs, conjunctions, adverbs or any other grammatical category.

In the children's system it is seen that the overt links dealt with are not simple conjunctions. In addition to their role as links the forms _go_, _se_, _mus_, _mek_ have verbal functions. There is therefore no discrete grammatical contrast between verb and conjunction. The use of the verb, or the occurrence of verbal elements in this function, cannot be regarded as simply incidental. Lower social class systems are generally verb-oriented, or action-oriented, but at the same time these systems are not simplistic. A common core of meaning to be expressed causes there to be a certain number of essential grammatical functions. In the children's system the verb is involved in a greater number of these functions than it is in several other systems.

Contrasting with the links that involve the verb are the links that are not overtly marked (∅ with linked motion verbs, ∅(=SE _that_) in the topicalizer). These links are not peculiar to or more typical of lower social class systems or creoles. They are of interest here because they have been shown to involve features that are not to be found in SE. Here again, in spite of the fact that the basic link is not overt, non-discreteness or duality is involved. In the Jamaican language situation in general the links in the motion verbs structure and in topicalization are not seen by the children to be unusual or special in any way (i.e., stigmatized or non-SE), and as a result of this the children do not manage the related SE structures when they are taught them as well as if the differences were more apparent.

Another reason that one could give to explain this non-discreteness in Jamaican speech is the absence of a history of normative grammar. Although to deal with the possible influences of normative pressures is more speculation than science, there are certain facts that can be pointed out.

The notion of being "grammatically correct" hardly enters the minds of JC speakers when they are conversing. This, among other more obvious reasons, is why a JC speaker thinks that his speech has no grammar. In a post-creole continuum the situation is even more pronounced because there is a greater possibility of shifting through several levels in the course of a conversation, a few sentences, a sentence, or a phrase, and this shifting may be from any one lect to any other. This is not to suggest that there is a chaotic situation in existence, but that the listener is prepared for anything and does not think in terms of "correctness", except in a situation of formality.

In a speech situation like that in Jamaica every (native Jamaican) speaker understands without great difficulty every other one, no matter where the two are on the continuum. This suggests that if there is a variable which has variants in all the lects from SE to JC and if there are categorical differences between the variants, these categorial differences do not have a great part to play in interpretation and furthermore these categorial differences are either all associated in the competence of the listener or at least not differentiated from each other.

One of the facts of grammar, both traditional and modern, is that there is emphasis on dissection and segmentation (as opposed to establishing relationships and showing combinatory possibilities). It is conceivable therefore that if there was a history of grammatical analysis in Jamaica, that is, the teaching in schools not so much of SE but more of JC, this would have led to segmentation and dissection according to categories and to a lessening of non-discreteness across categories. If it could be shown that generally there is more categorial non-discreteness in creoles than there is in standard languages, this might substantiate in some way what is now speculation.

NOTES

[1]The research on which this paper is based was made possible by a Ford Foundation grant to the U.W.I. The research was actually done in 1971 and 1972 and the informants were from a homogeneous lower working class community near the University. The informants were divided into two groups--one of younger children 5-1/2 to 7-1/2 years in age, the other of older children 12 to 15 years in age. The children were recorded in two distinct speech situations--one with an interviewer asking questions or provoking speech, the other with the children alone talking among themselves. The children were recorded in groups of three or four sitting at a table with a tape recorder concealed in front of each child. The children were generally unaware of the tape recorder. The recording took place in the school yard during school hours in an atmosphere that was relatively comfortable. The examples of the children's speech given in this paper are followed by a number and a letter (e.g., 5.B). The number identifies the child and the letter identifies the situation--A refers to the situation when the interviewer is present, B refers to the peer-group situation.

[2]Note that Allsopp (1962) (II/108-111) for Guyanese Creole makes no distinction between a topicalizer and a particle. Furthermore, he does not point out any connection between a and *iz*.

REFERENCES

Allsopp, S.R.R. 1962. The verb or expression of state and action in the dialect of English used in the Georgetown Area of British Guiana. A study and report to the Colonial Social Science Research Council.

Bailey, B. L.   1966.   Jamaican Creole Syntax: A transformational
approach.   Cambridge, Cambridge University Press.

Bickerton, D.   1971a.   Inherent variability and variable rules.
Foundations of Language 7:457-492.

_____.   1971b.   On the nature of a Creole continuum.   Language
49(3):640-669.   [Originally presented at the Caribbean Linguistics
Conference, U.W.I., Jamaica]

_____.   1972.   System into system.   Paper presented at Creole
Languages and Educational Conference, U.W.I. Trinidad.

Chomsky, N.   1965.   Aspects of the theory of syntax.   Cambridge, Mass.,
MIT Press.

_____.   1970.   Remarks on nominalization.   In: Readings in
transformational grammar, ed. by R. Jacobs and P. Rosenbaum.
Waltham, Mass.

_____.   1972.   Studies on semantics in generative grammar.
The Hague, Mouton.

Jackendoff, R. S.   1972.   Semantic interpretation in generative grammar.
Cambridge, Mass., MIT Press.

Lakoff, George.   1966.   Some verbs of change and causation.   In: Harvard
Computation Laboratory Report to the National Science Foundation on
Mathematical Linguistics and Automatic Translation, Number NSF-20,
Cambridge, Massachusetts.

Lees, R. B.   1960.   The grammar of English nominalisations.   The Hague,
Mouton.

Reisman, K.   1970.   Cultural and linguistic ambiguity in a West Indian
village.   In: Afro-American Anthropology, ed. by Whitten and
Swed, pp. 129-144.   New York, The Free Press.

Ross, J. R.   1969.   Auxiliaries as main verbs.   In: Studies in philosophical linguistics, ed. by W. Todd.

_____.   1972.   Unpublished paper handed out at LSA Summer School,
1972 [title page missing].

Williams, W. R.   1971.   Serial verb constructions in Krio.   Paper
presented at Second Annual Conference on African Languages, U.C.L.A.
Mimeo.

ON THE NOTION OF DECREOLIZATION AND

ST. KITTS CREOLE PERSONAL PRONOUNS

Vincent O. Cooper
Princeton University

St. Kitts is a former British colony located one hundred and twenty miles southeast of the United States Virgin Islands, in the Eastern Caribbean archipelago.[1] Some type of (West African) Pidgin English, forged in the contact situation between Africans and Europeans, was brought here by slaves during the seventeenth, eighteenth and nineteenth centuries and experienced those sociolinguistic developments associated with English-based (or English-directed) non-standard languages of the area. The history of this territory with its 48,000 people has produced a culture and a language that is outstanding for its fluidness, inherent variability and dynamism, and what Reisman says about the neighboring island of Antigua is just as applicable to St. Kitts:

> English-based Creole ... exists and finds its identity
> not in any system of bi- or multi-dialectalism (or
> lingualism), nor even in a system that can be character-
> ized as a simple scale or continuum. Creole plays its
> role as part of a more general way of handling cultural
> symbols which maximizes and plays with ambiguities of
> cultural reference and of expressive and moral meaning.[2]

Due to this patterning, cultural and linguistic, this systematic tension between Creole and English, we find here an intricate network of expression characterized by its capacity for "remodelling," in the words of Douglas Taylor (1963), the "new and the alien to suit its purposes." It is precisely this "remodelling" which we refer to as the process of decreolization.

Evidence for a Creole Continuum in St. Kitts-Nevis

By using the term 'decreolization', we are suggesting that there exists a Creole language in St. Kitts, which is evolving toward the St. Kitts variety of standard West Indian English.[3] Even though this process began after emancipation, approximately one and a half centuries ago, the interaction of social, psychological, economical, political and cultural forces has preserved the essential characteristics of the Creole. One example of this is the continued predominance of restricted codes over elaborated ones in what is (in spite of the efforts of the school, and the illusion of upward mobility for a small percentage of the community) still an agrarian culture.[4]

If, however, we were to limit our definition of a Creole to the idealized basilect, as Bailey (1966) and, I suspect, Craig (1971), and others have done, the bulk of the St. Kitts language would fall within the variation area, and so would the other "English-directed" West Indian Creoles.[5] In Bickerton's model, this would be the *mesolectal area* (Bickerton 1973); in Craig's it would be a combination of the *variants area* and the *interaction area*. Below is a diagram showing Craig's description of the dynamic linguistic situation in the "English-directed" Creole, or post-Creole continua, existing in the different West Indian territories today.

(Ia)

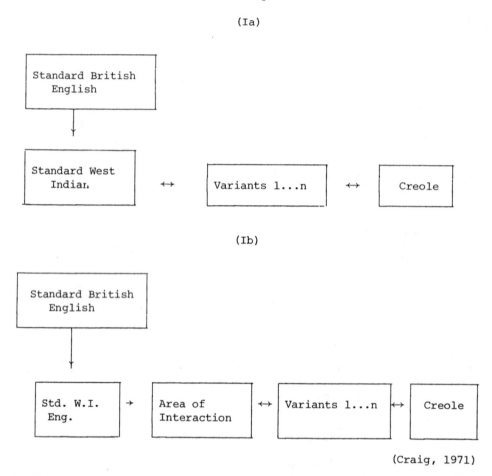

(Ib)

(Craig, 1971)

Before proceeding further, we would like to make a statement about the factual evidence upon which the paper is based.

The data used in this paper are of three different types. The first consists of narrative, and ordinary dialogue between an informant and myself, and was elicited by using the open approach. The second was obtained over a period of several months from random recordings of speakers coming from various parts of the territory, and belonging to different age groups. The third set of examples is representative of the casual speech of educated natives like myself. On the following pages we present examples of Guyanese Creole (GC) (Bickerton, 1973) matched by examples from St. Kitts Creole (SKC), in the different environments specified by Bickerton.

Pronoun/Copuloid Co-occurrence

Bickerton, in his study of the Guyanese continuum (1973), suggests five major developmental stages for West Indian 'English-directed'
Creoles. Stage one is characterized by the present of the basilectal
copulas, *a*, *Ø*, and *de*. *a* functions as a linking verb for the purpose of
equating NPs:

> 1. mi a wan gud romi
>   'I'm a heavy drinker' (GC)
>
> 2. mi a wan big uman
>   'I'm a big woman' (SKC)

in cleft and pseudo-cleft sentences,

> 3. a so abi yuus tu du land taim ...
>   that was the same thing that happened ... (GC)
>
> 4. a so i go
>   'that is the truth' (SKC)

in impersonal expressions:

> 5. if a tuutrii ayu, ...
>   'if there are two or three of you, ... (GC)
>
> 6. if a mo dan tuu a dem, no bada fait
>   if there are more than two of them, don't
>   bother to fight (SKC),

and also as the continuative/habitual aspectual marker:

> 7. mi a wok a bak
>   I'm working further inland (GC)
>
> 8. mi a wok a diibe
>   I'm working in Dieppe Bay (SKC)

Ø copula co-occurs with adjectival formatives:

> 9. mi trang
>   I'm strong (GC)
>
> 10. mi big
>   I'm big (SKC)

(Bickerton suggests that if we treated adjectives as predicates,
the Basilect would have no such thing as a *Ø* copula.) Finally, there
is the locative/existential marker, *de*:

> 11. abi de a striit
>   we are in the street (GC)

12. bwai, ũ baksaid de a paat
    boy, your rear is exposed (SKC)

13. mi de (reply to greeting, waapnin? 'what's happening?')
    I'm here, I'm making out, I'm so so (GC)

14. mi de (∿ a de de) same meaning as 13 (SKC)

The following represent the other four stages of copula development
through the mesolect to the acrolect: Stage two is characterized by
Ø copula; stage three, the acquisition of the past marker, *bin*; stage
four, by the acquisition of iz/woz, overgeneralized to indicate both
singular and plural number. The acrolectal and stage five witnesses the
introduction of the more elaborate distinctions between *am*, *ar*, *iz*, *woz*,
and *wor*.[6]

To anyone who looks at the data given above, the close kinship between St. Kitts Creole and the other English-based West Indian Creoles
becomes obvious. The SKC examples clearly indicate what may be inferred
from the history of former British West Indian territories (excluding the
special cases of Barbados and Anguilla)--they all share basically the
same linguistic system, in spite of certain regional lexical differences.[7] Because of this close kinship, we feel fairly safe in using
evidence from SKC to support, or challenge the conclusions, or 'conjectures' made about syntactic phenomena in Jamaican, or Guyanese Creole,
for that matter. Our immediate concern here is with Bickerton's conclusions or 'conjectures' on Guyanese pronoun/copuloid co-occurrence.
Some of these are presented below.

1. The synchronic spectrum of Guyana today merely
    reflects a diachronic cut through two centuries
    of its (GC) history.

2. For some speakers at least, the a/ai distinction
    is little more than a function of the difference
    between fast and slow speech-delivery, while the
    fact that the two items enter simultaneously arise
    from the use of *ai* as a carrier of stress, even
    before the *mi* has been definitely abandoned.

3. The critical factor in the timing of a/ai appearance
    may be the dropping of *a* both as continuative marker
    and equative verb, for there is an absolute restric-
    tion on their co-occurrence.

    15. mi a wan gud romi
        I'm a heavy drinker (GC)

    16. mi a wan big uman
        I'm a big woman (SKC)

    17. *a a wan gud romi (GC)

    18. *a a wan big uman (SKC)

19. mi a wok abak
     I'm working further inland (GC)[8]

20. mi a wok a diibe
     I'm working in Dieppe Bay (SKC)

21. *a a wok a bak (GC)

22. *a a wok a diibe (SKC)

4. The same would apply to the basilectal negator *na* in
    similar contexts.[9]

Let us now consider conclusion 1. Bickerton's attempt to bridge
the gap between synchronic and diachronic linguistics may very well
prove to be a much needed departure from the Saussurean doctrine. But,
as we are all aware, this is tricky business. For instance, it is
quite contrary to the teachings of John Lyons (1971) and others who
argue that: "Synchronic linguistic descripcion attempts [only] to formu-
late *systematic* 'rules' as they operate in the language of a particular
time" (emphasis mine). Lyons continues by warning that although it is
possible that the way the rules are integrated in the system of description will reflect particular historical processes in the development of
the language, this is not necessarily the case, nor is it a necessary
condition. This view is, however, given a paradoxical flavor by the
claim that, "From the microscopic, as distinct from the macroscopic
point of view, it is impossible to draw a sharp distinction between
diachronic 'change' and synchronic 'variation'" (Lyons, 1971). We find,
on the other hand, characterizations of diachronic linguistics as the
reconstruction of the particular steps by which a language changes, and
hypotheses about language change in general (Traugott, 1972).

Because of the potentially polemic nature of the synchrony/diachrony
relationship, any claim about the historical state or development of a
language that is based on synchronic analysis of presently existing linguistic rules, should attempt to avoid ambiguity.

Claim 2 is a case in point. Here we find what appears to be a number of inconsistencies. First of all, we would assume that an analysis
of this type is intended to capture *important generalizations* in a language by a process of hypothetical rules. But a statement that begins,
"for some speakers at least, the a/ai distinction is little more than
..." is ambiguous and does not seem directed towards systematic generalizations. What we need, I would think, is a hypothesis about the
systematic development or acquisition of *a* and *ai* in Guyana.[10]

Second, it seems slightly inconsistent to enter *mi* as 1, *a* as 2,
and *ai* as 3 (see Tables 1 and 2, column 3), while implicitly assuming
that *a* and *ai* belong, in virtue, to the same lect. We would suggest
instead, a categorical statement similar to that adopted by Bickerton,
on the nature of the idealized GC basilectal pronouns vis-à-vis those of
the other lectal levels or varieties on the continuum. Such a statement
would hypothesize that the sequence of first person pronoun development
is *mi, a, ai* respectively. (Note that oi ∿ ai in St. Kitts Creole, with

Table 1.   Singular-pronoun distribution (Bushlot)

Speakers	1	2	3	4	5	6	7	8
23			1	1				1
16				1	1	1		
7			1					1
20			1					1
24								1
9		1	1	1				1
25	1		1	1	1			1
14			1					1
10								1
28			1	1				1
12		1		1				
6			1					1
17				1				
13				1				
26								1 2
2			1					1 2
21			1	1				1 2
15	1	1	1	1				1 2
5	1			1	1	2	3	
11		1		1	1 2			
27			1	1 3				1 2
1		1 2						2
19			2	2 3				2

(Col. 1 = 1st per. poss. (1 = *mi*); Col. 2 = 3rd pers. masc. poss.
(1 = *i*); Col. 3 = 3rd per. neut. subj. (1 = *i*, 2 = *it*); Col. 4
= 1st pers. subj. (1 = *mi*, 2 = *a*, 3 = *ai*); Col. 5 = 3rd. pers.
mase. obj. (1 = *am*, 2 = *i*);   Col. 6 = 3rd pers. fem. poss. (1 = *i*,
2 = *shi*);   Col. 7 = 3rd pers. fem. obj. (3 = *shi*);   Col. 8 = 3rd
pers. neut. obj. (1 = *am*, 2 = *it*).   Scalability 100%.   No deviations.
Based on Bickerton 1973, Table 2.

ai occurring mainly in careful acrolectal speech).   This assumption is
further supported by the fact that the environments favoring the *ai*
occurrence are significantly more restricted than those favoring the *a*
(i.e., there is a preponderance of constructions with the *a* pronoun).
In fact (Bickerton himself would admit that) the basilectal *mi*, not *ai*,
is the typical carrier of stress, even in the semi-acrolectal varieties
(i.e., *ai* is more marked than *a*).

> 23.   a se m̀i iz a big (w)uman
>   I said that I'm a big woman   (GC & SKC)

> 24.   *a se ái iz a big (w)uman

    Finally, any characterization of the a/ai distinction as a func-
tion of the rate of speech-delivery, must take into consideration the
fact that creoles, or post-creoles, are spoken fairly rapidly.

Table 2.   Panlectal grid for Guyanese singular pronouns

Lects	1	2	3	4	5	6	7	8	9	Table 5 equivalent
1	1	1	1	1	1	1	1	1	1	A
2	1	1	1	1	1	1	1	1	1 2	B
3	1	1	1	1	1	1	1	1	2	C
4	1	1	1	1	1	1	1	1 2	2	-
5	1	1	1	1	1	1	1 2	1 2	2	-
6	1	1	1	1	1	1	2	1 2	2	-
7	1	1	1	1	1	1 2	2	1 2	2	D,E
8	1	1	1	1	1	1 2	2 3	1 2	2	-
9	1	1	1	1	1	1 2	3	1 2	2	F
10	1	1	1	1	1 2	1 2	3	1 2	2	-
11	1	1	1	1	1 2	1 2	3	2	2	G
12	1	1	1	1	2	1 2	3	2	2	-
13	1	1	1	1	2	2	3	2	2	-
14	1	1	1	1 2	2	2	3	2	2	-
15	1	1	1	2	2	2	3	2	2	E
16	1	1	1 2	2	2	2	3	2	2	I
17	1	1	1 2 3	2	2	2	3	2	2	-
18	1	1 2	1 2 3	2	2	2	3	2	2	J,K,L
19	1	1 2	2 3	2	2	2	3	2	2	M
20	1 2	1 2	2 3	2	2	2	3	2	2	-
21	1 2	1 2	2 3	2	2	2 3	3	2	2	N,O
22	1 2	1 2	2 3	2	2	3	3	2	2	-
23	1 2	1 2	2 3	2	2	3	3 4	2	2	-
24	1 2	1 2	2 3	2	2	3	4	2	2	P,Q
25	2	1 2	2 3	2	2	3	4	2	2	-
26	2	2	2 3	2	2	3	4	2	2	R,S,T
27	2	2	3	2	2	3	3	2	2	U

(Columns and indices as in Table 5.   Note: A complete panlectal grid for this area would have to include two more lects to accommodate the change from *shi* to *or* in Col. 5.   Our data gave no information on this change, but we may conjecture it would fall between lects 20 - 25 (cf. Section 5.3 above) (Bickerton, 1973).

25.   iz strang *a* strang, man

26.   iz strang *ai* strang, man
       Strength is what I have

27.   a (s) trang *a* (s)trang, man
28.   * (s)trang *ai* (s)trang, man.

This takes us to claim number 3:   "The critical factor in the timing of a/ai appearance ... co-occurrence."   This statement makes the wrong generalization.   First of all, as argued above, it is not clear that *a* and *ai* appear simultaneously, as suggested by the phrasing of the preposition. Second, the validity of this claim can be enhanced by restricting the scope of such an argument to a more specific environment, or set of environments. Indeed, for all the environments where the pronouns, *a* and *ai* co-occur with an equative verb (i.e., NP - equative verb - NP), Bickerton's observation that "there is an absolute restriction on their co-occurrence," is fully justified. (See examples 15 to 18.) However, we perceive no such "absolute restriction" where the continuative marker *a* is involved. (See examples 19 to 22.) If we assume, and there are empirical grounds for this, that there occurs in the process of decreolization, a hypothetical intermediary stage, a a wok abak; and that an attraction rule, and a deletion rule apply, i.e.,

> 29. a a wok abak $\Rightarrow$
> 30. aa wok abak $\Rightarrow$
> 31. a wok abak.
> 32 **aia wok abak

We would, it seems, be able to capture a useful generalization (which is further implied by the existence of the *na* vs. *nas* contrast in our discussion of claim 4). Evidence for such an intermediary stage exists, though somewhat elusively, in SKC and Jamaican Creole, and, I would suppose, Guyanese Creole.

> 33. aa taak tu yu[11]
>   I'm talking to you (SKC, JC)
>
> 34. *aia taak tu yu.

We also have the minimal pair:

> 35. bwei, aa taak tu yu
>   Boy, *I'm talking* to you
>
> 36. bwei, a taak tu yu
>   Boy, I *have spoken* to you (or, I spoke to you)

similarly, in cleft sentences we have:

> 37. a taak aa taak tu im
>   ... speaking to him--that's what I'm doing

versus:

> 38. a taak *a* taak tu im
>   ... speak to him--that's what I did.

Finally, we discuss Bickerton's fourth claim, which concerns the application of the basilectal negator, *na*. (Note the connection with the discussion of claim 3, and more indirectly, with that of claim 2.) Unless we are terribly mistaken, there is no "absolute restriction" on the co-occurrence between the pronouns, *a*, *ai* and the continuative marker, *a*, when the negative marker, *na*, is involved.

> 39. mi naa sing

40. a naa sing
    I'm not singing

41. *ai naa sing
is semantically distinct from

42. mi na sing

43. a na sing
    I did not sing (I have not sung)

44. *ai na sing (*ai no sing)

The same conditions hold for verbs like *studi* (study), *wok* (work),
dolzop (dress up), *tek* (take).

45. a *naa* tek it, yu no
    I'm not taking that, you know

46. *ai *naa* tek it.

47. a *na* tek it, yu no
    I did not take that, you know

48. *ai *na* tek it, yu no

More evidence, based on the actual speech of Kittitian and Nevisians,
can be produced to support our arguments. This could, however, involve us in issues beyond the scope of the present paper.

In summary of the points argued in this paper, we now suggest a
hypothetical model showing the development of the SKC personal pronouns,
mi, a, ai. This diagram is intended to reflect general linguistic
change in the St. Kitts-Nevis society as a whole, and does not attempt
to show socio-linguistic stratification.

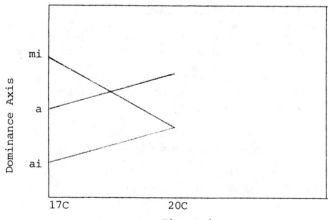

(The diagram assumes the dominance of, first, *mi* (in the seventeenth-nineteenth centuries), then *a*, and, predictably, *ai*, sometime in the future. *mi, a, ai* = Eng. 'I')

NOTES

[1]We use 'St. Kitts' to refer to the joint territory of St. Kitts and Nevis.

[2]Even though we do not adopt the ethnographic framework for our present analysis, it is, we suggest, an equally, if not more appropriate model for describing sociolinguistic variability. See Reisman (1971) and Bernstein (1964).

[3]See Fasold (1973) and Bickerton (1973).

[4]The British social psychologist, Basil Bernstein (1964) suggests that working class speakers are confined to restricted codes while middle class speakers are confined to (more) elaborate codes. The typical characteristics of the restricted code are summed up in terms of 'fast, fluent, speech with reduced articulatory clues.' Meanings are 'discontinuous, dislocated, condensed and local', there is a low level of vocabulary and syntactic selection and the 'unique meaning of the person would tend to be implicit'.

[5]St. Kitts Creole, Jamaican Creole, and Guyanese Creole share a basically common sociolinguistic history. For further discussion on this, see Cassidy's Introduction to the *Dictionary of Jamaican English* (Cassidy and Le Page 1967).

[6]These groupings are based on Bickerton (1973). Bickerton's data source includes the basilectal subcorpus of Bushlot, Guyana, with topics and circumstances of recording held constant; and 'random' selections of speakers from the 'main body' of the corpus. My 'preliminary' data are based on random selections from the rural speech of Kittitians and Nevisians, i.e., 'casual' as well as 'self-conscious' conversation at home, and on the streets etc. The role of rural Nevisian basilect is similar to that of Bushlot. The preliminary nature of this investigation, and the inaccessibility of adequate funds and equipment for more sophisticated field work, as well as the absence of any previous investigation of SKC would, perhaps, limit the thoroughness, but not negate the relevance, of the 'tentative' conclusions reached in this paper (emphasis mine).

[7]See Hancock (1971) for lexical correspondencies between Krio, JC, GC. To these we may safely add SKC since it contains these corresponding forms.

[8]Creole examples 1, 2, 7, 8 correspond to egs. 17, 18, 19, 20, respectively.

[9]For more detailed discussion on this, see Bickerton (1973).

[10]Traugott (1973:12-20) suggests that it is possible to explain pidginization and creolization largely in terms of acquisition.

[11]*aa taak tu yu* "I'm talking to you" vs. *a taak tu yu* "I spoke to you," is attested by different studies of JC, as well as by Jamaicans themselves.

REFERENCES

Bailey, Beryl. 1966. Jamaican creole syntax: a transformational approach. London, Cambridge University Press.

Bernstein, B. 1964. Elaborated and restricted codes: their social origins and some consequences. In: The ethnography of communication, ed. by J. J. Gumperz and D. Hymes, pp. 55-69. Washington, D.C., American Anthropological Association.

Bickerton, Derek. 1973. On the nature of a creole continuum. Language 49(3):640-669.

Cassidy, P. G. and R. B. Le Page. 1967. Dictionary of Jamaican English. London, Cambridge University Press.

Craig, Dennis. 1971. Education and Creole English in the West Indies: some sociolinguistic factors. In: Pidginization and creolization of languages, ed. by Dell Hymes, pp. 371-391. London, Cambridge University Press.

Fasold, Ralph W. 1972. Decreolization and autonomous language change. Florida Reporter, Spring/Fall 9-12, 51.

Ferguson, Charles A. 1971. Absence of copula and the notion of simplicity: a study of normal speech, baby talk, foreign talk, and pidgins. In: Pidginization and creolization of languages, ed. by D. Hymes, pp. 141-150. London, Cambridge University Press.

Hancock, I. F. 1971. A provisional comparison of the English-based Atlantic creoles. [A slightly enlarged version of a paper originally presented at the conference on Pidginization and Creolization of Languages.]

Lyons, John. 1971. Introduction to theoretical linguistics. London, Cambridge University Press.

Reisman, Karl. 1971. Cultural and linguistic ambiguity: some observations on the role of English-based Creoles in an Antiguan village. In: Pidginization and creolization of languages, ed. by Dell Hymes, pp. 409-410. London, Cambridge University Press.

Taylor, D.   1963.   The origin of the West Indian creole language:
     evidence from grammatical categories.   American Anthropologist
     65:800-814.

Traugott, E. C.   1972.   Diachronic syntax and generative grammar.
     In: A reader in historical and comparative linguistics, ed. by
     Allan Keiler, pp. 201-216.   New York, Holt, Rinehart and Winston,
     Inc.

Traugott, E. C.   1974.   Language change, language acquisition, and
     genesis spatio-temporal terms.   In: Historical linguistics,
     ed. by J. M. Anderson and C. Jones.   Amsterdam, North Holland.

THE CREOLE SITUATION IN THE CONTEXT
OF SOCIOLINGUISTIC STUDIES

Donald Winford
The University of the West Indies

The Problem:

One of the central concerns in creole studies has long been the
question of the relationship between a creole and its lexically related
standard language. Much of the discussion on this question in the past
has come out of the controversy over the origin of creoles, involving
the so-called monogenetic and polygenetic theories. One point that
seems to emerge from the monogeneticist view is that the "abstract
syntactic patterns" discoverable in creoles form a system distinct
from those of the related standard languages. (See Thompson 1961,
Whinnom 1965, etc.) More recently, Solomon has suggested that "the
grammatical structure of the dialect used in casual (Trinidadian)
speech is different from that of (standard) English" (1966:28). On the
other hand, some hold opposite views on the relationship between creoles
and their lexically related standard languages. Hall, for example,
argues that "abstract syntactic patterns" are not the only valid criteria for determining genetic affiliation, but that phonological and
morphological correspondences are just as relevant (1966:7). He
claims that there are "systematic correspondences in all aspects of
language structure--phonology, morphology, syntax, vocabulary" between Creole French and Standard French (1966:368). He concludes that
the admixture of non-European elements which all linguists acknowledge
to exist in European-based creoles (and pidgins) is to be regarded as
secondary to the basic "affiliation" between the creole and its "target" language (op. cit., p. 118).

There seems little doubt that the degree of similarity or difference existing between a particular creole and its related language
must be accounted for in some way. The difficulty involved is of
course compounded, in many cases, by the fact that the "creole" does
not exist as a homogeneous or isolatable linguistic system. The cases
in question are those where the official language is the same as the
"adstratum" language which forms the "base" of the creole, and where,
for various reasons, there is a continuing variation caused by increasing modification of the creole in the direction of the "model"
language. All commentators seem to agree that in these cases, there
develops "a continuous linguistic spectrum of speech varieties ...
which includes all possible intermediate varieties" (De Camp 1971:28).
Communities such as Jamaica and Trinidad in the West Indies are generally accepted examples of the post-creole continuum.

Situations such as that just described seem to all appearances
quite similar to those which have provided the testing ground for
recent developments in sociolinguistic description. The relevance of
such approaches to creole studies is obvious. One of the basic tenets
of sociolinguistic description is that "deviations" from a homogeneous

system are not all error-like vagaries of performance, but are to a high degree coded and part of a realistic description of the competence of a member of a speech community" (Weinreich et al. 1968:125). As a possible means to such a realistic description, Weinreich et al. envisage a model of language which has

> (1)   discrete, co-existent layers defined by strict co-occurrence, which are functionally differentiated and jointly available to a speech community, and

> (2)   intrinsic variables defined by co-variation with linguistic and extra-linguistic elements.

The task of the linguist, then, is "to determine the degree of social correlation which exists, and show how it bears upon the abstract linguistic system" (Ibid., pp. 185-186). The question that arises is whether such an approach, and such a model of language, are applicable to the study of post-creole continua.

The present paper will attempt to do two things:

> (1)   Demonstrate to what extent the variation characteristic of a post-creole continuum is amenable to sociolinguistic analysis.

> (2)   Discuss to what extent the results of such an analysis shed light on the nature of the "abstract linguistic system(s)" in operation in creole communities.

Central to this will be whether sociolinguistic analysis offers any answers to the problem of the relationship between the creole and the "model" language.

Grammatical Variables in Trinidad English

The following are examples of sentences commonly used by Trinidadians. Standard English sentences of equivalent meaning are listed opposite each. For convenience I shall use Standard English orthography:

(1) He does eat plenty	He (habitually) eats plenty
(2) He eatin	He's eating (now)
(3) He eat it	He ate it
(4) He done eat it	He has eaten it
(5) He did eat it	He had eaten it (rough equivalent)
(6) He go eat it	He will eat it
(7) He was go eat it	He would have eaten it
(8) I/He/You is a fool	I am/He is/You are a fool
(9) The man mad	The man is mad
(10) She in the garden	She's in the garden
(11) He was mad	He was mad
(12) He was in the house	He was in the house

The existence of these grammatical patterns in the speech of Trinidadians has led both Solomon (1966) and Warner (1967) to treat "colloquial Trinidadian English" as having a system of predication distinct from that of Standard English. Solomon suggests that the verb forms exemplified in sentences (1) to (12) constitute "deviations from Standard English" which seem to form a system of relationships among themselves" (1966:8). Similarly, Warner gives an outline of the "vernacular verb system" which she claims "differs from that of Standard Trinidadian" (1967:78). If we were to accept these claims for the moment, we could set up the following outline of formal elements and their functions for the vernacular used in Trinidad. The table is, of course, not intended to represent the entire system of predication.

Table 1. Finite Verb System

FORM	FUNCTION	EXAMPLE
(V) - ∅	Completive	I eat it.
(V) - ing	Continuous	I eating it.
does (V)	Habitual or Repeated	I does eat.
go (V)	Future or Intended	I go eat

The system of predication corresponding to that which exists in S.E. for the verb *to be* would be as follows:

FORM	FUNCTION	EXAMPLE
∅	Predicator in Env./N.P.-Adj., Adv., Prep Phrase	He mad
	(Present Context)	He here
is	Predicator in Env./N.P.-N.P. (Present Context)	I/He is a doctor
was	Predicator in Env./N.P.-Adj.,Adv. ⎫	I/He/They was sick
	-Prep Phrase ⎬ Past Context	I/He/They was
	-N.P. ⎭	In the house etc.

Underlying the above formulation are a number of assumptions which are by no means sound. The first is that the use of each form listed above is always restricted to the same function, This form/function correspondence, however, does not apply in a number of cases. For instance, use of ∅ verb forms is normal in sentences like

(13) First you have to dig three holes, then you
draw a line and *throw* your marble ....

Forms such as those in (15) may be referred to as having descriptive
or instructive function and seem neutral with respect to tense. Again,
-*ing* forms are often used by Trinidadians to denote future or intended
action, as in

> (14) I coming tomorrow.
> (15) They leaving next week.

In these sentences the meaning conveyed is not that of continuous action
in the present.

A second objection to Table 1 is the fact that it does not include
verb forms which are common to both Standard English and all varieties
of Trinidadian English, including the most colloquial usage. (I shall
refer to this as T., following Solomon.) For instance, the quasi-model
have to is used in both S.E. and T. to express obligation, e.g.,

> (16) I have to go tomorrow.

Another example of shared forms is *used to*, which expresses habitual
action in past context, e.g.,

> (17) I used to play cricket in those days.

Moreover, among the forms listed in Table 1 as belonging to the T. verbal
system are some which occur in other contexts where their use is common
to both T. and S.E. For instance, forms like *is*[1] are found in both
varities of English in clause final position, e.g.,

	(18) Tell me what that is.
in wh-questions, e.g.,	(19) What's the point.
and in cases like	(20) That is what I want.

Such examples suggest that the boundaries between T. and S.E. are by no
means as clearly-defined as Table 1 implies.

The third assumption behind the setting up of an autonomous verb
system for T. is that two varieties or "dialects" of English exist in
Trinidad, one with consistent use of the verb forms listed in Table 1.
Even if we restricted our attention to these forms alone, there is no
certainty that usage on any social level, even in the most spontanteous
speech, will not vary between T. and S.E. forms. Neither Solomon nor
Warner has adduced evidence to resolve this question. In fact, Solomon's
research showed not only that S.E. forms occurred in the spontaneous
speech of lower-status Trinidadians, but also that the incidence of these
forms increased appreciably in more formal style. Moreover, the "highly-
educated" informant he used as a control showed very frequent use of
S.E. forms in both styles for all but one of his grammatical variables.
Warner, for her part, points out that research done on the syntax of
Trinidadian English has not been sufficient to provide a basis for
"syntactic dialectal divisions." One of the aims of the present investigation will be to show that systematic variation in the use of T. and
S.E. syntactic forms occurs in the speech of Trinidadians, and that
this variation is conditioned by style and social status as defined in
this study.

In order to test this hypothesis, the following grammatical variables were chosen.

(a)   The variable (ED)   -   The presence or absence or "past" inflection in finite verbs in past context.
                e.g.:   -   *I kill/killed it yesterday*

(b)   The variable (DOES)   -   Variation between use of the T. form *does* (V) and use of S.E. forms to express habitual or repeated action in present contexts.
                e.g.:   -   *I does come/come here every day*

(c)   The variable (V-ING)[2] -   The presence or absence of forms of the verb "to be" before finite verbs with the suffix *-ing.*
                e.g.:   *I/I'm doing it now.*

(d)   The variable (COP-A)[2] -   The presence or absence of forms of the verb *to be* in the following environments in present contexts.

                (i)   NP - Adj.   e.g. *He/He's mad.*
                (ii) NP - Adj.   e.g. *He/He's here.*
                (iii) NP - Prep. Phrase.
                                e.g. *He/He's with us.*

(e)   The variable (GO)   -   Variation between use of the T. form *go* (V) and S.E. forms to express future or intended action;
                e.g.:   -   *I go/I'll tell you later.*

The grammatical variables above were chosen because they occur fairly frequently in conversation, and therefore provide adequate examples of informants' usage on which to base judgments about their use on different social levels and in different styles. They do not, however, account for the entire range of syntactic variation to be found in the speech of Trinidadians.

It is obvious that any attempt to discover whether the various T. verb forms add structures identified above form a system of relationships among themselves would require extensive work on all aspects of the T. system of predication--a task which it is impossible to undertake within the limitations of this study. The quantitative evidence to be presented later will not provide any final solution to this problem--or to the related problem of the relationship of forms peculiar to T. to forms used in the same environments in S.E. However, if we find that informants use the different T. forms consistently in some context, we can *infer* from this that the T. forms function as interrelated parts of a system of predication distinct from that of S.E. For the time being, I am assuming that it is possible to make identifications between certain structures which might be described as part of the T. system, and what appear to be equivalent structures in S.E. This is the basis of my choice of the grammatical variables discussed earlier.

The Sample and the Data

The data to be presented here are based on the quantitative mea-
surment of a number of grammatical variables as used by male informants
in St. James, a district in the capital city, Port of Spain. Recordings
were made of the speech of 33 informants in an interview setting, and
additional data were collected from five of these informants and seventeen others in a peer-group setting. The informants were ranked in
four socio-economic categories, on the basis of their income, occupation
and education.

For purposes of the analysis, it was decided to establish two
styles of interview speech for each informant--"Careful" (Style A) and
"Spontaneous" (Style B). In addition, informants of socio-economic
classes (S.E.C.) III and IV (Lower-middle and working class respectively) were recorded in peer-group interaction. The style of speaking
used in these group sessions was labelled Casual Style (Style C) (Labov 1966).

Class and Style differentiation of the variables

Table 2 gives the values for the grammatical variables in the
respective styles and socio-economic groupings. The figures represent
percentages of T. forms in the total occurrences of each variable.

We can now turn to the discussion of each variable as used by the
informants.

Differentiation of (ED):

The class and style differentiation of (ED) in St. James is
illustrated in Figure 1.

Though it appears to be, the pattern shown in Figure 1 is not a
regular structure, since Class I shows higher values than the lower-
status group, S.E.C. II. The reason for this is the relatively high
incidence of uninflected forms shown by one informant in Class I.
Without him, values for this group would be far lower than those for
Class II. It is perhaps inevitable that in a class containing only
four persons, as Class I does, the usage of one marginal informant will
affect the values for the entire group.

There is only one informant in the entire sample who always uses
S.E. forms to express "past" meanings. He belongs to Class I. All
other informants have at least a few instances of uninflected verbs.
The classes are therefore distinguished by the frequency with which
they show inflection. For classes I and II S.E. forms predominate in
both interview styles; for class III there is almost a one-to-one
correspondence between standard and nonstandard forms in Styles A and
B; nonstandard forms predominate in the usage of Class IV members in
all styles.

Style shifting is evident on all social levels, suggesting that
informants regard the use of inflected forms as more appropriate in

Table 2. Average Values of the Grammatical Variables in St. James

	Socio-economic Class			
	I	II	III	IV
(ED)				
STYLE A	19	15	37	63
STYLE B	36	26	49	79
STYLE C	--	--	88	97
(DOES)				
STYLE A	00	02	04	02
STYLE B	06	00	10	36
STYLE C	--	--	50	84
(V-ING)				
STYLE A	30	37	51	61
STYLE B	67	68	80	95
STYLE C	--	--	94	100
(COP-A)				
STYLE A	00	13	15	39
STYLE B	47	25	44	86
STYLE C	--	--	84	88
(G)				
STYLE A	00	14	00	04
STYLE B	00	21	18	15
STYLE C	--	--	55	80

formal speech. Of particular interest is the marked increase in the incidence of T. forms shown by members of classes III and IV in casual style (Style C).[3] For respondents of class III, the contrast is particularly marked, the incidence of T. forms in peer-group speech being almost twice as high as that in Style B.

Figure 1 provides no information on differences in usage of "regular" and "irregular" verbs, which are inflected in different ways to express past meanings in S.E. We can isolate the following four sub-classes of verbs in S.E.

    1a) - Regular verbs like *kill*, *pack*, *wrap*, etc., the
             inflected forms of which end in consonant clusters.

    1b) - Regular verbs like *fold*, *collect*, etc., to which
             /Id/ is added as a past tense marker.

(ED)

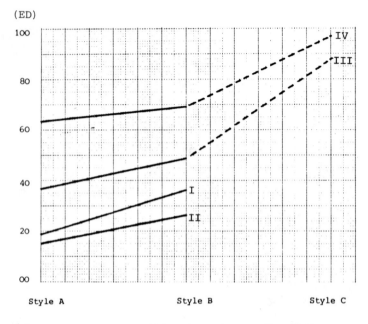

Fig. 1.   Class Stratification Diagram for (ED)

2a) - Irregular verbs like *hold*, *sit*, *come*, etc., where the
       past tense is signalled by mutation of the stem vowel.

2b) - Irregular verbs like *feel*, *tell*, etc., where both
       mutation of the stem vowel and final -*t*, -*d* signal
       the past tense.[4]

    Generally speaking, the highest incidence of S.E. inflected forms
is shown for irregular verbs with (KD);[5] then, for irregular verbs
without (KD); then for regular verbs without (KD), and the lowest,
finally, for regular verbs with (KD). A comparison of the four sub-
classes of verbs is presented in the T. forms in all occurrences of
(ED) in Style A.

Table 3.   Implicational Series for (ED) in four sub-classes of Verbs--
           (Style A)

	Class I	Class II	Class III	Class IV
Irregular, (KD) - (feel)	00	00	25	50
Irregular, No (KD) - (come)	00	7	29	55
Regular, No (KD) - (plant)	36	25	37	57
Regular, (KD) - (fill)	22	23	62	76

There are only one or two slight exceptions to the uniform pattern characteristic of an implicational scale. We can interpret Table 3 as implying that more tolerance is shown toward lack of inflection in regular verbs, while it is more socially stigmatized in verbs like *feel* and *come*.

For classes I and II in particular, it would seem that phonological constraints are responsible for the highest incidence of Ø in the past forms of regular verbs with (KD). For Classes III and IV, it seems futile to speculate on the comparative effects of phonological and grammatical[6] constraints on the incidence of inflected forms in Style A. It seems likely that both sources of interference are in operation in the speech of these groups. For Classes I and II, on the other hand, it seems to be phonological constraints rather than un-familiarity with S.E. forms which increases the incidence of Ø forms of *fill* etc. But even for these groups, the use of T. forms of *want*, *plant*, etc. where no phonological "interference" is evident, suggests that grammatical constraints are also in operation.

In the peer-group speech of Classes III and IV lack of inflection occurs just as much for regular verbs without (KD) like *plant*, as for verbs like *fill*. Moreover, the vast majority of irregular verbs are also uninflected. For the peer-group of Class IV (P.G. IV) there were only three instances of inflected forms, all involving irregular verbs like *come*. For the peer-group of Class III (P.G. III) there were 31 in-stances of inflected forms in a total of 232 occurrences of (ED). All but six of these involved irregular verbs, but most of the irregular verbs which occurred were in fact inflected.

Though no absolute norm of usage exists for either peer-group, the behavior of each strongly suggests use of a grammatical category distinct from that of Standard English. This supports the view that for many informants the S.E. category of "past tense" is not part of their native system of predication.

The acquisition of standard forms appears to be dependent on the intensity of social pressure exerted upon persons of different socio-economic strata. Class IV respondents show least capacity to produce these forms, even in formal speech. For Class III there is a consider-able range of variation in the use of (ED) from formal style to peer-group speech. In the latter, their use of uninflected forms is almost without exception, and closely parallels the behavior of Class IV respondents.

Differentiation of (DOES):

Figure 2 is a class stratification diagram for the second of the variables, (DOES). The index measures the percentages of occurrences of the T. form *does* in the total number of possible occurrences of the variable.

As can be seen, there is a certain amount of class stratification in Style B, where Classes III and IV are differentiated from each other

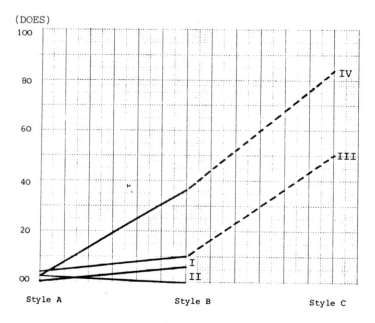

Fig. 2   Class Stratification Diagram for (DOES)

and from Classes I and II. The latter groups are undifferentiated, only one occurrence of *does* being recorded in each case for both Styles A and B combined. In Style B, Class III has only ten occurrences of *does* out of a possible 95, while Class IV has 24 out of a possible 66.

In Style A, though the number of possible occurrences is almost double that of Style B for each group, the percentage of *does* is almost zero for all classes so that no stratification is evident. The use of *does* appears to lend itself easily to conscious suppression, as opposed to use of T. forms of (ED). Its near absence in Style A suggests that it is a highly stigmatized form.

Stylistic variation within the interview is restricted to Class IV. The rise in the incidence of the T. form in peer-group speech for Classes III and IV is considerable, though differences between the two social levels are still quite marked--the members of peer-group IV using *does* over 80% of the time, as compared with only 50% for peer-group III. This appears to reflect the use of *does* in interview speech, and to support the conclusion that *does* is a highly stigmatized form.

In spite of the marked increase in the use of T. forms in peer-group speech, the frequent occurrence of what appear to be S.E. forms prevents us from regarding *does* as the norm for either group.

The relatively low incidence of T. forms for this variable, particularly in interview speech, suggests that Standard English forms replace occurrences of *does*. My data show, however, that the forms substituted for *does* by informants were not generally standard forms. This applies only to occurrences of finite verbs with third person singular subjects. In Standard English, such verbs are "marked" for the present by the morpheme -Z (realized as *IZ*, -Z and -s). In the usage of many informants in this survey, however, -Z was not consistently used when the verb occurred with third person singular subjects. This suggested that informants were not generally familiar with the S.E. "rule" governing subject-verb concord in such cases. To test this hypothesis, the variable (Z) was set up to examine the incidence of unmarked third person singular verb forms in the speech of informants.

The population for this variable includes all cases where S.E. requires use of -Z with finite verbs. This means that forms which were not included in the population for (DOES) are included here. Among these are cases like the following:

> (21) If he come(s) he can see it.
> (22) When the man return(s) I'll ask him.

Occurrences of *does* were not included in the population for (Z), though all other occurrences of the variable (DOES) with 3rd person singular subjects, were. The reason for this is simply that the focus of interest in our investigation of (Z) is the presence or absence of S.E. subject-verb concord as expressed by -Z. This morpheme does not co-occur with the T. form *does*.

Social Differentiation of (Z):

Figure 3 is a class stratification diagram for (Z). The index measures the percentage of -Z absence in the total occurrences of the variable.

As can be seen, there is a regular structure of class and style stratification, with Class I showing most frequent use of the suffix, and Class IV the least frequent use.

Style shifting is quite marked for all social strata indicating that informants are aware that -Z is used to express present tense concord with third person singular subjects. The Stylistic variation also suggests that a certain amount of prestige is attached to use of -Z. However, the fact that none of the classes[7] approaches consistent use of -Z even in formal style may mean that S.E. rules of concord lack stability on all social levels.

The relatively high incidence of -Z absence shown by Classes II to IV in Style B suggests that the everyday usage of these informants is characterized by the use of non-standard forms. This conclusion is reinforced by the values shown in peer-group speech. The members of peer-group IV show complete absence of -Z, while those of peer-group III have only a few occurrences of the variable. We can conclude that S.E. rules of concord are at best an unstable part of the basic grammar which respondents use.

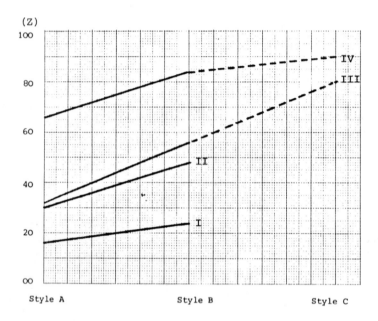

Fig. 3:   Class Stratification Diagram for (Z)

Another possible explanation for the use of unmarked forms of the
verb with 3rd person singular subjects is that it is due to "interference" from the T. system of predication. This will apply only to
certain occurrences of the variable, viz, in subordinate clauses introduced by temporal conjunctions like *when* etc., and by conditionals like
if etc. (See sentences (21) and (22) above.) It will be recalled from
our earlier discussion that the unmarked form of the verb in T. (or more
precisely, Ø) can be interpreted as carrying the meaning "completive"
(aspect). In the occurrences of (Z) listed above, it is quite likely
that the Ø forms of the verbs are due to interference from this grammatical rule of the T. system. The implications of this do not end
here. It may be the case that even when informants appear to be using
S.E. constructions, they may in fact be employing the abstract grammatical category of completive aspect from the T. system--as for example, in: (23) *When you come I'll show you.* The same phenomenon may
also occur in other areas of the systems in question. Thus Solomon
(1972:2-4) argues that even when Trinidadians appear to be using
Standard English verb forms like *could have + - en, had + - en* etc.,
they may in fact be subject to the influence of certain conceptual
distinctions and categories that really belong to the T. System.
These, of course, are matters for independent enquiry and analysis.

Social Differentiation of (V-ING)

The stratification of informants by (V-ING) is illustrated in Figure 4. The index measures the percentage of times Ø is used in preference to forms of the S.E. verb *to be* (BE).

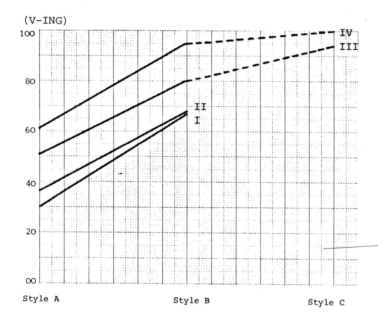

Fig. 4:   Class Stratification Diagram for (V-ING)

Figure 4 shows that a near-regular structure of social and stylistic variation exists for this variable. This resembles the pattern shown for (Z) in many respects, though in the latter case Classes I and II were more widely separated, and Classes II and III were less differentiated than they are for (V-ING).

As in the case of the other grammatical variables, there is marked style shifting between Styles A and B, indicating that the use of BE is accepted as more appropriate in formal speech. However, the generally high values shown even in Style A suggest that there is a great deal of tolerance of Ø on all social levels.

In peer-group speech, members of Class IV use T. forms without exception, while there are only 13 instances of BE forms in 299 occurrences of the variable for peer-group III. Nine of these standard forms occurred in the speech of one respondent. Absence of BE can justifiably be regarded as the norm for all respondents in conversation with their friends. Before we arrive at any further conclusions regarding the use of (V-ING), we can investigate the other structures in which forms of BE alternate with Ø in the speech of Trinidadians.

Social Differentiation of (COP-A):

Figure 5 is a class stratification diagram for (COP-A). The index is identical to that used in the case of (V-ING).

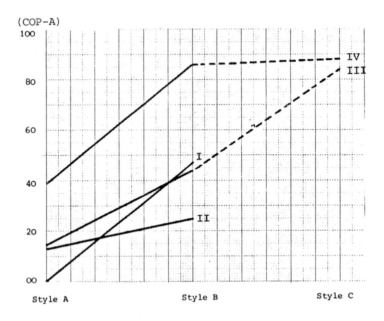

Fig. 5: Class Stratification Diagram for (COP-A)

We can observe a clear pattern of class stratification in more formal style, but in Style B the high value shown by Class I distorts what would otherwise be a regular structure. This high value for Class I is due to the same informant who was singled out in the case of (ED).

There is sharp stylistic shifting for (COP-A) in interview speech, especially by Classes I and IV. In formal style, Class I in fact uses BE without exception. BE occurs in all styles for all groups. In peer-group speech, there is only a marginal difference between Classes III and IV, T. forms predominantly in both cases. However, a fairly sub-stantial percentage of standard forms is to be noted even in this style. In all of these respects, the contrast between the patterns for (COP-A) and (V-ING) is quite noticeable.

Further conclusions on (V-ING) and (COP-A):

The variables I have identified as (V-ING) and (COP-A) were also found by Labov (1968 et al.) and Wolfram (1969) to be part of the systematic variation between standard and non-standard forms in the speech of

Black Americans. For Labov, however, all occurrences of (V-ING) and
(COP-A) were to be regarded as belonging to the population for a single
variable. His study of "deletion, contraction and inherent variability
of the copula" therefore investigates the use of "finite forms of the
copula before noun phrases, predicate adjectives, locatives, negatives,"
as well as "before the verb with progressive suffix, and before *gonna*,"
which he regards as one of the various reduced forms of *going to* (Labov et al.
1968:174).

Labov regards all of these structures as "containing" the same
grammatical element, the "copula," which is variously realized as Ø and
as forms of the verb *to be*. One of the main reasons he gives for this
approach is the evidence of "related sentences in which the forms of
be are never deleted by any speaker" (Ibid., p. 174). He cites eleven
examples of such grammatical constructions in which forms of BE regularly appear in non-standard Negro speech (N.N.E.). These include the
use of *was* and *wasn't* in past tense, the maintenance of *I'm*, the use of
the infinitive *to be* after modals, and so on (Ibid., pp. 177-184).

In Trinidadian English we can identify a number of grammatical constructions which appear to be related in Labov's sense to the structures identified for the populations of (V-ING) and (COP-A). For
example, there is the use of BE in embedded questions, with modals,
after *that* and *what*, before Noun Phrases, and in "past tense." Very
often, however, forms which appear to be realizations of BE occur in
environments where their use would not be tolerated in S.E. For instance *is* occurs with all persons before predicate nominals, as in the
following examples.

     (24) I/You/He is a fool.
     (25) We/They is funny people etc.

Similarly, the form *was* is invariant with all subjects in sentences
like:

     (26) I/You/He was a fool.
     (27) We/They was here yesterday, etc.

On the basis of such occurrences, it could be argued that forms like
is and *was* belong to a system of predication distinct from that of S.E.,
and are therefore not necessarily related to S.E. forms of the verb *to
be*. It would be difficult to argue along similar lines in cases where
use of BE appears to be common to both T. and S.E., for instance in
embedded questions, after *that* and *what*, and with modals.

One point not yet made is the fact that in (V-ING) and (COP-A)
structures, Ø can occur with all subjects, including *I*, in T.E.[8] This
is in marked contrast to the N.N.E. system, where *am* or *'m* occur regularly with the first person pronoun in such grammatical constructions.

The main conclusion to be drawn from all of these points is that,
until a thorough analysis of the structures in which BE occurs has been
made, the relationship between the T. and S.E. systems in this respect
must remain open to doubt. As I have already pointed out, the evidence

of quantitative patterns of variation can only act as a guide to an investigation of the grammatical processes at work for (V-ING) and (COP-A)
in Trinidad English.

The difference in incidence of BE shown in our results above for the
two variables suggests that they are distinct for all informants.   Indeed, the results strongly support the interpretation that -*ing* belongs
to a T. system of tense and aspect which applies to all finite verb
forms.   It seems likely that for many Trinidadians *BE* does not function
at all in this system.[9]   Indeed, even in S.E. there is reason to doubt
that forms of *BE* when used before verbs with the "progressive" suffix
bear anything but phonetic similarity to *BE* as used before noun phrases,
predicate adjectives and locatives.

Social Differentiation of (GO):

Figure 6 is a class stratification diagram for (GO).   The index
measures the percentage of times *go* is used to indicate future or intended action in the total occurrences of the variable.

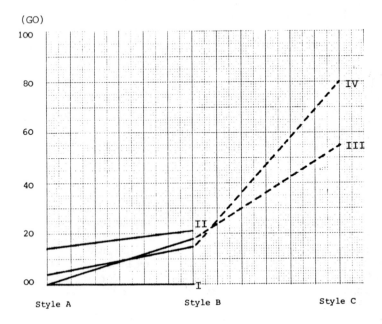

Fig. 6:   Class Stratification Diagram for (GO)

Despite deliberate attempts during the interview to elicit (GO)
variants, the number of occurrences of the variable was quite small for
each informant.   The data for interview speech may not therefore constitute an adequate basis on which to judge the social differentiation
of (GO).   But a number of observations can still be made.

The use of *go* appears subject to a greater degree of conscious suppression than we found for *does*. The patterns shown in Figure 6 do not make this clear. For instance, the percentage of 21 shown for Class II in Style B represents only 3 uses of *go* in 14 occurrences of the variable.

The only conclusion that we can reach for interview speech is that there is no differentiation between Classes II, III and IV in the use of (GO). Class I is isolated from these by having no instances of *go* in any style.

The values shown in peer-group style support the view that *go* is subject to a high degree of conscious suppression in interview speech. In fact, Group IV members use *go* five times more often than persons of equivalent status did in Style B, while the value for peer-group III is three times that recorded for S.E.C. III in Style B. There are noticeable differences between the two groups in Style C. Peer-group IV uses the T. variant 80% of the time, while peer-group III uses it only 55% of the time.

The number of occurrences of the variable in peer-group speech was far more substantial than in interview speech. There were 49 occurrences for P.G. IV, an average of 8 per person, and 83 occurrences for P.G. III, an average of 5 per person. We can therefore claim that our peer-group data are a more reliable indication of the usage of respondents in this setting, than our interview data were for Styles A and B.

There were only two respondents in the two groups combined who used *go* without exception. Variation between T. and S.E. forms occurs for all other persons, so we cannot claim that *go* is the norm for either peer-group.

Summary of Conclusions:

Our discussion has revealed a number of clear patterns of class differences in the use of the grammatical variables. Some conclusions are as follows:

Social Variation: The following variables are the best indicators of social class: (ED) (Z), (V-ING) and (COP-A). No differentiation in use of (DOES) was found for Classes I to III in interview speech, but Class IV displayed a relatively high incidence of the T. form *does* in Style B. (GO) failed to provide any pattern of differentiation among informants in the interview, except for the fact that Class I had no instances of *go* while the other classes used the T. form a few times. Socio-economic factors seem to condition linguistic behavior even in the peer-group sessions. Thus, peer-group III has lower values than peer-group IV for all variables, differences being quite marked for (DOES) and (GO) but marginal in other cases.

Stylistic Variation: Stylistic shifts of varying sharpness were recorded for most of the variables in interview speech. The exceptions were (DOES) and (GO) for which informants showed a high incidence of S.E. forms in Styles A and B. For all other variables, the higher percentage of S.E. forms in Style A indicated that all informants regarded these as more appropriate in formal speech.

The classes differed to varying extents in their capacity for con-sistent use of S.E. rather than T. forms. For (ED), (Z) and (V-ING), Classes I and II were the only groups that consistently showed a higher frequency of S.E. than of T. forms in formal style. Class III followed this usage only in the case of (ED) and (Z), Class IV used T. forms much more frequently than S.E. forms for all variables except (DOES) and (GO). In peer-group speech, Classes III and IV generally showed a much higher incidence of T. than S.E. forms--sometimes approaching consistent use of the former.

Norms of Usage: It is difficult to draw any firm conclusions from the above points regarding norms of usage. For interview speech, it was only in the case of (DOES) and (GO) that we found relatively consistent use of S.E. forms on all social levels. This was also true to a lesser extent of the use of (COP-A) by Classes I to III. Apart from these cases, variation between T. and S.E. forms is the rule for all speakers in the interview setting.

For all the variables, values are considerably higher in the peer-group speech of Classes III and IV. Non-standard variants are used almost without exception for (ED), (Z) and (V-ING). Even in these cases, however, a number of standard forms were used. For (COP-A), T. forms make up the vast majority of occurrences of the variable; but the percentage of S.E. forms is substantial in the speech of many respondents. (DOES) and (GO) behave rather differently from other variables. The incidence of T. forms for these variables is balanced by an almost equal incidence of standard forms for both peer-groups.

The findings from peer-group data reinforce the conclusion that any norm we isolate for the T. system of predication would have to be an abstraction from the actual behavior of respondents. Variability seems to be an inherent part of the language used even in settings in which the minimum attention is given to monitoring of speech.

It is of course possible that we have not succeeded in isolating the basic vernacular in our peer-group recordings. Perhaps the effects of systematic observation are still responsible for the presence of standard forms. It may even be possible that data from much younger informants, say pre-adolescent children, will not be characterized by the degree of variability we have noted here.

At any rate, if we wish to account for the language used by per-sons of various ages and socio-economic backgrounds in the community studied, it seems evident that we cannot speak in terms of "pure" systems with categorial rules for the use of any grammatical form.

The Creole Situation in the Context of Socio-linguistic Studies:

This study represents one of the first attempts to apply socio-linguistic methodology to the investigation of a creole situation.

From a sociolinguistic point of view its primary aim has been to demonstrate that the types of correspondence between linguistic and sociological phenomena which have been shown to exist by Labov and other
researchers in more "typical" dialect situations also apply to creole
communities such as that investigated here. From a linguistic point
of view its chief purpose has been to show that the creole language
matrix is not made up of invariant, homogeneous linguistic systems,
either "creole" or "standard", as other researchers have assumed.

Both of these aims have been achieved, to a certain extent, in the
present investigation. In the first place, it has been shown that linguistic features show a regular distribution over socio-economic groups.
Secondly, each social group shows regular style shifting in the same
direction, indicating that the values associated with the various linguistic features are quite uniform in the community. Finally, we have
demonstrated that the varieties of English used by the socio-economic
groups are not differentiated from one another by discrete sets of
features, but rather by differences in the combinations of features, and
in the frequency with which they occur in everyone's speech.

Some studies of creole situations have avoided facing the facts of
heterogeneity by appealing to the notion of "co-existent systems" (Fries
and Pike 1949). Similar approaches have been made in studies of multilingualism (Gumperz 1958, Bright and Ramanujan 1964), and of diglossia
(Ferguson 1959). The differences between these and creole situations
is that clearly identifiable stata can presumably be isolated in the
former, but not in the latter. At any rate, the notion of co-existent
systems does not in itself clarify our understanding of the specific
relations which hold between the linguistic subsystems within a creole
complex.

Such relations are two-fold. On the one hand they involve the
purely linguistic rules which relate varieties of language to one
another. On the other, they concern the rules which state when, where
and how the speaker adjusts his behavior in the direction of one system
or another. Each of these aspects of variation poses difficult problems
for the creolist. It is worthwhile to consider each in turn.

Problem One:

There have been a few attempts in recent years at constructing an
adequate model of a differentiated language which applies to the entire
speech community. One of these is that outlined by Weinreich et al.
(1968), as mentioned earlier. This model of language has

1) "discrete, co-existent layers defined by strict
   co-occurrence which are functionally differentiated
   and jointly available to a speech community.

2) intrinsic variables, defined by co-variation with
   linguistic and extra-linguistic elements." (1968:185)

But the above model poses difficult questions for the creolist. The
most important of these is how to decide when we have cases of "discrete

co-existent layers defined by strict co-occurrence," and when we have cases of "intrinsic variables." Weinreich et al. seize on the Jamaican Creole construction *a tired im tired* as an instance of a "code or system conceived as a complex of interrelated rules or categories which cannot be mixed randomly with the rules or categories of another code or system" (Ibid., p. 167). The J.C. construction is opposed to the Standard English *he's tired, that's all*, and the point made that a sentence like *a tired he's tired* (involving mixing of rules of 2 codes) is impossible. There may indeed be various cases of this sort of co-occurrence restriction (in Weinreich et al.'s sense), but there are many examples in T.E. of precisely the sort of "mixing" or rules that they regard as unlikely. E.g.,

(29)   IZ tired he tired/it's tired he's tired.
(30)   it have/it has (="There is/are")
(31)   John an' dem/John and them/they.
(32)   Look he here/Look him here/Look at him here.

Similar comments might be made on various aspects of the system of predication. Indeed it is arguable that even certain cases of what appear to be "hypercorrections" are really cases of the mixing of systems mentioned above (see Winford, 1972:303-306, 311-312, etc.).

Another model aimed at accounting for heterogeneity is that proposed by De Camp (1970, 1971). He suggests that

> The linguistic diversity within any speech community
> may be factored into a small set of socio-linguistic
> structures each of which may be represented by a simple
> mathematical function (a line, a circle, etc.) and by a
> corresponding schema of binary features which, if they
> are incorporated into a generative grammar, can result
> in the grammar's generating those aspects of the lin-
> guistic diversity which are attributable to that struc-
> ture.   (1970:166)

In one sense the models of both Weinreich et al. and De Camp must cope with the problem of whether there exist syntactically different systems in the creole complex, and how these are related to each other. To elaborate this point, let us consider the rather different question of phonological variation. As DeCamp (1971) shows, by establishing base forms, a generative approach points out not only the correspondences between phonetic elements as such, but also the correspondences between their distribution in lexical forms. The former types of correspondence can be established on the basis of common phonic features. But, as other researchers have pointed out before, grammatical features which may also vary in a language community have no such real common denominator for comparison. (See Klima 1964:2.) Two major questions have therefore been posed, which arise from the concept of language as a system with orderly heterogeneity:

(a)   In what manner and to what degree may linguistic
      structures differ from each other and yet be in-
      corporated into the same grammar?

(b)   What is the criterion on which we base our
      identification of one structure, or feature,
      with another?

The criterion used in defining the grammatical variables and their
variants for this study was impressionistic. We grouped together in the
same variable, forms which offered alternative means of "saying the same
thing," and which were "jointly available to all members of the community." It is obvious that in a formal model of variation, the relationships between such forms would have to be specified in a far more
explicit way.

In the past, creolists have tended far too much to assume the truth
of propositions concerning such relationships, without any real empirical proof. For instance, Solomon (1966), while sticking to the
Saussurean-Bloomfieldian notion that "any given form in a given
utterance can only be part of one system," claims that in post-creole
continua "items inter-related in one way at one point in the evolution
of the language come to be interconnected in another way at a later
point, and ... the period of evolution to this later point is very
short" (1966:56). Whether for Solomon this interrelationship can extend to identification of a "creole" structure with a "standard" structure, is difficult to say. But for De Camp such an identification comes
easily:

> Even if we do not go so far as to agree with some
> theorists that phrase structure branching rules are
> universals, it is still clear that Standard English
> and Creole, even the extreme variety of Creole des-
> cribed by Bailey, are identical in phrase structure.
> The differences are entirely in the lexicon and the
> transformations. (1968:35)

It is precisely these types of assumptions whose validity needs to
be tested and verified before further fundamental advances can be made
in creole studies. We need to return to basic principles, and basic
questions like (a) and (b) above. I do not pretend to have any answers
to such questions, involving as they do not just a theory of grammars,
but a theory of differences between one grammatical system and another.
But guidelines have been established which can be taken up. For example, some of the remarks made by Katz concerning "semi-sentences"
might be modified and adapted to the study of creole situations. He
points out that

> There are no procedures of formal manipulation
> that suffice to determine ... what relations between
> well-formed parts of a string and ill-formed parts of
> that string allow the string to be understood by
> speakers, and what relations do not. (1964:402)

The main point of interest for the creolist is his proposal that the
task of discovering such relations involves methods of:

> distinguishing between those phrase-structure rules
> which develop phrases, those which develop word-
> classes, and those which develop word-classes or
> word subclasses that cross-classify words. (Ibid.,
> p. 413)

Such an approach, modified if necessary, may prove quite fruitful in
probing the nature of the relationships between sub-systems in creole
continua.

Alternatively we might attempt to adapt for our purposes tests of
linguistic similarity or diversity such as those proposed by Ervin-Tripp
(1971). Such tests are concerned with questions like

(a)   Whether there are "shared categories of meaning so
      that speakers will attend to the same features of
      the referent materials."

(b)   Whether there is "shared lexicon identifying the
      significant referents, attributes, relationships,
      and actions," and whether there are "shared central
      meanings for this lexicon."

(c)   Whether the shared lexicon is recognizable (in terms
      of its morphophonemic realizations).

(d)   Whether there are "shared order rules for the basic
      grammatical relations" (viz, "subject-verb, verb-
      object, and modifier-head"). (Ervin-Tripp 1971:63-65)

Some such procedure is required if we are to probe in depth the nature
of a creole speaker's interpretation and use of the heterogeneous structures which are basic to his language.

Problem Two:

The models proposed by DeCamp and Weinreich et al. both aim at formalizin
the relationship between linguistic variation, and the extra-linguistic
factors which condition it. Two main objections can be made to such
attempts. In the first place, we have had ample evidence in this study
that co-occurrence of linguistic features does not fall into the neat
implicational patterns that De Camp assumes to exist in creole situations. Certain features are far more subject to variation than others,
and certain individuals vary in their usage far more than others, even
when the extralinguistic factors which may be influencing their behavior
appear constant. Any implicational ordering we might establish on the
basis of the findings of this survey would undoubtedly be an abstraction from the facts of linguistic variation. Labov has criticized De
Camp for "using categorical invariant rules as if speakers always used
a particular form in a given system, and relying on the old notion of
code-switching to explain the variaton" (DeCamp 1970:171). Such
criticism appears quite justified. As has often been pointed out, anyone who works with the language creole speakers actually use will be

faced with dozens of "switches" in relatively short stretches of speech, which have no apparent motivation.

It is also difficult to incorporate a hierarchical ordering of rules into any description of a creole language matrix because social signifi- cance is not equally distributed over all elements of the system, nor are all aspects of the system equally marked by regional variation. The attachment of "prestige" or any other value to a linguistic feature is often arbitrary. For such reasons, Weinreich et al. (1968) decide that the primary task of the linguist must be to

> determine the degree of social correlation which
> exists and show how it bears upon the abstract
> linguistic system. (p. 186)

In their scheme, quantitative analysis of the covariation of linguistic and sociological phenomena is only a preliminary, though an essential one, to the problems of "purely" linguistic analysis.[10]

The variable rules employed by Labov to account for the hetero- geneity in linguistic systems are the closest he comes to a formaliza- tion of social correspondences with variation in language. Such rules are not predictions about individual utterances of individual speakers, because "a large number of small effects contribute to a base level of fluctuation which makes such predictions impossible" (Ibid., p. 173). Rather, they are rules which belong to grammar of the speech community. But though the value of each variable is represented as a function of several social and linguistic factors, it is clear that the variable rules are concerned primarily with interpreting relationships between purely linguistic features.

The differences between Labov's and DeCamp's approaches outlined above have to do with methodological techniques rather than theoretical principles. Both share the view that a single underlying representation and a single set of grammatical rules form the basis of interdialectal communication. It may be that this is true of creole situations as well. But there is need for considerable refinement of the techniques used in analysis of dialectal variation before we arrive at a formal- ization of the creole language continuum.

NOTES

[1] It might be argued that the forms *is* and *was*, when used with the functions illustrated in Table 2, are not the same as the S.E. forms since they are invariant, and show no number concord as do S.E. forms.

[2] Labov et al. (1968) treats the variables I have labelled (V-ING) and (COP-A) as one in his study of non-standard Negro English in New York City. He describes this "dialect" as characterized by "omission of finite forms of the copula ... before noun phrases, predicate adjectives, locatives, negatives ... and verbs with progressive suffix" (Labov et al. 1968: 174). It seems to me, however, that structures involving verbs with

-ing must be treated as part of the finite verb system, distinct from structures like those for (COP-A).

[3]The broken lines which connect these values to those shown in Styles A and B by the informants are intended to indicate that the members of the peer-group involved are not the same as the members of the respective classes, though they share the social characteristics of the latter.

[4]In fact, I make only a token distinction between verbs like *feel*, in which the past is signalled by both mutation and final *-t*, *-d*, and verbs like *hold*, for which only mutation is used to mark the past tense. In each case, the final consonant clusters are subject to "reduction" (see Winford 1972:206-212). The presence of mutation in verbs like *feel* etc. was therefore taken as sufficient indication of an S.E. inflected form.

[5](KD) represents the variable whose variants are simply the presence or absence of /t/ or /d/ in final position in monomorphemic words like *fact*, *bold* etc. (KD-MM) and in bi-morphemic words like *packed*, *killed*, etc. (KD-P). Regular patterns of both class and style differentiation exist for these variables (see Winford, op. cit., pp. 206-212).

[6]"grammatical" in the sense of "arising from a different grammatical system."

[7]It must be pointed out, however, that all the instances of *-z* absence recorded for Class I occurred in the speech of one informant. The other three members of this group used S.E. forms consistently.

[8]Labov considers "zero copula realization" to be a phonological process (i.e., deletion) which operates on the *-z*, *-s*, or *-r* which are the result of contraction. In the case of T.E., no independent evidence can be adduced to support a phonological interpretation of the absence of *am*, *are*, or *is* (see Winford 1972:318-319).

[9]We would still however have to account for cases like the following, where the idea of habitual or repeated action and the idea of continuous action are both expressed:

(28) Everyday I does be coming down the road the same time
     as he.

[10]In this connection, Solomon's comment seems quite justified:

> I think it might be more appropriate to ... say
> that quantitative methods, while adequate for the
> description of language viewed as behaviour, are in-
> effective in accounting for the differences between
> linguistic codes. (1972, p. 8)

REFERENCES

Bright, W. and A. K. Ramanujan. 1964. Sociolinguistic variation and
    language change. In: Proceedings of the 9th International Congress
    of Linguistics, ed. by H. Lunt. The Hague, Mouton. Pp. 1107-1112.

DeCamp, David. 1968. The field of Creole language studies. Mimeo.

DeCamp, David. 1970. Is a sociolinguistic theory possible? In:
    Report of the 20th Annual Meeting on Linguistics and Language
    Studies. Washington, D.C., Georgetown University. Pp. 157-173.

DeCamp, David. 1971. Toward a generative analysis of a post-creole
    continuum. In: Pidginization and creolization of languages, ed.
    by D. Hymes. Cambridge University Press. Pp. 349-370.

Ervin-Tripp, Susan. 1971. Sociolinguistics. In: Advances in the
    sociology of language, ed. by J. Fishman. Vol. I. The Hague,
    Mouton. Pp. 15-91.

Ferguson, C. A. 1959. Diglossia. Word 15:325-340.

Fries, C. and K. Pike. 1949. Co-existent phonemic systems. Language
    25:29-50.

Gumperz, J. J. 1958. Dialect differences and social stratification in
    a North Indian village. American Anthropologist 60:668-682.

Hall, R. A. Jr. 1966. Pidgin and creole languages. New York, Cornell
    University Press.

Katz, J. J. 1964. Semi-sentences. In: The structure of language:
    Readings in the philosophy of language, ed. by J. A. Fodor and J. J.
    Katz. Englewood Cliffs, N.J., Prentice-Hall, Inc. Pp. 400-416.

Klima, E. S. 1964. Relatedness between grammatical systems. Language
    40:1-20.

Labov, W. 1966. The social stratification of English in New York
    City. Washington, D.C., Center for Applied Linguistics.

Labov, W., P. Cohen, C. Robins and J. Lewis. 1968. A study of the
    non-standard English of Negro and Puerto-Rican speakers in New
    York City. Vol. I. Final Report. Co-operative Research Project
    No. 3288, Office of Education.

Solomon, Denis. 1966. The system of predication in the speech of
    Trinidad--A quantitative study of de-creolisation. Unpublished
    M.A. thesis, Columbia University, New York.

Solomon, Denis. 1972. Form, content and the post-Creole continuum.
    Paper presented at the Conference on Creole Languages and Educa-
    tional Development, University of the West Indies, Trinidad. Mimeo.

Thompson, R. W.   1961.   A note on some possible affinities between the
    Creole dialects of the old world and those of the new.   In:
    Creole language studies II--Proceedings of the conference on
    creole language studies, ed. by R. B. Le Page.   London, MacMillan
    and Co., Ltd.   Pp. 107-113.

Warner, M.   1967.   Language in Trinidad with special reference to
    English.   Unpublished M.Phil. Thesis, University of York.

Weinreich, U., W. Labov and M. Herzog.   1968.   Empirical foundations for
    a theory of language change.   In: Directions for historical
    linguistics--A symposium, ed. by W. P. Lehmann and Y. Malkiel.
    University of Texas Press.   Pp. 95-188.

Whinnom, K.   1965.   The origin of the European-based creoles and
    pidgins.   Orbis 14:509-527.

Winford, Donald.   1972.   A sociolinguistic description of two communi-
    ties in Trinidad.   Unpublished D.Phil dissertation, University of
    York.

Wolfram, W. A.   1969.   A sociolinguistic description of Detroit Negro
    speech.   Washington, D.C., Center for Applied Linguistics.

HOW DOES *DOZ* DISAPPEAR?[1]

John R. Rickford
University of Guyana

Introduction

In Guyana Creolese, sentences like the following can be heard frequently:[2]

(1) dI gjal dəz traI tə sma:t di baI, an dI baI
     dəz traI tə sma:t di gjal.

The girls usually try to outsmart the boys, and
the boys usually try to outsmart the girls.

Unlike Standard English *does*, the *doz* in sentences of this type occurs with weak stress, and is clearly not an emphatic but an iterative marker, signalling that the action referred to in the verb occurs repeatedly or habitually.

Not only does *doz* occur with high frequency, but it shows up in the speech of a wide range of social or "sociolinguistic" types. *Doz* would have to be defined as a mesolectal marker, insofar as there exist alternate means of marking the habitual or repeated occurrence of an action which are on the one hand, closer to Standard English (acrolectal), and on the other, even more different from it (basilectal). The basilectal marker is *a* (also used for continuative aspect), and the acrolectal system involves the use of the Verb stem alone or the S.E. Present tense.

But the mesolectal span of *doz* is particularly broad. For instance, basilectal speakers are distinguished from mesolectal ones, not by the fact that they use no *doz*, but that the relative frequency of *doz* in their speech is less than that of *a*.[3] Here for example, are the relative frequencies of iterative *doz* and *a* in the speech of Granny, an old East Indian woman now retired after working for over fifty years in the canefields (weeding, thrashing cane, etc.). Her output is typically basilectal:

$a = 57$ (81.4%) $doz = 13$ (18.6%)

We find the same relationship in Table 1 in Bickerton which displays the basilectal outputs of twenty Guyanese speakers. This table is reprinted below as Table 1. Note that there are only five speakers whose tape-recorded speech does not include any *doz* tokens. The other fifteen all have some *doz*, but regularly use more *a* than *doz*; the total frequencies are *doz* = 100, *a* = 732. Note though that *doz* does occur with some frequency--more often than the truly basilectal *bin* (49 tokens) and *bina* (35), for instance. There is a valid explanation for this--as Bickerton (1975:27) points out, these latter markers are used only in contexts which are rare in ordinary discourse. But the point remains that *doz* is the second most frequent non-standard marker in this

TABLE 1.   *Basilectal Outputs of Twenty Guyanese Speakers*
        (=Table 2.1 in Bickerton 1975:25)

Speaker	-s	-ed	(be)	-ing	doz	don	bina	bin	a
2				3	1	1		1	21
9			1	2	21	7	2	3	128
15			1	1	7	3	1		26
24							1		18
25				1		1	1		31
27		2	8	2	2	2		4	42
28					14	5		4	55
118							2	3	28
129							2	4	16
137		1	2	3	3	1	7	6	9
148	2		1				1	4	22
168		1	6	1	5	3			44
170				1	8	2		1	11
172				1	2	9			15
176					12	6		1	39
178				1	6	3		5	56
186		1	13	10	1		2		38
188					9	3	9	9	94
198				1	8		2	10	15
219				1	1		5	1	24
TOTAL	2	5	32	28	100	46	35	56	732

Total standard forms: 67   Total nonstandard forms: 969.

NOTE: -s = 3rd pers. sing. non-past -s; -ed = past morphemes for all
   verbs except *have* and *be*; (*be*) = all forms of verb, inflected or
   otherwise; -*ing* = verbal, adjectival and nominal forms, but excluding *going to* or equivalents.

basilectal sample. While it is used less frequently than *a* by basilectal
speakers, it cannot be ignored or cast aside.

    At the other extreme are acrolectal speakers, who more frequently use
the S.E. present tense for expressing habitual aspect (often with
iterative adverbs), as in

    (2)   They *go* home everyday.

But these acrolectal speakers also use *doz*. Somewhat like the basilectal
speakers, it is the lower frequency of *doz*, relative to some other means
of signalling iterative aspect ("present tense" in this case) which distinguishes them. Here for example are the frequencies of *doz* versus
present tense forms used for iterative aspect in the speech of Ustad, an
educated and respected member of his village, in a fairly formal interview.

> *doz*: 15 (17.4%)   present tense: 71 (82.6%)

In fact *doz* is very tenacious indeed. Of the five non-standard markers
represented in table 1 (*doz, bin, bina, don* and *a*), *doz* is the only one
which acrolectal or upper mesolectal speakers will continue to use quite
freely in their informal speech, while avoiding all the others.

So far I have been trying to establish the frequency with which *doz*
occurs in Guyana. But *doz*-usage is not confined to Guyana. The form has
been reported for Barbados (Collymore 1965), Trinidad (Solomon 1968) and
the Bay Islands (Ryan 1973). My own investigations have revealed that
it is alive and well in the South Carolina Sea Islands, in Antigua, St.
Kitts, Nevis and Belize. I am sure that it can be found elsewhere in
the Caribbean. In Alison Shilling's paper for this conference, for
instance, we learn that it is also current in the Bahamas! We may
safely conclude then that *doz* is a well-attested and important creole
feature in the English-speaking Caribbean.

However, while *doz* may be a household word in these creole communities, it has not yet become so in creolist circles. The form received
passing reference only in Collymore (1965), Solomon (1968) and Ryan
(1973), although it was treated in somewhat more detail in Bickerton
(1972) and Rickford (1974). It is certainly not generally considered one
of the classic features of an English creole--on a level with *bin* or *mi* or
a--and this despite the fact that it may well enjoy wider currency than
these other features.

This brings us to the question of why *doz*--so central a feature in
creole communities--has been thus ignored.

One possible answer is of course to say that *doz* is only one of
several fascinating creole features (*sa, neva, did, again* are others)
that have suffered from the paucity of descriptive creole studies in the
field. Contrary to what many people seem to feel, we still have a great
deal to discover about what features individual creoles exhibit, quite
apart from all the very interesting speculation about where they came
from, where they're going to, and so on.

Another possible explanation may have to do with the fact that most
of the active work on Caribbean English creoles has taken place in
Jamaica. Now I still have not ruled out the possibility that *doz* may
turn up in Jamaica, but so far I haven't received any evidence that it
is current there. If *doz* does not in fact show up anywhere in Jamaica,
this would be an interesting discovery, leading us to question in the
first place the extent to which we could continue to view Jamaican
Creole as the proto-typical Caribbean creole, and in the second, to seek
out the historical and other factors which might explain this unique
situation.

But there is surely more to this issue than the coincidence that
the crowd was at one place and the action at another. There *have* been
scholars interested in language in other parts of the Caribbean (certainly there has been no shortage on the S. Carolina Sea Islands). And

they have brought back the usual creole treasures--the tokens of *bin* and *mi* and *da* and *a*.

However, the treasures which creolists seek, and find, in creole communities, have always been the most basilectal items possible--the real "raa taak", the varieties furthest removed from the standard language. In fact, many of us conceive of the term "creole" as referring only to some invariant conglomeration of basilectal items.[4]

Given this kind of attitude and approach, it is easy to see how *doz* might have been ignored, in the light of the existence of basilectal *a*. But as I hope this paper has already made clear--in neglecting *doz*, we would be neglecting a crucial aspect of the linguistic competence of the creole community.

Another reason why *doz* may have been overlooked is that it often occurs in phonologically reduced forms--əz, *Iz*, and even z. Out of a total of 215 *doz* tokens examined for this paper, *doz* was realized in its full form only 62 percent of the time. Furthermore, many of the occurrences of əz or *Iz* reduced from *doz* might easily be mistaken for instances of the English copula.

Surprisingly enough, very little work has been done on the nature of phonological reduction or morphological condensation in creole communities. The reduction of *doz* is only one instance of a tremendous amount of phonological reduction and loss which is typical of everyday speech in creole communities. It is this general phenomenon which makes creole speech virtually unintelligible at times--even when the syntactic and lexical levels are fairly standard.

But if we cannot hear reduced forms of *doz* as *doz*, reduced forms of *bin* or *gonna* as *bin* and *gonna*, we can hardly do any "fully accountable" descriptions of creole syntax, not to mention phonology.[5] An understanding of the principal types of phonological reduction which obtain in creole communities would clearly be of considerable practical as well as theoretical value. But few papers have been written on this subject.

The point should also be made here that the condensation of *doz* seems to be more than the automatic consequence of rapid speech, and seems to provide for more than an enrichment of the range of stylistic possibilities.[6] It systematically provides a means of approximating the prestigious standard dialect or acrolect with a minimum of effort, yielding intermediate and final forms which seem closer to the desired goal while at the same time can be related to and used like their nonstandard source. For instance, *Iz*, a reduced variant of *doz*, seems more standard than *doz*, because of the fact that it is phonetically identical with the 3rd person singular form of the English copula. But it still functions both syntactically and semantically just like *doz*. The more a speaker reduces *doz*, the more he is able to "pass" as controlling the formal machinery of a higher lect, while being able to draw at the same time on the semantic and expressive machinery which "lower" lects provide.

Just as one might utter a taboo word in condensed or virtually inaudible form, thus meeting requirements of propriety while still feeling to oneself that the expressive purpose had been served, I think the phonologically reduced forms of *doz* permit more self-conscious speakers to use the morpheme without doing so blatantly and obviously, and in a way that might find accommodation among "higher" lects.

On this point, I think it is no accident that upper mesolectal speakers more frequently condense *doz* than basilectal or lower-mesolectal ones. For instance, Johnny Wade, an upper mesolectal speaker, realizes his *doz* tokens in full form only 20 percent of the time, while Uncle, a basilectal speaker, produces his *doz* tokens in full form 83 percent of the time. The upper mesolectal speaker, in a sense, tries to pass his non-standard *doz* off as a more "standard"-looking *Iz* or *z*. But the basilectal speaker is typically less concerned about trying to disguise or conceal his resources, and is more prepared to simply call a *doz* a *doz*. If all of this is true, then it is clear that an understanding of how decreolization proceeds would require an understanding of how processes of phonological condensation like those attested for *doz* actually operate.

With these motivating considerations in mind, let us turn now to a more detailed examination of the reduction of *doz*.

The d- undoing of doz

We shall concentrate most heavily on the "undoing" of the initial *d* in *doz*--the process by which it is deleted, often through assimilated intermediate forms (*nəz*, *ləz* etc.). There are well-known precedents in many English dialects for the reduction of the *əz* which would remain after the *d* is removed, to *z* and even *∅*--the reduction of the English copula *Iz* to *əz*, prior to contraction and deletion, for instance. (Cf. Labov [1969] for a detailed examination of these processes in English in general, and Black English in particular.)

But there are no equally well-known precedents for the deletion of initial voiced stops in English dialects. The closest parallel to the deletion of the initial *d* in *doz* is found only in words like *this*, *that*, *those*, *the*, *them*, etc. in which an initial *ð* becomes *dð* or *d* before being removed, often through assimilation to the preceding element (Cofer 1973).[7]

As we shall soon see, however, the removal of the initial *d* in *doz*, far from being an isolated phenomenon, is part of a general rule affecting initial voiced segments in creole auxiliaries or tense-aspect markers. But before we come to this general pan-creole rule, let us more modestly attempt to work out the rules which would provide for the undoing of *d* in *doz*.

Table 2 displays the frequency with which *doz* (varying in full form between *dʌz* and *dəz*, sometimes *daz* and *das*) was realized without the initial *d* in a total of two hundred and fifteen tokens. One hundred and ninety-six of them were taken from tape-recorded interviews with

twenty-one Guyanese Creole (GC) speakers, and nineteen from interviews
with two Sea-Island Creole (SIC) speakers in South Carolina.[8]

TABLE 2.   *Frequency of d-less forms of doz by Preceding Phonological
Environment*

Speakers	Pause	Vowel	Obstruent	Sonorant	Total
SIC	--	4/13=31%	1/1=100%	5/5=100%	10/19=53%
GC	0/6=0%	43/138=31%	3/8=38%	25/44=57%	71/196=36%
Combined total	0/6=0%	47/151=31%	4/9=44%	30/49=61%	81/215=38%

Note: "Sonorant" in column 5 refers to sonorant consonants only
(i.e., nasals and liquids).

On the whole, the SIC speakers display a higher rate of d-deletion
than the GC speakers (53% as against 36%), but since the SIC community
is at a more advanced stage of decreolization, this would accord with
what I have already said above about upper mesolectal speakers reducing
doz more often than their basilectal counterparts.

On the surface, the SIC speakers also appear to have a simpler
and more clear-cut rule than the GC speakers: delete ##*d* variably after
vowels, and categorically after consonants.   But the simplicity of this
pattern is probably due to the paucity of data in consonantal environments (only six tokens).   From other SIC data not tabulated here, SIC
speakers *do* have some d-retention in consontal environments, as in:

(2)   ju no--sɔ̃ pipl dəz kʌm ovə jer...
You know--some people come over here

Their real pattern would thus appear to be quantitatively rather than
qualitatively different from that of the GC speakers.

Ignoring for the present this and other minor differences between
the two communities, we shall refer from this point on to the combined
totals in table 2, exploiting all the data at our disposal.

The overall picture of the contrasting effect of preceding phonological environments shown in table 2 is simple enough to explain.   Since
we are dealing with the removal of a *consonant*, we would expect consonantal environments to favor the rule, and a preceding vowel or pause
to disfavor it.   (Compare the final *t, d* deletion rule, or the rule for
deleting the remaining *z* once contraction has applied to the English
copula, in Labov et al. 1968).   Furthermore, nasals are more typically
involved in homorganic assimilation processes with neighboring segments
than non-nasal consonants, and if this assimilative weakening is a prelude to *d*-loss itself, this might explain why *d*-loss is highest after
sonorant consonants.

We may represent this general picture by a variable rule of the following form:[9]

RULE I: *d*-undoing of *doz*

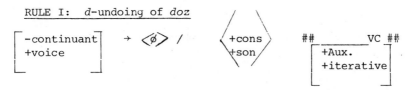

$$\begin{bmatrix} \text{-continuant} \\ \text{+voice} \end{bmatrix} \rightarrow \langle\phi\rangle \; / \; \begin{pmatrix} \text{+cons} \\ \text{+son} \end{pmatrix} \; \#\# \underline{\qquad} \text{VC} \; \#\# \; \begin{bmatrix} \text{+Aux.} \\ \text{+iterative} \end{bmatrix}$$

While this is an accurate overall characterization, we find intermediate forms which allow us to establish the process of d-undoing in finer detail when we consider the preceding segments individually. Preceding sonorants--nasals in particular--furnish the richest set of intermediate forms, and we shall deal with them first, and in greater detail than the others.

PRECEDING SONORANTS (NASALS AND LIQUIDS)

The following different realizations of *doz* occur in nasal environments:

(3) m##dəz: sʌm dəz ste an pak ap.
     Some stay and pack up

(4) m##{$\overset{\text{əz}}{\text{Iz}}$}: demIz gat arkestra de.
     They (usually) have orchestras there.

(5) n##dəz: dɛn dəz plant stʌmp lang taɪm.
     They used to plant stumps long ago.

(6) n##nəz: sʌmtaɪm di *lan* nəz hard.
     Sometimes the land is (be) hard.

(7) ø##nəz: *dɛ nəz* pʌŋ əm.
     They (usually) pound it.

(8) n##{$\overset{\text{əz}}{\text{Iz}}$}: di*gravn*ɪz drɔ əm.
     The ground draws it.

(9) ŋ##nəz: di *t*Iŋ ŋəz spIn.
     The thing spins.

As example (3) indicates, one possibility is for *doz* to remain in its full form without any compensating changes in the preceding nasal. But one other alternative (illustrated in (5) in which the underlying subject pronoun is dɛm) is for the *doz* to remain in full form while the preceding nasal assimilates to the coronal articulation of the initial *d*. This may be handled by the rule:

RULE II: *Nasal assimilation to point of articulation of following segment*

$$[+\text{nasal}] \rightarrow \begin{bmatrix} \alpha \text{ anterior} \\ \beta \text{ coronal} \end{bmatrix} \Big/ \underline{\hspace{2cm}} \#\# \begin{bmatrix} \alpha \text{ anterior} \\ \beta \text{ coronal} \end{bmatrix}$$

This fairly general rule of English, which produces *ribm bo* from 'ribbon bow' and aŋgənə from 'I'm going to' in a number of English dialects (see Labov et al. 1968:252 for a discussion of the latter), will also handle the specific case of (5) with which we are concerned.

The other possibility, represented by (6) and (9), in which the initial stop of *doz* is itself assimilated to the preceding nasal, is unusual in English, and must be represented by a more restricted rule:

RULE III: Assimilation of stop to preceding nasal

$$[-\text{continuant}] \rightarrow \begin{bmatrix} + \text{ nasal} \\ \alpha \text{ coronal} \\ \beta \text{ anterior} \end{bmatrix} \Big/ \begin{bmatrix} + \text{ nasal} \\ \alpha \text{ coronal} \\ \beta \text{ anterior} \end{bmatrix} \begin{matrix} \#\# \quad VC\#\# \\ \begin{bmatrix} + \text{ aux} \\ + \text{ iter} \end{bmatrix} \end{matrix}$$

The outputs of RULE III may be further reduced, as examples (4) and (8) indicate, by the more general rule:

RULE IV: Simplification of geminates

$$X_i \rightarrow (\emptyset) \Big/ X_i \quad \#\#\underline{\hspace{1cm}}$$

Example (7) is especially interesting. The subject pronoun (dɛm) has lost its final nasal. (The lone nasal in the subject auxiliary sequence is clearly part of the habitual auxiliary). We could account for this by a possible RULE IV' applying to the output of II or III:

RULE IV': Alternative simplification of geminates

$$X_i \rightarrow (\emptyset) \Big/ \underline{\hspace{1cm}}\#\#X_i$$

The most obvious objection to this rule is that it would have the exact opposite effect of RULE IV as it stands: i.e., it would remove the *first* of two adjacent identical segments rather than the *second*. But apart from the ad hoc nature of such a formulation, RULE IV' would not allow speakers to produce *either* (7) *or* (8), as speakers in fact do.

A better way of accounting for (8) is by RULE V:

RULE V: Resyllabification of nasal

$$\begin{matrix} \text{dɛN} & \$ & VC \\ [+\text{pro}] & & \begin{bmatrix} \text{aux} \\ +\text{iter} \end{bmatrix} \end{matrix} \rightarrow \begin{matrix} (\text{dɛ} & \$ & NVC &) \\ [+\text{pro}] & & \begin{bmatrix} \text{aux} \\ +\text{iter} \end{bmatrix} \end{matrix}$$

RULE V would allow for the generation of (7) without excluding the possibility of (8) (by RULE IV), and is further justified by the fact that dɛm and dɛ are normal pronominal variants in mesolectal levels of both GC and SIC. It appears that, given the output of RULE IV (e.g., dɛn əz), and somehow still feeling the need for an initial consonant on what was originally *doz*, speakers resyllabify--transferring the nasal from the pronoun to the iterative marker. This option is made possible by the independent existence of dɛ as a pronominal variant.

Here are some sample derivations for underlying dɛm##dəz, which can go two possible routes, and for underlying lan##dəz, which can only go one. Note that while dɛm##məz and dɛ##məz are not actually attested in the recorded data, dɛm##əz is attested, and the former two, which would precede and follow this in the derivation, seem intuitively possible where something like *la##nəz does not.

	dɛm##dəz	dɛm##dəz	lan##dəz
RII	Option not taken	dɛn##dəz	Vacuous application
RIII*	dɛm##məz	dɛn##nəz	lan##nəz
RIV	dɛm##əz	dɛn##əz	lan##əz
RV	*dɛ##məz	dɛ##nəz	Not applicable

In the case of preceding liquids, we find evidence for some of the very processes which operate in nasal environments. In no event is the subject NP affected (as in (9) above), but *doz* itself may be modified as in:

(10) l##ləz: pipl ləz plenti he.
There are usually plenty of people here.

(11) l##{Iz/əz}: pipl iz bi baIjIn sun.
People usually start buying soon.

(10) may be accounted for by amending RULE III to provide for assimilation of the stop to a preceding sonorant instead of a nasal. (11) requires no further modification of RULE IV.

PRECEDING OBSTRUENTS (STOPS AND FRICATIVES)

Preceding stops and fricatives simply do not provide enough data to allow us to work out finer processes with any reliability. Two *d*-less forms of *doz* occur after stops:

(12) dem wId strɛŋk ŋʌz wʌk.
Those with (the) strength work.

(13) Gad əz drim i waIf.
God makes his wife dream...

In view of examples like (9) above, (12) could probably be derived by allowing RULE III to operate as a distant assimilation rule. From

(13), and the fact that all the full forms of *doz* are preceded by *t##* (*naɪt dəz; paːt dəz, wat dʌz*), we must assume that *d*-undoing takes place most often in stop environments by a process of geminate simplification, when the preceding stop happens itself to be *d*.

In the fricative environments, no intermediate forms of *doz* (**səz *zəz* for instance) are attested, and we are not therefore justified in positing any modified form of the assimilation rule III for fricatives. However, in both cases in which the *##d* is deleted, the preceding fricative is a sibilant (*aːlwɪz ɪz, perənts əz*), suggesting that sibilants perhaps trigger *d*-undoing more often than other fricatives.

PRECEDING VOWELS

No finer rules can be established as to how preceding vowels function in the *d*-undoing of *doz*. Tense vs. lax, front vs. back--none of these nor any other distinctions seem to correlate with any greater or less deletion. There is at least one case of an initial ð instead of *d* in *doz*, and several cases in which the *d*- is more tenuous (which we might write as ᵈəz). These suggest that a process of weakening often takes place as a prelude to, or instead of total deletion. But beyond this we can say little more.

The deletion of initial stops in auxiliaries--a pan-creole rule:

We have now covered the general, and as far as possible, the specific processes by which the initial *d* in *doz* is removed. As was mentioned before, the deletion of an initial voiced stop seems at first like a rare phenomenon in English dialects. But in English creoles and decreolized dialects such as Black English, we discover several other similar cases.

In Sea-Island Creole, for instance, the basilectal continuative/habitual marker is normally *da*, as in:

> (14) shi mʌsi *da* hʌnt hʌzbən.
>   She must be hunting (for a) husband.

However, *da* alternates with *a* after *bɪn*, as in:

> (15) bai, andi bina hala.
>   Boy, Andy was hollering.

Note that *bɪn* ends in a *nasal*, and as we have already seen in the case of *doz*, preceding nasals provide one of the most favorable environments for the deletion of the initial stop via assimilation.

In Guyana and Jamaica today, only *a* is used for the basilectal continuative/iterative marker. It is very likely that this *a* is a derived form of an earlier *da*,[10] and that the complete loss of *##d* was preceded by a *da/a* alternation such as still exists in SIC.

Bɪn, a marker of anterior aspect or past tense in almost all the Atlantic creoles, provides another example--the first to suggest that the deletion rule is not limited to dentals or alveolars, but extends to all voiced stops. The form occurs as *mIn* in Antigua and St. Kitts, *wen* in Hawaiian Creole, and *en* in Jamaican Creole. The variants themselves suggest the diachronic processes which might have been involved: nasalization of the initial *b*, lenition to a glide, complete deletion of the initial segment.

It should be added here that the pronominal morphology of creoles is likely to have played some part in the development of these processes, given that the effect of a preceding nasal is always so strong. Unlike the S.E. subject pronouns, *none* of which ends in a nasal at least one (*dem*--third person plural) and frequently another (*Im*--third person singular, as in Jamaica) of the creole subject pronouns and in nasals. Add to this the fact that in our data pronouns are the most frequent NP before the auxiliary, and that third person pronouns occur with particular frequency, and it can be seen how the process of initial stop assimilation and deletion might have been facilitated by the regular occurrence of favorable environments.

GC and SIC furnish yet another example of initial stop deletion in the alternation of *bi* and *i*--most widely demonstrated in the use of *mʌs##i* for "must be", as in (14) above. I have also been told that an alternation between *go* and *o* exists in Sranan, a well-known English creole in Surinam. There is a similar alternation between future *gun* and *un* in GC.

The final three examples come from Black English. The fact that they are peculiar to Black dialects in the U.S. has frequently been noted, but no explanations have been offered for their idiosyncracy.

Labov et al. (1968:255-257) point out that the use of *ain't* for *didn't*, and the realization of *don't* as simply a nasal vowel (ɔ̃ or ũ or ɔ̃), differentiate Black non-standard dialects from White non-standard ones. But they offer no rules for such alternations, stating that this would require "further investigations." Undoubtedly it does. But it seems clear that to provide for the use of *ain't* for *didn't* and a nasal vowel for *don't*, we would require rules deleting the initial voiced segment-- the same phenomenon we witness in the Caribbean creole auxiliaries. Note too that where the GC basilect has *no* or *na*, the GC mesolect uses *en*, *ɛn*, *In*, *ən*, or *ņ* for the acrolectal forms *didn't* and *don't*. The B.E. situation is therefore not as unfamiliar as it might at first appear.

Black English furnishes an additional example that the deletion rule might apply to all kinds of voiced stops: *##b*, *##d* and *##g*. The example in question is the possible reduction of "(I) *am going to*" in B.E. to *mən*, *mnə* and *mə*. Ignoring the earlier stages which are irrelevant to this discussion, we may enter the derivation provided by Labov et al. (1968:251-252) at *mgənə*. The authors point out that the B.E. sub-path on the reduction route from this point on "is unusual, involving as it does, the assimilation of the stop to the nasal--unusual in English, but the rule in other languages such as Korean."[11] The derivation for the B.E. sub-path runs as follows:

(16) *mgənə*
(17) *mmənə* : assimilation of stop to nasal
(18) *mənə*   : simplification of geminates
(19) *mnə*   : ə - elision
(20) *mmə*   : assimilation of nasal to preceding nasal
(21) *mə*   : simplification of geminates

We do not need to turn to languages as distant as Korean for precedents for this kind of derivation, however. Note how closely the processes involved in (16) to (21) parallel Rules II to IV devised for *doz* above.

Each of these cases merits further individual investigation to see what specific role phonological environments play in the deletion of their initial segments. But we can capture the general nature of the phenomenon in a preliminary way (much as we did with RULE I above) by the following pan-creole rule:[12]

RULE VI: Deletion of initial voiced stops in creole auxiliaries

$$\begin{bmatrix} -\text{contin.} \\ +\text{voice} \end{bmatrix} \rightarrow (\emptyset) \ / \ \#\# \underset{[+\text{ aux}]}{\underline{\hspace{1cm}}} V(C) \ \#\#$$

We still need to find out a lot more about the possible application and non-application of RULE VI. (For instance, why no single creole seems to allow it to apply to *all* the cases discussed in this section; or why certain possible candidates for this rule, like anterior or past *dId* seem never to be affected in *any* creole.) But the need for some rule of this type seems incontrovertible.

Loss of the Vowel in (d)oz:

Let us now return to the specific case of *doz*. We have provided now for the removal of its initial segments, after which the variant forms remaining consist of *Vz* (*əz* and *Iz* are the most common realizations).

But further condensation can occur. The lone vowel can itself be removed, leaving a vestigial *z* to mark iterative or habitual aspect. Our discussion of this step will not be as involved as our discussion of the removal of initial *d*, because the patterns represented here are much more transparent. Table 3 for instance, displays the relative frequency of *z* out of all *z* and *Vz* tokens, according to preceding phonological environment (i.e., the relative frequency of *z* out of all forms in which the initial segment has been removed) in the speech of the seven Guyanese speakers I recorded myself.

The pattern revealed in table 3 is totally unambiguous: further reduction of *doz* to *z* occurs only after a vowel. Not only are *z* forms unattested in the other environments in the data, but intuitively they seem quite unlikely: While *də brɛd əz hard* or *di pipḷ əz wʌk* have iterative interpretations ("The bread is usually hard" and "The people work"), *də brɛdz hard* could only mean "The bread is hard", and *di pipḷz*

TABLE 3.   *Relative Frequency of z Out of Vz + z Tokens in GC,*
           By Preceding Environment

VOWEL_____ : 74% (n=42)   CONSONANT_____ : 0% (n=11)

Note: No data were available in this sub-sample on the effect of
        PAUSE_____ .

wʌk "the people's work". That is, the z in these cases cannot come, it
seems, from an underlying iterative *doz*.

Since we are dealing here with the removal of a *vowel*, it is natural
to expect that an immediately preceding vowel would favor removal. But
the apparent impossibility of any such reduction after consonants is not
what we might normally expect. The restriction on the reduction of *(d)oz*
to z to vocalic environments effectively helps to distinguish the iterative marker from the English copula, which *can* be contracted in consonantal environments albeit less frequently than in vocalic environments.

In the condensation of iterative *doz*, then, we see the deceptiveness
of first appearances. The removal of the initial voiced stop seemed at
first to be an unprecedented phenomenon, but turned out to be part of a
widespread process in the English creoles. The reduction of iterative *Iz*
or əz seemed at first to involve nothing more than the processes involved
in the widely attested contraction and deletion of the English copula,
but turns out to be subtly different.

Within the category of preceding vowels, I have not as yet been
able to establish any internal constraints on the reduction of *(d)oz*
to z . So we must simply account for this kind of reduction by the
optional RULE VII.

RULE VII: Vowel elision in iterative Vz forms

$$\begin{bmatrix} -cons \\ +syll \end{bmatrix} \rightarrow (\emptyset) \ / \ \begin{bmatrix} -cons \\ +syll \end{bmatrix} \ \#\# \underline{\quad} z \ \#\# $$
$$\begin{bmatrix} +aux \\ +iter \end{bmatrix}$$

The final disappearance of doz

If the lone z remaining after RULE VII has applied, or the z remaining when RULE VII does not apply, were to be deleted, the effect
would be the complete disappearance of iterative *doz*. And in cases where
the *doz* had preceded an invariant verb-stem, as in (22):

   (22) hi *(ə)z go der*

the verb-stem by itself would be left to signal the meaning of a habitual or repeated action:

> (23)   hi *go* der

Now in cases like (23) in which there is a third-person singular subject, it is theoretically possible to differentiate between the signalling of habitual aspect by a lone verb-stem (remaining after a preceding *doz* has been wiped out), and the signalling of habitual aspect by means of the SE present tense,[13] since the latter would require the third-person suffix on the verb, as in:

> (24)   hi *goz* der

However, with *first* and *second* person subjects, or third-person *plural* subjects, in which the verb is not marked with a present tense suffix, it would be impossible to differentiate verb-stem forms (from deleted *doz*) from present tense forms. Even with third-person singular subjects the distinction would be more theoretical than practical, because mastery of the third-person present inflection is character- istic of only the very highest lects in a creole continuum. (Note that only one speaker in table 1 has any -*s* tokens.) Essentially, there- fore, we must conclude that in practice it is difficult to distinguish between cases in which an underlying *doz* is deleted on the surface and the verb stem is left as the sole habitual marker, and cases in which there is no underlying *doz* and the SE present tense is used to mark habitual aspect.[14]

Problematic though this may be for the linguist, note how it facilitates the native speaker in the process of decreolization. To achieve the present tense forms used for the expression of habitual aspect in standard English, he does not need to master an entirely new system, but simply to extend the condensation processes which have been nibbling away at his old habitual marker *doz*, allowing them now to swallow it altogether.[15]

The synchronic problem for the linguist also has its diachronic counterpart: in those creoles or dialects which currently use verb- stem as habitual marker, can we infer earlier stages in which *doz* was used, but subsequently deleted? Without documentary or other evidence, such an inference might be difficult to justify.

In American Black English, however, there seems to be good justifi- cation for positing the earlier existence of *doz*, in the light of the present-day use of invariant *be* as a habitual or iterative marker. I have argued this position at length elsewhere (Rickford 1974), so will offer only a brief summary here. Essentially, the argument is as follows. Sentences like "He *be* working", "He *be* sick", and "He *be* in the club", which occur with iterative meaning in Black English, would result automatically if *doz* were deleted completely from the antecedent creole structures "He *doz be* working", "He *doz be* sick", and "He *doz be* in the club". In most urban settings, one finds only the iterative *be* structures, but among Black Americans on the S. Carolina Sea-Islands,

one finds both iterative *be* and *doz be*, the latter often in the reduced
forms discussed above in this paper. When the *doz* disappears completely,
the habitual or iterative function is carried solely by the remaining *be*.

An interesting question is why invariant *be* has not, as far as I
know, been adopted as an iterative marker in "decreolized" lects outside
of American Black English. In Guyana, I have collected this single
example, which seems to be derived from a deleted *doz*:

> (25)   These days the sun *be* down fast. But August i gon
>   steady back. "In these days (i.e., in the month
>   of November) the sun goes ("does be") down fast.
>   But in August it will become steady again (i.e.,
>   it will go down later)".

But *be* never becomes a stable part of the grammar, attested on a general
scale. One reason for this may have to do with the tenacity of *doz*--if
only in highly condensed form--among Guyanese speakers. I think a pre-
condition for the emergence of invariant *be* as iterative marker would be
that *doz* is completely deleted so often in the community, that the "dummy"
be could be reinterpreted as the real iterative signal. This is not
(yet?) the situation in the Caribbean creoles, although it is more so on
the Sea Islands, where *be* is rapidly replacing *doz be*.

Another explanation may be that in some creole environments, there
is not always a "dummy" *be* to take over the habitual function of *doz* if
the latter is lost. GC adjectives, for instance, often behave more like
verbs than true adjectives, and frequently occur after *doz* (and other
auxiliaries) without *be*, as in:

> (26)   Shi doz sIk plɛnti.   "She gets sick often"

Obviously, if there is no *be* in such environments when *doz* is present,
no iterative *be* can emerge after the *doz* is deleted.

Concluding Remarks

I have attempted, in this paper, to shed some light on the phonological reduction processes to which *doz* is subject in two English creole
communities. In the process, we have unearthed a subtle but widespread
pan-creole rule by which initial voiced stops in auxiliaries are deleted,
and have seen some of the *grammatical* effects of the *phonological* reductions, and some of the contributions they make to upward style-shifting
and decreolization. There is more to be learned about and from the
reduction of *doz* than I have been able to set out above. And there is
even more to be learned about and from reduction processes in creole
communities in general. Hopefully this paper has provided a hint of the
value to be derived from this kind of learning, and will encourage other
creolists to join in the quest for it.

NOTES

¹This paper is substantially the same as that prepared for the
Hawaii creole conference in 1975; changes made were primarily updatings,
corrections, and modifications of wording. The reader familiar with
Rickford (1974) will notice some similarities between this paper and
that one; the major difference is that this concentrates on the reduction processes which are only dealt with in passing in the earlier paper,
and also makes use of an expanded data base. The origin of Black English
be--central to the earlier paper--is marginal in this one, although the
question of why iterative *be* does not emerge in other English creoles or
ex-creoles is explored for the first time in this paper. For their helpful comments on a 1973 draft, I wish to thank C. J. Bailey, Derek
Bickerton, William Labov and William S. Y. Wang, while disassociating
them from any of the defects of the present paper.

²Sentences will be recorded in a broad phonetic transcription. I
continue to use the form *doz* adopted by Bickerton (1972) when making
general reference to the iterative morpheme. In fact however, the
phonetic realizations of this morpheme are dəz, dʌz, sometimes *das*,
daz. Of these dəz is the most frequent in the data, and I shall therefore use the schwa in derivatives, and when making reference to condensed forms of *doz*.

³Basilectal and lower-mesolectal speakers are also frequently distinguished from upper mesolectal ones by the fact that their *doz* is unmarked for time or tense. Whereas mesolectal speakers typically use
doz only for iterative non-past events (and *useta* for iterative past),
basilectal speakers have no such restriction. For instance, in response
to the question, "What kind of work you used to do when you were small?",
Baby Sookhia responds: watə dam bed, ken tap--den dʌz plant stʌmp laŋ
taIm, an ju watə stʌmp an tIŋ. "Water dam beds, cane tops--they *used to*
plant stumps long ago, and you had to water the stumps and so on."

This difference in the tense marking of *doz* is an interesting subject, but is not really pertinent to this paper, and will not be discussed further.

⁴In this regard, folk-usage may provide a more realistic and
useful model. In Guyana, for instance, "Creolese" is used to refer to
a wide range of varieties short of the acrolect or most standard-like
variety.

⁵Labov (1971) cites the extreme difficulty which researchers working
on Hawaiian Creole experienced in trying to transcribe auxiliaries which
occurred in reduced form: "Condensation of the auxiliaries is so extreme
that the outside listener often does not perceive the relevant bits of
sound, and thinks that he is hearing zero forms ..."

⁶I am alluding here to an intriguing suggestion made by Labov (1971)
that one reason for the replacement of adverbs of time by tense auxiliaries in many creoles is that the latter, appearing in a wider range of
variant condensed forms, offer more scope for *stylistic* variation.

[7]C. J. Bailey (personal communication) has pointed out that examples like ənə for "on the", ɔlə for "all the" (where *n* and *l* are interdental) are quite frequent in "standard American colloquial English".

[8]Forty-one of the GC tokens are from interviews with fourteen Guyanese speakers conducted by Derek Bickerton and his field assistants. I am indebted to him for the opportunity to draw on these data. The remaining one hundred and fifty-five GC tokens are from longer interviews with seven Guyanese speakers which I conducted myself between July and September 1974. The SIC data are from recordings which I made on one of the S. Carolina Sea-Islands in summer 1972.

[9]As is customary, the angled brackets around the output signify that this is a variable rule, its probability of application depending on the presence or absence of the favoring variable constraints--also within angled brackets--in the environment. In this case, for instance, rule application is most likely when the preceding environment is [+cons, +son], less when it is [+cons, -son], and even less when it is [-cons, +son]. Features within square brackets must be present for the rule to operate at all.

[10]When I first made this claim that GC and JC *a* might be a derived form of an earlier *da* (at the 1975 Hawaii conference), I was using only the comparative evidence of SIC and the phonological inference permitted by the pan-creole initial stop deletion rule. However, I have since found textual support for this claim, for GC at least, in McTurk's (1881) short story, "A Case in Court", in which the following sentences occur, the first with iterative *da*, the second continuative:

    (i)   sometime dem fowl *da* lay, too . . .
          "Sometimes those fowls used to lay, too . . ."

    (ii)   you ebba see um *da* waak wid razah?
          "you ever see it walking with razor?"

Support for the additional claim that the loss of *da* might have been preceded by *da/a* alternation is provided in the same text, in the fact that *a* is also used therein for iterative and continuative functions:

    (iii)   an' som time dem duck *a* lay . . .
           "and sometimes those ducks used to lay . . ."

    (iv)   you see da man *a* call me liah.
          "You see that man is calling me a liar."

Note finally that the text provides evidence only of *bin a* and not *bin da*, precisely as in modern-day SIC:

    (v)   me does see he *bin a* watch dem.
          I used to see him watching them.

Another piece of textual evidence for an earlier *da* is in proverb 689 in Speir's (1902) Guyanese collection, although it seems to have a possible future interpretation as well as a continuative one:

> (vi)   Nobody go beg w'en rain *da* come.
> "Nobody will beg when the rain is coming."

I am grateful to Ian Robertson, U.G., for drawing my attention to this example in Speirs (1902), and would be happy to receive similar textual evidence for earlier varieties of *Jamaican* Creole.

[11]C. J. Bailey has drawn my attention to examples like *plen(t)y*, *twen(t)y*, *cen(t)er* and *win(t)er* in some varieties of American English, suggesting that the assimilation of the stop to the nasal is not in fact unusual in English. But these examples do not involve progressive assimilation across a morpheme or word-boundary, and seem less close to the case of "I am going to" in B.E. than the examples of creole reductions discussed in this section, all of which involve members of the auxiliary.

[12]Since there are no auxiliaries in the English creoles or B.E. which begin with an affricate, [-continuant] will suffice to cover the actual cases with initial voiced stops. Alternatively, we could use Schane's (1973) feature, [-delayed release], to exclude affricates, but this feature does not appear to be as well-established or agreed upon.

The role of Aux. in the rule (i.e., the fact that all the forms to which the rule applies occur in preverbal positions, and may be treated as members of the auxiliary) is not entirely clear, but probably relates to the weak stress which auxiliaries typically receive. (Cf. Labov 1971.)

[13]As Charleston (1955) and others have pointed out, the so-called present tense of English usually indicates the general or habitual occurrence of an action, and only in specialized speech-events like sports-commentaries does it refer to an action taking place at the moment of speaking without any habitual or iterative sense. Of course, the habitual sense is most explicit when the present tense forms co-occur with such adverbials as "usually", "sometimes", and "often".

[14]The problem of circularity also bedevils the suggestion made in Bickerton (1975:136), and informally discussed by Jerrie Scott and myself at the 1973 Linguistic Institute, that the last stage of *doz* reduction might involve the hopping over of preverbal z to postverbal position. Confronted with examples like *hi goz der*, or even *wi goz der*, it is virtually impossible to decide whether the z in these cases represents the transferred remnant of an originally preverbal *doz*, or an attempt to use the English present tense. Since the present tense normally expresses habitual aspect anyway (see fn. 13 above), it is also impossible to establish that what is often regarded as "hypercorrect" *-s* insertion in B.E. or the English creoles is in fact an attempt to express habitual aspect instead of present tense, as argued in Roberts (1976).

[15]In a comment on an earlier draft of this paper, Derek Bickerton raised the question of whether the phonological attrition of *doz*, or the realization that it is a non-standard form, should be held responsible for its final disappearance in the upper mesolect. However, I

don't think that there is any crucial opposition between these two possibilities. Granted a realization that *doz* is non-standard, a speaker may decreolize most simply, as I argue in this paper, by allowing his condensation and reduction rules for *doz* to apply more extensively.

REFERENCES

Bickerton, D. 1972. System into system. Paper presented at the Conference on Creole Languages and Educational Development, St. Augustine, Trinidad. Mimeo.

_____. 1975. Dynamics of a creole system. Cambridge, Cambridge University Press.

Charleston, R. 1955. A reconsideration of the problem of time, tense and aspect in English. English Studies 36:263-278.

Cofer, T. M. 1973. A variable rule for DH. Paper presented at the Thirty-fifth summer meeting of the LSA, Ann Arbor, University of Michigan. Mimeo.

Collymore, F. 1965. Notes for a glossary of words and phrases of Barbadian dialect. 3rd ed. Bridgetown, Barbados, Advocate Company.

Labov, W. 1969. Contraction, deletion, and inherent variability of the English copula. Language 45:715-762.

_____. 1971. On the adequacy of natural languages: I--the development of tense. Mimeo.

Labov, W. P. Cohen, C. Robbins, and J. Lewis. 1968. A study of the non-standard English of Negro and Puerto-Rican Speakers in New York City. Vol. I, Final report to U.S. Office of Education (Co-operative Research Project No. 3288). Columbia University. Mimeo.

McTurk, Michael "Quow". 1881. A Case in Court. In: Essays and fables in prose and verse, written in the vernacular of the Creoles of British Guiana. Georgetown, Argosy Press. Reprinted in: Rickford, John R. (ed.) 1978. A festival of Guyanese words. 2nd ed. Georgetown, University of Guyana.

Rickford, J. R. 1974. The insights of the mesolect. In: Pidgins and creoles: current trends and prospects, ed. by D. DeCamp and I. Hancock, pp. 92-117. Washington, D.C., Georgetown University Press.

Roberts, Peter. 1976. Hypercorrection as systematic variation. Paper presented at the conference on New Directions in Creole Studies, Georgetown, Guyana.

Ryan, J. 1973. Blayk is White on the Bay Islands. University of
    Michigan Papers in Linguistics, vol. 1, no. 2.

Schane, S. A. 1973. Generative phonology. New Jersey, Prentice
    Hall.

Solomon, D. 1966. The system of predication in the speech of
    Trinidad: a quantitative study of decreolization. M.A. thesis,
    Columbia University.

Speirs, James. 1902. The proverbs of British Guiana. Demerara, The
    Argosy Company.

FROM PREPOSITION TO COMPLEMENTIZER

IN CARIBBEAN ENGLISH CREOLE*

William Washabaugh
University of Wisconsin-Milwaukee

My intention here is to add to this growing list of studies in creolization which support the hypothesis that abstract, grammatical categories develop from concrete spatio-temporal categories (Sankoff and Laberge 1974; Sankoff 1975; Traugott 1974). I will show that, in the formation of Providence Island Creole (PIC), the *grammatical complementizer evolved from a locative or directional preposition*. More specifically I will demonstrate that the non-finite sentential complementizer *fi* evolved from a locative preposition.

Before presenting evidence in support of the hypothesis, I must point out the *fi* as a surface morpheme performs a number of syntactic functions, not all of which have been thoroughly described and analyzed in studies of Caribbean English. First, *fi* serves as a general dative preposition:

(1) *ai me fried fi i sniek.*
I was afraid of the snake.

Besides marking datives, *fi* serves to mark possession:

(2) *dem brienz fi im bettaz.*
They fooled his betters.

Also, *fi* serves as a non-finite complementizer as in (3), and as some sort of marker of obligation (4). Neither of these two functions is well described in the literature (Bailey 1966; Cassidy and LePage 1967).

(3) *ai mek fi stan op.*
I tried to stand up.

(4) *ah me fi aks dem if dem neva gi im no nurishment.*
I was supposed to ask them if they gave him any food.

The hypothesis that the complementizer *fi* evolved in creolization from a locative use of the proposition *fi* implies the broader claim that all these other functions of *fi* in PIC have similarly evolved from that preposition *fi*. A strong and empirically falsifiable claim is being made here, that all the uses of *fi* are evolutionarily related to the locative preposition. Should any one of the above uses of *fi* be found to be structurally or historically unrelated to the original preposition *fi*, that finding would be sufficient to nullify the hypothesis.

My support for the strong claim will be entirely indirect. Unlike languages like Tok Pisin or Hawaiian English, PIC has long since been completely creolized. No speakers are available who are making the sorts of syntactic extensions which would support this hypothesis. Given this lack of firsthand data, my approach will be to present evidence from surface syntactic structures of PIC which indirectly supports the hypothesis.

The conclusion which will be drawn from these indirect data is that there is no good case for any other explanation besides the claim that the *fi* complementizer evolved from the *fi* preposition. The indirect data support the proposed hypothesis, and lend no support to any alternative, e.g., that the preposition *fi* evolved from the complementizer *fi*.

Sentences (5-7) each contain an enigmatic syntactic structure. The resolution of the enigma will provide the empirical support for the proposed evolutionary relationship between preposition *fi* and complementizer *fi*.

> (5) *im drap bred skrumz fi dey fala di trak.*
>   He dropped bread crumbs so that they could follow the track.

> (6) *iz nowier fi mieri plant soka.*
>   There isn't anyplace for Mary to plant suckers.

> (7) *ah prei fi nat a suol kom.*
>   I prayed that no one would come.

The enigma may not become apparent until (5-7) are compared with (8) which exemplifies the normal Jamaican Creole (JC) subject complement construction (Bailey 1966:124), and until that JC complement construction is understood. In the JC sentence, the complement clause

> (8) *i wuda nais fi jan fi go.*
>   It would be nice for John to go.

contains a NP head which is preceded by a *fi*. A second *fi* stands to the immediate left of the non-finite verb. This double *fi* complementizer looks to be a reflex of the SE *for...to* complementizer. If we can show that this resemblance is deeper than surface syntax, then the existing analyses of English complement constructions will also serve as analyses of the JC *fi* complement construction.

It does in fact seem that all those transformations posited by either Rosenbaum (1967), Lakoff (1968) or Bresnan (1970) apply not just to English but also to JC. These syntacticians all agree that the English non-finite sentential complement is marked on the surface by a double morpheme complementizer, *for...to*. The head NP of the complement clause is transformationally removed to an oblique case as object of the preposition, like *for*, and the *to* is placed immediately to the left of the VP to mark its subjectless character. The JC sentence structure exemplified in (8) has all these central features of the parallel English construction. The double morpheme complementizer is *fi...fi*, hereafter specified as *fi-1...fi-2*. As in the English construction, the head NP of the complement clause in (8), *jan*, is transformationally placed in an oblique case as object of *fi-1*. *Fi-2* stands before the subjectless verb. Just as in the English complement construction, if the head NP of the complement clause were to be deleted by an equivalent NP deletion transformation (EQUI) (such a derivation is shown in (9), then *fi-1* must also be deleted by a later transformation.

> (9) (jan waan fi jan fi go) →
> (jan waan fi ∅ fi go) →
> (jan waan ∅ ∅ fi go)

Furthermore as in English non-finite complement clauses such as those in (10), verbs of perception are followed by an infinitive clause from which the infinitive morpheme *to* is often deleted. Sentence (11) shows that the same constraint on deleting the infinitivizing morpheme applies to JC.

> (10) I heard him speak (Bolinger 1968:125).

> (11) *im see him waak da town.*

We have, then, a description of the JC non-finite complement construction arrived at by comparing PIC complements to English complements. This description helps point out the strangeness of PIC (5-7). The fact is that PIC speakers regularly employ sentences like (5-7) rather than sentences like (8). The interesting feature of sentences (5-7) is that one, not two, *fi* morphemes appear. A comparison of the structures of sentences (12) and (13) suggests that the single *fi* in (5-7) is *fi-1* rather than *fi-2*.

> (12) ((im tel im) (no fi go raki paint))
> He told her not to go to Rocky Point.

> (13) (mek ah put (fi i no wiel mi))
> Let me place it so it won't leave wails on my skin.

Sentence (12) contains a complement clause which, on a parallel with English complements after the verb *tell,* has raised the NP head of the complement clause to the position of object of the main verb. *Fi-1* must therefore have been deleted following EQUI. The remaining *fi* which separates the negative particle from the non-finite verb must therefore be *fi-2*. In sentence (13), as in the sentences (5-7), the *fi-2* has been deleted while the *fi-1* has been retained.

Of course, it is not always the case that *fi-1* is retained in a complement clause and *fi-2* is deleted. Sentences (14 and 15) should make it clear that where the head NP of the clause has been deleted, *fi-1* is also deleted and *fi-2* is retained as the infinitivizing morpheme. *Fi-2* is deleted and *fi-1* is retained only where the head NP of the clause has not been deleted from the subordinated clause.

> (14) *an di paggl, i haad fi brok.*
> And the paddle was too strong to break.

> (15) *ai fiil fi piipi.*
> I want to pee.

This construction which appears in (5-7) is now adequately described, but some account of its transformational derivation is still required. Such an account is particularly necessary in view of the fact that PIC complement structures seem to parallel English complement structures in all but this enigmatic construction. It is not enough to say that a sentence like (16), parallel to (5-7), does not occur in English. Such a sentence is not just ungrammatical, but is flagrantly ungrammatical, and is deserving of a double asterisk. A complete analysis of PIC (5-7) should account for their acceptability in view of the unacceptability of (16) in English.

(16) **It is difficult for John to ask Oscar to keep his
     dogs at bay.

Such an accounting must have little to do with the underlying form or placement of the complementizing morphemes. We have already seen that both English and PIC have a double morpheme complementizer in corresponding underlying positions. So the different constructions must depend more on the function of the morphemes than on their form or position. As it happens, there is little agreement among authorities on English complement structures (Rosenbaum 1967; Kiparsky and Kiparsky 1970; Lakoff 1968; Bresnan 1970) regarding the function or underlying semantic value of the complementizing morphemes.

Regarding the *for* morpheme of the complementizer pair, there is disagreement over whether it is transformationally placed and therefore semantically empty (Rosenbaum 1967), or derived from a category in deep structure (Bresnan 1970). There is further argument over the surface and underlying function of that *for*. Rosenbaum (1967) sees *for* as a purely structural marker which accidentally assumes a prepositional role in the surface sentence. Kiparsky and Kiparsky (1970) suggest that *for* consistently functions as a preposition from deep through surface derivations. Bresnan (1970) and Lakoff (1968) see *for* to have a complementizer function in underlying structure but that function changes to a preposition function in surface structure. In summary there is a controversy over the semantic value of *for* and over its functioning as a preposition or as a complementizer.

There is somewhat more concord regarding the function of the *to* morpheme of the complementizer pair. Most of these syntacticians, except Rosenbaum (1967), seem to agree that *to* is dependent for its placement upon *for* (Bresnan 1970:300) and that it is placed in a string following upon and in response to the removal of the head NP of the complement clause to an oblique case. The function of the *to* then is to fill the empty subject slot and indicate the infinitival character of the VP.

Given the structural similarities between the form and placement of *fi-1...fi-2* and *for...to*, it is reasonable that the arguments for the particular functions of *for...to* should also apply to *fi-1...fi-2*. Among all these arguments, Bresnan's (1970) analysis seems to best account for the semantic distinctiveness of the *for...to* complementizer (see Bolinger 1968), and it also explains both the surface prepositional character of the *for* as well as the category relationships between the *for...to* and other complementizers. Therefore it is reasonable to argue for the extension of Bresnan's account to PIC *fi-1...fi-2*.

However, there is a major difference between the grammar of English and the grammar of PIC which precludes such a straightforward extension of Bresnan's account. PIC as a creole language possesses a grammar which has recently undergone rapid expansion the symptoms of which are still obvious in a number of grammatical irregularities (Roberts 1975; Voorhoeve 1975; Koefoed 1975). The implication of this recent expansion is that the grammatical structure of a creole language can be built upon piles driven deep into abstract structures. In recently elaborated creole languages there exists synchronic evidence for postulating deeper and more abstract structures than can be postulated for more stable languages in which processes of regularization have erased the evidence of such evolutionary developments. With regard to the *fi-1...fi-2* complementizer, this means that we can expect to look beyond Bresnan's postulation of a deep structural complementizer category, a node labeled COMP. The evidence from creoles allows us to derive that COMP node from yet deeper sources.

Such a very deep level accounting can begin by pointing out the structural and functional parallels between deep level prepositions and Bresnan's COMP category. Deep level verbs are subcategorized according to the prepositions which normally follow them, e.g., *certain of*, *blame on*, *eager for*, but not *eager of*. Similarly deep level verbs are subcategorized according to the complementizer which normally follows them, e.g., *want for*, *mean that* but not *mean for* (Bresnan 1970:304). Also deep level prepositions mark the relationship of an underlying NP to other structural units of the string. In fact Fillmore (1969) has suggested that at some very deep level, *every NP* is accompanied by a preposition which serves to relate that NP to other units of the string. Such very abstract prepositions are often realized as surface prepositions, but some are also regularly deleted depending on the function of the NP in the sentence in the particular language being analyzed. For example, the prepositions governing surface subjects and objects in English are regularly deleted. Like deep level prepositions, complementizers also function to indicate the relationship of potential underlying constituents to other units of the sentence; the difference is that a complementizer is realized just in the case where the constituent is a clause.

Mindful of these structural and functional parallels between deep level prepositions and COMP, I propose that COMP might well be considered to be a specific type of deep level preposition, namely, one which introduces an NP which is expanded into a sentence, and marks the relationship of that expanded NP to other constituents of the sentence. In short, I argue that COMP, and specifically the *for* complementizer, derives from a deep level preposition.

I have no intention of pressing this argument for the derivation of the complementizer *for* in English syntax, but there is evidence for such a derivation of the complementizer *fi* in PIC. Specifically when such an analysis is applied to PIC *fi-1...fi-2*, it seems to account for the acceptability of all the example sentences including (5-7). All uses of *fi* in PIC ultimately derive from the abstract preposition (fi).

The surface prepositional morpheme *fi*, as in sentences (1 and 2), derives without alteration of the function of that abstract category. The surface form *fi-1* undergoes a change of function in derivation, i.e., from prepositional function to complementizing function. However in the sentences of PIC that alteration of function has not gone to completion. *Fi-1* in (5-7) still performs both a prepositional and a complementizing function. In other words the one morpheme *fi-1* is simultaneously a preposition, taking the head NP of the complement clause as its object, and also a complementizer, which serves to relate the complement clause to the matrix sentence.

This extension of prepositional function to complementizing function began historically during creolization; this extension process is still being completed. The result is that one morpheme *fi* can perform two syntactic functions simultaneously. Such incomplete extensions are characteristic of recently expanded creole languages. Roberts (1975) points out a similar incomplete extension of the syntactic functions of the JC morphemes *go, se, mus, mek*. And again the morphemes *bai* and *ia* are undergoing a change of function in Tok Pisin such that for some speakers, these morphemes each perform at least two syntactic functions simultaneously.

The (fi) preposition acquires a complementizing function in creolization, thereby creating morpheme *fi-1* with a double function. In a later step in the creolization process, the complementizing function is transferred from *fi-1* to the *fi-2* morpheme, thus reducing the functional load on *fi-1*. Just as in English the *to* acquires a complementizing function from *for*, on which it depends, leaving *for* the sole function of preposition, so in the same way the *fi-2* acquires an infinitivizing complementizer in PIC. *Fi-2* takes over the complementizer function from *fi-1*.

It is not unreasonable to claim that the development of a *fi-2* infinitivizer occurs later in creolization than the development of *fi-1*. When the data from the various forms of Caribbean English are compared, it is found that everywhere the presence of a *fi-1* morpheme is predictable when the head NP of the subordinate clause has not been removed. However the presence of a *fi-2* in such cases is not predictable. *Fi-2* rarely appears in PIC and Sranan, but it regularly appears in *JC* and *Gullah*. It is reasonable to claim that the more predictable form developed earlier than the variable form.

Now we are in a position to understand the flagrant unacceptability of English (16). The *for* morpheme in English derives from an underlying complementizer node, but it assumes a purely prepositional function in English surface sentences (Kiparsky and Kiparsky 1970; Bresnan 1970). The *to* morpheme, originally dependent upon the underlying complementizer *for*, has acquired the complete task of complementizing from that *for*. Therefore surface sentences like English (16), in lacking a *to*, lack a complementizing morpheme and are therefore extremely difficult to interpret. The English derivation of the complementizer *for...to* can be characterized as having completed a shift of function. *For* completely shifts from an underlying preposition with a complementizer function to a surface preposition evidenced by the fact that the surface *for* can no longer serve as a complementizer and that the complementizing morpheme *to* is required. In PIC *fi* there is a partial and incomplete shift of function. *Fi-1* acquires a complementizing function and maintains its underlying prepositional role. Since *fi-1* can perform two surface tasks simultaneously, the *fi-2* is not necessary for interpreting the sentences (5-7).

Sentence (17) provides additional empirical evidence that the *fi-1* morpheme, while obviously functioning as a preposition, also performs a complementizing function. In the false start, the speaker of this sentence uses a *fi* morpheme which, since a head NP is missing, must be a *fi-2* infinitivizing morpheme.

(17) *im kom fi gi im--fi mi gi im uol stuori.*
He came to give him,--for me to give him old stories.

Realizing that she has encoded the wrong meaning the speaker restarts the sentence with a *fi* morpheme, presumably the same *fi* morpheme as in the false start, and she continued with an NP and a VP. The point is that the *fi* in the restart must now be a *fi-1* which evidently still carries the same complementizing function which it performed in the false start.

Some further evidence is to be found in the general construction in sentences (18 and 19). The gerund in PIC and in JC is not overtly distinguished from the infinitive, and so can only be identified where the verbal forms stand as object of a preposition. The preposition *fi* together with its variant *tu* is what is of interest in the gerund constructions in (18 and 19).

(18) *ai ken biit you fi daiv.*
I can beat you at diving.

(19) *ai gat di jab tu kliin aut jan pen.*
I have the job of cleaning out John's pen.

In most instances the preposition *fi* varies with the form *for* in the post-creole continuum. But here in (18 and 19) and regularly throughout both PIC and JC, the preposition *fi* varies with the form *to* when it introduces a gerund. That is, as PIC and JC progressively come to approximate English, *fi* varies with *to* just where the *fi* stands immediately to the left of a verb functioning as a noun. This idiosyncratic feature of decreolization is a result of hypercorrection. Speakers extend the prepositional function of *fi* to a complementizing function in one situation too many. Seeing that the *fi* preposition stands before the non-finite verb, a gerund, they interpret that *fi* as an infinitive marker. In decreolization they vary the form of that *fi* with *tu* which is the SE infinitive marker. Therefore again it is apparent that *fi* performs a double function in the mind of PIC speakers.

The History of *fi*

The evidence adduced to this point allows us to make two statements: (1) the *fi-1* morpheme in PIC performs two functions simultaneously, i.e., it does the work of a preposition and of a complementizer; and (2) the function of the *fi-1* morpheme is prior to and more basic than the function of the *fi-2* morpheme. Beyond these two statements I suggest that the prepositional function of *fi* is derivationally prior to the complementizing function. That is, an analysis of the functions of the categories underlying *fi-1* suggests that the category complementizer is derived from the category preposition.

This proposal, that the complementizing function of *fi* derives from the prepositional function of *fi*, is supported by comparative data from the language cognates of PIC. Data from PIC, JC, West African Pidgin English (WAPE), Sranan, and Twi provide sufficient material from which to reconstruct the path of historical development for the Caribbean English *fi-fo-fuh*. That path of historical development will be shown to correspond to the hypothesized direction of synchronic derivation, namely, from preposition to complementizer.

Twi, though distantly related to PIC, has been suggested as a possible source of the PIC *fi* morpheme. Edwards (1974) suggests that *fi* most likely evolved from a Twi verb *fi* which had a very flexible but clearly directional meaning, loosely to *come or go out or from* (see Christaller 1933:124). Most of the Twi meanings for *fi* imply some direction, location or reference:

> (20) *mi fi háyi*.
> I am from here.

> (21) *mé ná asém yu fi me*.
> This matter is from me (Christaller 1933:124).

Twi *fi* was the model for the development of a preposition in a pidgin which was ancestral to PIC. That preposition must have resembled WAPE *fo* since, according to Cassidy (1964, 1971), WAPE is probably similar to the pidgin from which PIC and JC evolved. Sentence (22) illustrates the use of *fo* in WAPE. The meaning of *fo* can be considerably more concrete and local than the prepositional meanings of PIC *fi*. These directional and local meanings are probably the original meaning of *fo* since the Twi verb from which *fo* derives is directional and local.

> (22) *meri tek nati com fo maket* .
> Mary came to the market at night (Agheyisi 1971:103).

In the New World Creole Sranan , we find a similar local and directional use of the preposition *fo* as shown in (23).

> (23) *dan ala den anansi kom opo fo na godo*.
> Then all the spiders came out of the gourd (Herskovits and Herskovits 1936:158).

But besides the locative uses of *fo*, *fo* is also used in both WAPE and Sranan to mark embedded sentences as in (24).

> (24) *plenti pipu di kom fo wash-am*.
> Many people are coming to wash clothes (Schneider 1966: 103).

It is interesting to note that both Schneider (1966) and Hall (1948)
would categorize the *fo* in this last sentence as a preposition.

The extension of the function of a preposition to mark infinitives
is consistent with what we know of the processes of pidginization and
creolization. In pidginization the vocabulary is reduced with the result that only the most essential semantic relations are overtly marked
(Kay and Sankoff 1974; Voorhoeve 1964:239). These most basic semantic
categories are concrete and locative rather than abstract. Moreover as
the communicative needs arise the basic vocabulary items in the pidgin
are subjected to a variety of recombinations in order to express a mul-
tiplicity of different concepts. The reason for the manipulations and
recombinations is that in pidginization "as in first language acquisition,
semantic structure, as distinct from the syntactic structure of expressive
mechanism, ... develops prior to the expressive means," and as a result
"new functions are first expressed by old forms" (Dennis and Scott 1975:
13). The new function in the case of WAPE and Sranan is infinitivizing
complementizer; the old form is the preposition *fo*. In creolization such
an extension of old forms to new functions continues to the point where
the extensions become cemented and ossified. Speakers no longer perceive
the *fo* with the new infinitivizing function to be related to the older
fo as preposition.

It is therefore consistent with the nature of cognitive development,
Fillmore's (1969) deep syntactic analysis of prepositions, and with comparative evidence from the reconstruction of the history of PIC *fi* to
claim that the *fi* complementizer has evolved from a *fi-fo* preposition.

Discussion

This argument for the prepositional provenance of the PIC complementizer *fi* is not new. It was originally proposed in Washabaugh
(1975). During the time since that first proposal, a number of analyses of creole complementizers have appeared. Some of these analyses
criticize, some of them corroborate, but none of them falsify this
argument.

The most serious criticisms are offered by Bickerton (1979). He
argues that there are no non-finite sentences in Caribbean English
Creole, concluding, quite gratuitously, that "if there are no nonfinite
sentences in PIC, then we can assume that *fi* (where it introduces a
sentential complement) is in fact a modal auxiliary" (Bickerton 1979:9).

In the course of his arguing, Bickerton admits that not "every
occurrence of *fi* in PIC is a verb." There are obviously prepositional
uses of *fi* which have probably derived from a primordial verb *fi* by a
process like serial verb reanalysis. But, he does argue that the
development of *fi* prepositions from verbs is quite independent of the
development which allows the *fi* auxiliary verb to introduce sentential
complements. Finally, Bickerton argues that true infinitive complementizer develops from the auxiliary verb *fi* during the process of decreolization.

Bickerton's observations are valuable in two respects, yet in each respect his arguments are flawed. First, his conclusion, that Caribbean English Creole basilect lacks nonfinite sentences, is probably correct; but his arguments toward that conclusion are faulty (see Washabaugh 1979). The critical sentence on which he bases his conclusion, *mi sii am a kom*, is ungrammatical, but not because the subject has been raised out of the complement sentence. This sentence is ungrammatical because, after the subject has been raised, the aspect marker remains in the complement sentence, thus violating the "specified subject condition," a putative universal constraint on the movement of particles out of embedded sentences. Thus, the sentence does nothing to demonstrate the absence of raising transformations in creoles or the absence of nonfinite sentences. But, in the end, his arguments and its flaws are unnecessary, because my description of *fi* complement clauses, which is presented here, is consonant with the observation that Caribbean English Creole lacks nonfinite sentences. My argument for the developmental priority of the *fi-1* morpheme is tantamount to an argument for the absence of nonfinite *fi* sentences in the basilects of Creole. All sentences like (5-7), in which only a *fi-1* morpheme appears, are finite sentences.

Second, Bickerton's argument that all PIC *fi*'s are developed ultimately from a verb is plausible and consistent with other developments in creolization. But his ordering of particular aspects of this developmental process is arbitrary and not well motivated. His argument that the *fi* preposition is developed through something like the reanalysis of a serial verb—perhaps a verb akin to the Twi verb *fi*—is well supported by work like Voorhoeve's (1975). But there is no equivalently solid ground for his arguing that the *fi-1* morpheme in (5-7) developed directly from the primordial verb rather than from the newly developed preposition *fi*. Bickerton's claim that the complementizer derived directly from a verb rather than from the preposition *fi* is supported only by some circumstantial evidence (such as the development of Caribbean English *go*, *kom*, and *gan* complementizers from directional verbs (Washabaugh, forthcoming), or the development of a Haitian Creole *pu* modal verb independently of the *pu* preposition (Koopman and Lefebvre 1979)). Moreover Bickerton's argument for the independent development of the *fi* complementizer from a *fi* verb fails to account for facts which corroborate the link between complementizers and prepositions in creoles. Nichols (1975) and Woolford (forthcoming) demonstrate, for Gullah and Tok Pisin, that particles which end up as infinitive complementizers exhibit close structural links to particles which serve as prepositions.

In summary, Bickerton's arguments, as well as the descriptions of complementizer developments in Washabaugh (forthcoming) and Koopman and Lefebvre (1979), require us to withhold the earlier claim, which appeared in Washabaugh (1975:130), that *all* infinitive complementizers derive from prepositions, but they do not falsify the well-supported argument that the *fi* infinitive complementizer in PIC is derived from a preposition.

NOTE

*This paper is a short version of the paper which was presented at the International Conference on Pidgins and Creoles, Hawaii, 1975, and which subsequently appeared in Vol. 17 of the Working Papers on Language Universals, 1975. I am grateful to NIMH for funding the research through which these data were collected, and to Fred Eckman, Jane Hill, Pieter Muysken, and William Stewart for their comments on the conference paper.

REFERENCES

Agheyisi, Rebecca. 1971. West African pidgin English: Simplification and simplicity. Doctoral dissertation, Stanford University.

Bailey, Beryl Loftman. 1966. Jamaican Creole Syntax: A transformational approach. Cambridge, Cambridge University Press.

Bickerton, Derek. 1979. Decreolization and the creole continuum. Paper presented at the Conference on Theoretical Orientations in Creole Studies, Virgin Islands.

Bolinger, Dwight. 1968. Entailment and meaning structures. Glosses 2(2):119-127.

Bresnan, Joan. 1970. On complementizers: Toward a syntactic theory of complement types. Foundations of Language 6:297-321.

Cassidy, F. G. 1964. Toward the recovery of early English African pidgin. Symposium on Multilingualism. (Brazzaville 1962.)

_____. 1971. Tracing the pidgin element in Jamaican creole. In: Pidginization and Creolization of Languages, ed. by Dell Hymes. Cambridge, Cambridge University Press.

Cassidy, F. G. and R. LePage. 1967. Dictionary of Jamaican English. Cambridge, Cambridge University Press. Pp. 203-221.

Christaller, Rev. Johann. 1933. A Dictionary of the Ashante and Fante Language called Tshi. Basel, Basel Evangelische Missionsgesellschaft.

Dennis, James and J. Scott. 1975. Creole formation and reorganization. Paper presented at the International Conference on Pidgins and Creoles, Honolulu, Hawaii.

Edwards, Jay. 1974. African influences on the English of San Andres Island. In: Pidgins and Creoles: Current Trends and Prospects, ed. by D. DeCamp and I. Hancock. Washington, D.C., Georgetown University Press. Pp. 1-26.

Fillmore, Charles. 1969. Towards a modern theory of case. In: Modern Studies in English, ed. by D. Reibel and S. Schane. Englewood Cliffs, New Jersey, Prentice-Hall. Pp. 361-375.

Hall, Robert. 1948. The linguistic structure of Taki Taki. Language 24:93-116.

Herskovits, Melville and F. Herskovits. 1936. Surinam Folklore. New York, AMS Press.

Kay, Paul and G. Sankoff. 1974. A language universals approach to pidgins and creoles. In: Pidgins and Creoles: Current Trends and Prospects, ed. by D. DeCamp and I. Hancock. Washington, D.C., Georgetown University Press. Pp. 61-72.

Kiparsky, Paul and C. Kiparsky. 1970. Fact. In: Progress in Linguistics, ed. by M. Bierwisch and K. Heidolph. The Hague, Mouton. Pp. 143-173.

Koefoed, Geert. 1975. A note on pidgins, creoles, and language universals. Paper presented at the International Conferences on Pidgins and Creoles, Honolulu, Hawaii.

Koopman, Hilda and C. Lefebvre. 1979. Haitian Creole pu. Paper presented at the Conference on Theoretical Orientations in Creole Studies, Virgin Islands.

Lakoff, Robin. 1968. Abstract Syntax and Latin Complementation. Cambridge, Massachusetts Institute of Technology.

Nichols, Patricia. 1975. Complementizers in creoles. Working Papers on Language Universals 19:131-136.

Roberts, Peter. 1975. The adequacy of certain theories in accounting for important grammatical relationships in a creole language. Paper presented at the International Conference on Pidgins and Creoles, Honolulu, Hawaii. [See also pp. 19-38 this volume.]

Rosenbaum, Peter. 1967. The Grammar of Predicate Complement Constructions. Cambridge, Massachusetts Institute of Technology.

Sankoff, Gillian. 1975. The origins of syntax in discourse: Some evidence from Tok Pisin. Paper presented at the International Conference on Pidgins and Creoles, Honolulu, Hawaii.

Sankoff, Gillian and S. Laberge. 1974. On the acquisition of native speakers by a language. In: Pidgins and Creoles: Current Trends and Prospects, ed. by D. DeCamp and I. Hancock. Washington, D.C., Georgetown University Press.

Schneider, Gilbert. 1966. West African Pidgin English. Athens, Ohio, University Press.

Traugott, Elizabeth C. 1974. Language change, language acquisition, and genesis spatio-temporal terms. In: Historical linguistics, ed. by J. M. Anderson and C. Jones. Amsterdam, North Holland.

Voorhoeve, Jan. 1964. Creole languages and communication. Symposium on Multilingualism. (Brazzaville 1962.)

_____. 1975. Serial verbs in creole. Paper presented at the International Conference on Pidgins and Creoles, Honolulu, Hawaii.

Washabaugh, William. 1975. On the development of complementizers in creolization. Working Papers on Language Universals 17:109-140.

_____. 1979. Brainstorming creole languages. Discussion presented at the Conference on Theoretical Orientations in Creole Studies, Virgin Islands.

_____. Forthcoming. Pursuing creole roots. Generative Studies in Creole Languages, ed. by Pieter Muysken.

Woolford, Ellen. Forthcoming. Tok Pisin syntax and semantics. Generative Studies in Creole Languages, ed. by Pieter Muysken.

A CREOLE ENGLISH CONTINUUM AND THE THEORY OF GRAMMAR

Dennis R. Craig
University of The West Indies, Jamaica

Abstract

Previous studies of continuum situations have adopted
grammatical formulations that are incapable of representing the linguistic knowledge of speakers in such
situations. What is required is a grammar that is
capable of representing the invariant conceptual elements that can underlie syntactic and lexical variation,
and that is capable of showing the relationships between
variant syntactic and lexical forms. Some proposals are
made towards such a grammar and some implications are
discussed in relation to studies of variation and studies
of socially determined differences in the use of language.

Introduction:

1.1 If it comes to making a tentative theoretical stand most of
us would probably say, like Labov:

> (1973, p. 43)
> "We will adhere for the present to the Chomskyan notion
> that the grammar might represent the knowledge that the
> native speaker needs to produce and understand the lan-
> guage in native fashion..."

[margin handwritten note: but this isn't what Chomsky believes]

> (1971, p. 465)
> "... we can use Chomsky's insights and profit tremendously
> from generative grammar, but not if we allow him to define
> for us the limits of linguistics and the shape of linguistic
> rules ..."

What is surprising is that after this vigilant and selective acceptance,
most of us proceed, contradictorily, to accept without question the most
fundamental and at the same time the most limiting of Chomsky's (1957,
1965) proposals, namely, that a grammar begins with a base component
of the specific kind suggested by Chomsky.

1.2 Bickerton (1973) for example, referring to some of the most
striking additions to sociolinguistic knowledge, makes proposals for
polylectal grammars; in form, such grammars are shown as having a
Chomskyan base component, except for a difficult-to-justify peculiar-
ity (partly derived from Ross 1969) which allows *be* as a higher predicate with its complement as a lower predicate, although there is the
simultaneous, and apparently contradictory suggestion that the copula
does not exist in deep structure; where the grammar departs from a

standard generative model is really at the level of morphophonemics, a relatively superficial level, where "spelling rules" are permuted and combined in a "rule shift" component that would account for lectal variation.

1.3 The impression is given that what we have learned about continuum speech communities: the simultaneous processing by the speaker of overlapping systems of syntax and lexis, implicational hierarchies, intra-idiolectal variation, and so on offer no new possibilities for more explanatory descriptions of the form-meaning structure of language, except at a level of description where fundamental linguistic relationships and necessary inferences about the underlying knowledge of the speaker have already been established, and all that is left to be done is the listing and ordering of the superficial markers of such relationships and knowledge. In this respect, the latter impression is probably observable in the comment of Fraser (1973:11) that:

> "... variable rules describe the observable language
> behaviour but do not explain this behaviour in any
> sense of the word 'explain' ... to stop with variable
> rules is to be satisfied with data collection and not
> explanation, much the same as demographic information
> describes but doesn't provide an explanation."

One gets the impression that although only variable rules are mentioned, the comment might also refer to implicational scales and those portions of polylectal grammars that are particularly polylectal.

1.4 It is to be noted, however, that Fraser's example of how formulations such as the latter might be given greater explanatory adequacy merely involves relating them to the general syntagtactics and phonotactics of language conceived as a static system. The possibility does not seem to be envisaged that facts relevant to variation and continuum situations might themselves justify changes in our conception of the more general or abstract grammar of language, and that it might not be wise at this stage of our knowledge to assume that variation has implications only for the ends of generative grammars.

1.5 It is to the discussion of the latter possibility that this paper seeks to make a contribution. The specific question is: what does a language continuum, as such, have to suggest about the structure of the native speaker's linguistic knowledge, and about how this structure might be represented in a grammar?

2. *Non-existence, deletion, and variable representation*

2.1 In an interview with Peter Roberts* who would normally be regarded as a teacher (--the children referred to him as "Sir"), two

---

*The Creole-language data herein referred to were collected and transcribed by Peter Roberts in the Language Education Research Project funded by the Ford Foundation at the University of The West Indies, Jamaica, and directed by the writer between 1971 and 1975.

Jamaican 12-year olds, of urban low-socioeconomic status, answered the
question: "What you would like to be when you leave school?" They
replied:

> 1) ai waan tiicha / tiicha / sor   12/1/A
>   (I want (to be/turn a) teacher, Sir)

> 2) ai waan nors.   12/1/A
>   (I want (to be/turn a) nurse)

After further conversation, the interviewer went away, and the first
child, talking to her peer (with whom she was then completely alone
except for a third child and a concealed tape recorder) remarked:

> 3) enihou ai di hier di siem taim di-man-dat
>   (Anyhow I heard the same time that man
>
>   taak bout se dat wi na-a *torn nors*/
>   (talk about, - say that we'l not turn nurse(s)
>
>   aid sie no chilron in sevn-yu kyanot
>   (I'd say no children in 7U cannot
>
>   *torn nors* / biko -
>   (turn nurse(s), because -

(And the third child interjected at this point)

> 4) wat dem gain tek *torn it*?
>   (What are they going to take and *turn it*? (i.e.
>   What are they going to do in order to *turn*
>   *nurses*?)   12/1B

The presence of /ai (instead of /mi/), /aid/, /sie/ (instead of /se/)
and other indications mark this language as mesolectal to some extent.
These children would however experience no problem in conversing with
a basilect Jamaican Creole (JC) speaker, whatever the basilect is, and
no problem either, except for unfamiliar lexis, if such occurs, in conversing with a standard English (SE) speaker. It may be said that these
children can operate quite comfortably in the Jamaican speech continuum
and respond to any speaker, so long as they themselves are left free to
produce their own brand of preferred language.

2.2 What is significant for us at the moment is the similarity
of the VP's in 1 and 2, and the difference between the latter and the
VP's italicized in 3 and 4. It is to be noted that 3 is produced by
the speaker of 1 who, in the first instance used the same VP construction as the speaker of 2, but who subsequently reinterpreted the statement of the speaker of 2 and supplied the item:

> 5) /..torn.../
>   (to turn a...)

which was originally absent in both 1 and 2.

2.3   One might ask the reason for the realization of /torn/ in 3, and its non-realization in 1 and 2.   One answer might be that the speaker of 3 had no choice at all to do otherwise.   'Become' which is synonymous in this case with 'turn' is not in the basilectal repertoire of JC and is rare even in the mesolect, and there was no item like /waan/ in 1 and 2 that could render the surface realization of /torn/ unnecessary.   But one can still ask why /torn/ can be assumed to be unnecessary in 1 and 2; it is to be noticed that the item is strictly obligatory in the SE gloss.   The answer lies in the fact that in JC, there is a rule which states as follows:

> 6)   Nouns that denote persons by occupation (which will here be taken as being in a general category of 'function-defined' nouns) become abstract nouns, denoting occupation itself when the meaning of the verb requires it.

The fact that this rule exists in JC is independently attested by the fact that function-defined nouns can often be found as direct objects of verbs which leave no possibility at all that the person rather than the occupation could be intended.   Witness for example:

> 7)   Shi lorn tu duu *taipis*   12/25/A
>   (She learn∅ to do *typist*.)
>
>   i.e. "She learned typing."

2.4   It is therefore clearly evident that so far as the speakers here relevant are concerned, the VP's in 1 and 2 could simultaneously have two surface-level representations in the acrolect, as shown in 8 and 9.   Indeed, there is a third possible representation, 10, which is ruled out only because of the discourse context.

> 8)   .... want (to do) teaching/nursing
> 9)   .... want (to be/turn a) teacher/nurse
> 10) .... want a teacher/nurse

But the behavior of the speakers gives no indication whatsoever that the deep structural representations, i.e. the meanings, of the VP's at 8 and 9 are similarly ambivalent.   Nevertheless, the speakers them-selves shift between the different surface-level representations; one shift is seen when the speaker of 1 produces /torn/ in 3; and another shift of an even more complex kind is probably seen when the third child, interrupting the speaker of 3, produces 4.   The latter sentence, although copying the verb /torn/ which requires the person rather than the occupation complement, yet contains the *tek + NP* construction that would have the SE meaning:

> 11)   With what will they turn it?

Where *tek+NP* is the normal JC representation of the SE instrument phrase.   Person and occupation together here seem to take on a com-bined significance.

2.5 To describe the linguistic knowledge of speakers who will produce 1, 2, 3 and 4 in the same discourse and at the same time understand
their SE equivalents, a grammar that can do the following things is needed.

   12) a) For a given sentence, like 2, the grammar must be
         able to specify the actual conceptual elements or
         meanings contained in 2.

       b) It must be able to show that the conceptual elements
         contained in 2 are the same as those contained in 8
         and 9.

       c) It must be able to show the relationship between the
         syntactic form of 2, and those of 8 and 9.

There are other things additionally that the grammar would need to be
able to do, like specifying the determinants of the selection of one
surface form rather than another, but these other things need not hold
our attention at the moment. It is also to be noted that, so far as
references to deep structure and surface structure in the required
grammar are concerned, the question of whether there is a formally dis-
tinguishable level of deep structure, discussed for example in Lakoff
and Ross (1967), McCawley (1968), and Chomsky (1972), would here need
to be regarded as a pointless one that should rightly be assigned, as
Bedell (1974) explains, to a controversy about grammatical notation and
terminology; 'deep structure' is what the theorist uses in order to
describe the knowledge which a speaker must have before the occurrence
of a meaningful linguistic output or the comprehension of such an output; a problem occurs only when one tries to restrict this conception
to somebody's prejudices for a specific theoretical formulation.

2.6 If a grammar can provide the specifications suggested in 12,
it might account incidentally for some paraphrase relationships of the
kind stated in Chomsky (1965) as being unaccounted for in grammatical
models at that time, and that still remain unaccounted for after the
passing of the 1970s. It is not yet clear whether such a grammar might
earn the stricture stated in Bickerton (1973:22) of committing creoles
unjustifiably to the Indo-European camp, although it is to be noted
that in the particular continuum here relevant, the unified and smoothly
integrated movement of individuals between basilect and acrolect means
that the individual has an implicit and very active knowledge of the
correspondence between whatever is in his basilect and whatever is its
representation in the Indo-European camp. The possibility is that the
latter and all other possible camps might be closely unified in terms
of the knowledge of any speaker.

3. *The minimal SVO sentence*

3.1 In the search for a grammar that might be able to do the
things just stated, certain characteristics of the continuum that seem
to have a bearing on base-level sentence structure ought possibly to be
investigated. The present discussion can examine only one set of these

characteristics: some alternative forms of the SVO sentence, but it is
hoped that this will provide a direction for further investigation.

3.2   In JC (cf. Bailey, 1966), there is a passive voice which is
not separately marked morphologically so as to be distinguished from the
active, and there is no 'by'-passive phrase.   Bailey (1966:81) does not
refer to it as a passive voice at all, but regards it as resulting from
an optional transformation by which the direct object becomes subject
as a preliminary to the verb becoming adjectivalized.   However, since
there is a structure with which it might be compared at the opposite
pole of the continuum, we will here retain the term 'passive voice'.
Examples are as follows:

    13)   it tek out   12/5/B
        (It has been taken out)

    14) shi ..... get chruu wan shaat-kot we sel fish
        (She..... got through a short-cut where fish is sold)
                            12/12/B

    15) shi mus gyet biit   12/28/A
        (She must be beaten)

3.3   One might ask how the basilectal speaker/hearer distinguishes
between active and passive.   The answer is that he/she makes that distinction solely by the presence or absence of direct objects and by the
animateness restrictions that are obligatory in the subjects or objects
of transitive verbs.   Thus, a passive voice interpretation is obligatory for (13) because no direct object is present.   In (14), the antecedent of /we/ is /shaat-kot/ which can be regarded as the subject of
/sel/; this means that the subject being not only -animate but also
impossible as agent of /sel/, and the direct object /fish/ being present
in the sentence, it becomes obligatory to interpret the verb as being
in the passive voice, since an active-voice interpretation is nonsensi-
cal in that context.

3.4   By similar conventions, a sentence such as:

    16)   Bari lik ; (lik = 'hit')

would be difficult to interpret in JC, because it could be active or
passive unless there was some elucidatory context.   Nevertheless it might
still receive some interpretation because some exclusion of unlikely
meanings is still possible.   If the sentence was intended to mean "Barry
hits" (i.e. habitually or usually), it would most likely be:

    17)   Bari lik piipl
        (Barry hits people)

and if a passive-voice meaning was intended, the sentence could possibly, though not obligatorily be:

18) *Either* (a)   Bari get lik
                 (Barry was hit.   Literally: Barry got hit)

     Or   (b)   dem lik Bari
                 (Barry was hit: Literally: They hit Barry)

However, if the subject of 16 was changed so as to give a sentence like this one:

19)   di guot lik
     (the goat was hit)

it is practically certain that the sentence would receive an immediate passive-voice interpretation, without any context being necessary, since the nature of the subject 'goat' and its animateness status makes such an interpretation practically obligatory.

3.5   These facts about the JC passive concern *activity* as distinct from *stative* verbs.   In the former (i.e. activity) verbs what seems very important, and what seems to underlie the speaker's reliance on animateness restrictions and the presence or absence of likely subjects and direct objects, is the concept 'do' in its activity as distant from its auxiliary-verb sense.   This activity 'do' concept seems very strong in the relevant verbs as the well-known SE restriction seen in 20 and 21 shows:

20)   What Barry did was hit the goat
21)   *What Barry did was like the goat

In the examples the activity 'do' concept, which is focussed upon, is present in (20) but not in (21), hence the respective well-formedness in one   case and deviance in the other.   It could be said then that in JC the interpretation of a passive voice is possible only if the subject of the verb is incompatible, for one reason or another, with the inherent activity--'do' concept of the relevant transitive verb.

3.6   From these facts, it seems possible to describe the meaning of an activity, SVO, sentence such as

22)   Bari lik di guot
     (Barry hit the goat)

as consisting of two separate components. The first component would consist of an NP linked to the activity- 'do' concept and the second component would consist of another NP linked to a concept or a set of concepts that is stative in its meaning (as a passive-voice verb is) and that embodies the result of the activity in the first component. The linkage between the two components, in order to embody the meaning that the activity in the first component is 'causal' or directed toward achieving the state in the second, needs to be more than just coordinate linkage.   It is suggested therefore that the linkage between the two components is of the same kind as that indicated sometimes by the complementiser 'that' when it follows the deictic or rudimentary manner-adverb

'so' in natural language.   The components may be diagrammed as in (23),
where stative-VP can possibly be a complex of coordinately-linked
stative VP's in the form: *stative-VP and VP and VP .....*:

23)   (NP$_1$ activity-'do so' (NP$_2$ stative-VP))

Since the level of the representation of (23) is a conceptual one, it
seems best at the moment that the concepts be labelled as shown, to
avoid misunderstandings.

3.7   The deep structure shown in (23) can provide a derivation for
varied surface-level results depending on whehter the speaker has the
deep-level intention of topicalizing NP$_1$ or NP$_2$.   Topicalization (TOP)
is here conceived as an 'intention', similar in its grammatical status
to Q, Imp and other indicators of the speaker's purpose commonly used
in current grammatical models.   It is conceived that an ordered set of
topicalizations is, at least in SE, possible within the same sentence.
Possibly, one deep-level difference between JC and SE is that JC does
not allow secondary topicalization as shown in (24c) below, while SE
does.   The conception of the role of topicalization here suggested is
not incompatible with that stated in Fillmore   (1968, 4.4) for example,
although the conclusions about the necessary form of a grammar are
different.   The surface results of the varied placing of topicalizations on the elements in (23), using the lexical content of (22), are
shown in (24).

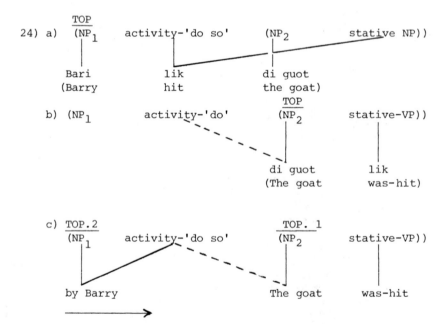

3.8   It is well known, although it is generally ignored in current grammatical models, that the active and passive voice forms of the
apparently same sentence do not have exactly the same meaning.   The
difference in meanings lies in the topicalization intent of the speaker
as here suggested.   It is further suggested that the varied placing of

topicalizations on the verb elements in the conceptual, base sentoids, as well as the possibilities for all types of topicalization to be affected by the specific contexts of sentences, would result in some of the different forms of 'split' sentence that are well known. Inherent in these proposals is the suggestion that increased explanatory adequacy in a grammar requires that a single base-level representation must be capable of giving rise to a variety of surface derivations in such a way that each separate surface result might be shown to originate in some specific motivation, like topicalization or focus or question for example, of the speaker.

   3.9   One might ask how the proposal in (24) would apply in the case of stative, transitive verbs, from which the activity-'do so' concept is obviously missing, as illustrated in (21). It is very significant that the JC basilect allows no passivization of stative verbs. For example:

   25) They liked Barry
   26) Barry was liked (by them).
   27) /dem laik Bari/.
   28) * /Bari laik/; * /Bari get laik/
   29) They liked the ice cream
   30) The ice cream was liked (by them).
   31) dem laik di ais kriim
   32) * /di ais kriim laik/

where, although (25) and (27) in one instance and (29) and (31) in the other are parallel acceptable sentences at opposite extremes of the continuum, their passivizations (26/28) and (30/32) respectively are not. Because of this, it would not be justifiable to suggest a deep structure approximately to (24) for stative, transitive verbs; that this should be so is not surprising because surface differences of the kind relevant here between stative verbs and other verbs ought to have deep structural origins or consequences (whichever term is preferred); to indicate the latter by the device + *stative* is probably description, but certainly not explanation. The required deep structure would need to reflect the fact that a stative, transitive verb generally represents some affective or sensory characteristic of its subject, and the relationship of subject-NP to object-NP is generally no more than that the latter is in existence as the topic of the sensory or affective characteristics of the former. These facts may possibly be captured within the format of the two-sentoid configuration used in (23), and illustrated as in (33) using the lexical content of (29).

33) a)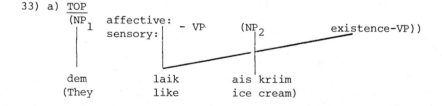

b) *JC procedure with topicality on NP$_2$*

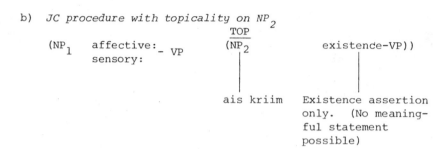

c) *SE procedure with topicality on NP$_2$*

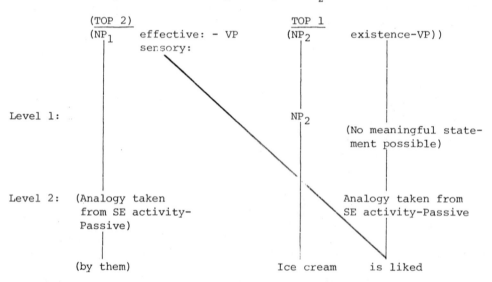

3.10   The illustration is intended to suggest that the sentence in (33 a) can occur at both ends of the continuum, but that the basilectal speaker, if he/she seeks to topicalize NP$_2$, as shown in (33 b) will find a blockage because the deep level VP that is related to NP$_2$ gives no possibility of a meaningful statement; the basilectal speaker will be forced to choose some other communication alternative. The acrolectal speaker, on the other hand, finding the same blockage, is permitted by the conventions of his language to take an analogy from the format of the activity-Passive, as shown in (33 c), with the result that a passivization of the affective/sensory-VP of the first sentoid takes place. It is possible that the acrolect allows this freedom to choose a structural analogy merely because it possesses a greater quantity of near-surface structural devices, while the basilect, on the other hand, cannot do the same because its surface structures remain closer in form to the general conceptual base underlying language.

3.11   Many other facts about transitive and intransitive-verb behavior at polar extremes of the continuum seem explainable within this framework. For example, Fillmore (1968:4) mentions the difficulty of explaining the deviance in (37).

34) John ruined the table
35) John built the table
36) What John did to the table was ruin it.
37) * What John did to the table was build it.

Apart from the pragmatic reality mentioned by Fillmore that whether
the object existed before or after the action has something to do with
the deviance, there is also the related fact of the conceptual difference between 'do' and 'do to'; the former represents a link between the
subject and the verb, and can apply irrespective of whether the object
existed before the action; the latter, on the other hand, represents a
link between the activity - 'do so' concept and the object itself, and
needs the prior existence of the object before it can be realized. This
fact is diagrammed in (24 b) and (24 c) by the broken line which links
the activity - 'do so' concept of the first sentoid to the NP of the
second sentoid. This link would of necessity be absent conceptually
in verbs like 'build', and it would also be absent in stative verbs
like 'like', as is suggested in the diagrams at (33). An extension
of this single explanation takes care of another kind of transitive-
verb behavior that does not seem adequately explainable in current
grammatical models: this is the difference in meaning between different forms of those transitive verbs (otherwise, causative verbs) whose
direct objects can become subjects of the verbs with or without passivization as in (38, 39, 40). In basilect JC, all three of the latter
sentences would be expressed as in (41).

38) The stick broke

39) The stick was broken (i.e. it is known that
    someone broke the stick)

40) The stick was broken (i.e. the stick was found in
    a broken state)

41) JC: /di stik brok/.

3.12 The relevant extension of the explanation is as follows:
For (38), the speaker entertains no activity - 'do so' concept at all
and 'broke' is practically stative in its meaning. If it is to be
diagrammed, it would need to be shown as having the same form as the
right-hand (or second) sentoid of (23), standing alone without a first
sentoid; but in its context (i.e. discourse context), there would need
to be some indication that someone witnessed the 'breaking'. The deep
structure of (40) would be similar, except that the discourse context
would have to exclude a witness. Example (39) however, would have a
deep structure similar to (24 b), necessitating two sentoids with the
NP of the first being indefinite and with a link between the activity
- 'do so' and 'stick'. So far as (41), the JC surface representation
is concerned, the deep structures would vary in the same way as just
explained, although the surface form would remain invariable. It
might be additionally pointed out that the explanation here given of
(39) and (40) applies not just to 'causative' verbs of the 'break/
burn/roll' variety, but to the passive forms of all transitive verbs
which permit a similar ambiguity (e.g. "The door was shut") not so

far adequately explained in current grammatical models. Although
Hasegawa (1968) takes them into account in his treatment of the passive which involves also a complementised second sentoid at a base
level, he does so without any splitting into component concepts as
is suggested here.

3.13 The preceding proposals can easily accommodate an account
of the instrument phrase that is optional with transitive verbs.   In
this respect, it is very significant that in the JC basilect, the
acrolectal *'with'* + *Instrument NP* is most often expressed as /tek/ +
NP as in (42).

> 42) shi tek tamrin wip an biit di children   12/28/A
>
> (She took a tamarind whip and beat the children
> i.e. She beat the children with a tamarind whip)

It is not at all unlikely that this basilectal form should represent
the deep structural origin of the instrument phrase, which at a surface level in the acrolect would become represented as a preposition-
phrase; and in grammatical terms, it would mean no more than the
addition of a single sentoid to the two that would normally represent
a single SVO sentence without the instrument phrase. The deep structure of (42) may be diagrammed as in (43) for example.

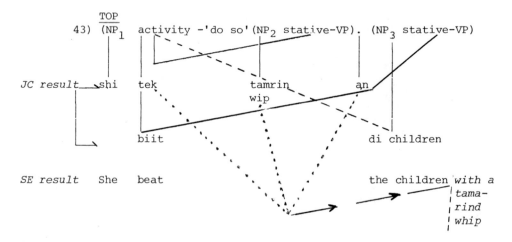

3.14 It seems deserving of more than a passing note that both agentive
'by' and instrumental-'with', the preposition phrases that obligatorily
need to be taken into account in the grammar of the transitive verb,
have been reduced within the present proposals to a common origin in
deep-level sentoids. Without further discussing the question at this
time, the strongly intuitive difference between the latter propositions
(i.e. 'by' and 'with') and other prepositions can therefore be accounted
for. It will also be noted that the well-known possibilities of the instrument NP taking on the role of subject are well accommodated within
the present proposals, since the sentoids containing the instrumental
and object NP's can combine to produce an SVO sentence having the form

of (23) except that the first sentoid would not in this case contain
activity- 'do so'; the fact that activity- 'do so' would thus be absent
however would be reflected in surface structure by the tendency towards
deviance which is observable in (44b) when understood in conjunction
with (44a) and (44c), taken from Fillmore (1968:22). What Fillmore
labels as case relationships is here dissected so as to show the conceptual constituents of such relationships.

> 44) a) John broke the window with a hammer.
>   b) **What a hammer did was break the window.
>   c) A hammer broke the window.

3.15   One of the facts about a sentence like (44a) which does not
seem to have been particularly noticed in previous treatments is the
lack of communication in the sentence about what the subject NP (in this
case 'John') really did. In purely pragmatic terms, he must have held
the hammer and imparted force to it, but after that he might either have
continued holding it or he might have thrown it. All that we know is
that he must have done something or other (i.e., activity- 'do so'), and
it was the hammer really (together with the window) that was really
directly involved in the pragmatic result that we label 'broke'. In the
present treatment, these pragmatic necessities, which after all must be
the basis of conceptualization and language, seem to be correctly represented by the fact that it is in the sentoids of the instrumental and
object NP's that the content of the verbs reside, and in the 'stative'
form that a pragmatic result would necessarily be in; the 'active'
principle, on the other hand, which needs to merge with the 'stative' one
to produce the full meaning of a transitive verb, resides in the sentoid
of the agent or subject.

3.16   The preceding proposals seem capable of providing a basis for
describing the deep grammar of transitive, partially transitive and intransitive verbs according to the ways they function at both extremes of
the continuum. In the case of the partially transitive and intransitive
verbs, one necessary modification in the structural description would be
that the NP in the second sentoid would be a repeat of the one in the
first. However, there are a number of verbs of several different kinds
that would need to be described by more complex extensions of the basic
two-sentoid pattern so far suggested, but the scope of the present paper
forbids a more detailed discussion. What has emerged so far in relation
to the Creole-English continuum is as follows:

> 45) a) An explanation of the simultaneous processing of
>   multiple surface-level representations of an in-
>   variant underlying meaning or concept requires
>   that a grammatical base consisting of primitive
>   conceptual elements, all selected from natural
>   language, should first be postulated.
>
>   b) The behavior of the minimal SVO sentence in the
>   Creole-English continuum suggests that stative
>   verbals (including some classes of affective and
>   secondary verbals), the concepts 'and', 'do' and
>   'so', the 'that'-clause relationship between sen-
>   tences, a number of *intentions* (*Top*, Q etc.) which

speakers are known to express, the concept 'not',
the concept NP (or in non-syntactic terms 'entity'),
and the combination of *NP ('be') Verbal* are some of
the primitive conceptual elements in the grammatical
base.

c) Specific combinations of the conceptual elements of
the grammatical base or, in other terms, segments of
base sentences, can be lexically re-labelled so that
the conceptual elements of the base remain as the
ultimate meanings of the lexical terms.

4.   *Hypotheses towards a grammar*

4.1   The preceding conclusions, while suggesting the possibility of
analyzing the internal content of verbals into component conceptual elements, have made no similar suggestion about nouns.   In relation to nouns,
the same possibility is implied, nevertheless, not only by what has so far
been said here, but by the well-known fact that the selectional restrictions of nouns are themselves stative predicates, and that they create
the practical effect of making nouns, in ordinary grammar, appear to be
no more than a syntactic category symbol (in this case NP, a mere concept of 'entity') followed by certain defining predicates in the general
form:

46)
NP (be-)count *and* (be-)animate *and* (be-)male *and* ...
        mass   inanimate   female
        singular
        plural

Katz and Fodor, in their well-known formulations, suggested in effect that
all the meaning of any given noun might be represented by the isolation of
additional features, whether syntactic or semantic.   The latter suggestion however has never become practicable, for the important reason that,
as suggested in Bolinger (1965) for example, a potentially infinite number of features would need to be determined.   On the surface, this fact
would seem to militate as well against the present proposal.   On further
consideration, however, it becomes evident that the potential ininfinity
of semantic features comes from the fact that the dictionary definition
of the noun can interact with a potentially infinite number of contextual
elements and create the illusion of a potentially infinite number of
semantic features within the noun.   In short, the potential infinity
lies in external contexts, and not in the internal features of the noun.
This discussion, again, cannot be taken further on this occasion, but
sufficient has been said to indicate the general directions of the
present hypotheses, quite apart from the validity or invalidity any
proposals of a different kind such as those in Bach (1968), for example.

4.2   Another area that needs some incidental clarification before
the form of a grammar can be outlined is that which concerns the distinction between stative and active verbals.   Schachter (1973), for
example, questions the empirical basis of the distinction and suggests
that the three criteria, acceptability of the imperative, the *do-*

something contribution, and the progressive, by which the stative-active distinction is supposed to be determined, do not give consistent results with assumedly stative or active items. In support of this contention Schachter cites (47, 48 and 49):

47) a. Be here at six o'clock.
    b. What you'll do is be here at six o'clock.
    c. *You're being here at six o'clock.

48) a. *Miss the parade.
    b. What you'll do is miss the parade.
    c. You're missing the parade.

49) a. Remember to write.
    b. *Don't remember to write.
    c. Forget to write.
    d. Don't forget to write.

These examples, however, contrary to Schachter's suggestions, provide no evidence against the consistency of the stative-active distinction since in each case the critical lexical item in the starred sentence is semantically different from its counterpart in the unstarred sentences, although it shares a common phonological shape. In each case, what distinguishes a genuinely stative meaning of a given phonological shape from an active meaning of the same phonological shape is that the stative meaning cannot be regarded as referencing any behavior that is within the voluntary control or subject to the will of the subject of the verbal. Schachter understood this and stated it in effect, but he did not consider shifts of meaning from one example to another.

4.3 With the use of conventional symbols so far as possible, the rules of the proposed grammatical base may now be outlined as follows:

50)

$$S \rightarrow [NP \ VP(S)] \ (and \ S)$$

$$NP \rightarrow \begin{Bmatrix} I \\ something \\ S \end{Bmatrix} \ (and \ NP)$$

$$VP \rightarrow \left(not \begin{Bmatrix} (be) \begin{Bmatrix} Adj \\ Pred. \ Adv. \\ Deictic \\ S \end{Bmatrix} \\ V \ [S] \end{Bmatrix} \right) \ (and \ VP)$$

Adj.→ <u>Sensation</u>: black, blue ... bitter, sweet ... good
<u>Shape, size, number, quantity</u>: broad, deep ... big, little ... more, less ... one, two ... many, several ... first, second ... some, all ...

```
Pred. Adv.  →  Location:   somewhere, everywhere ... in, on ...
                           belong ...

               Time:       now, then ...

   Deictic  →  Manner:     so

      V     →  Sensation:  feel, hear, see ... sound ...

               Psychological:  afraid, angry, pleased ... hat,
                               like, want ... believe, know, think ...
                               mean ...

               Activity:   do (so)
```

4.4   Apart from being consistent with the conclusions earlier reached, the constituents of the proposed grammatical base reflect a certain funda- mental relationship between language and human cognition which has never, so far, been reflected in grammatical formulations, despite Chomsky's repeated assertions to the effect that language is a part of human psychol- ogy. If the latter assertions are true, then linguistic structure must in its fundamental aspects be parallel to the structure of conceptualiza- tion, and must be based upon the details of human sensory perceptions and human cognitive abilities. It seems extremely significant that lexical labels for such perceptions and abilities are marked in a special way by the *stative* characteristic, and it ought to be natural that those lexical items and the relationships inherent in them (like the relationships of NP VP, VP[S], and 'and') should represent the base of the human faculty of language, as is here suggested.

4.5   A natural-language sentence represented in terms of the suggested base would of necessity appear as an apparently cumbersome string of possibly numerous two-part sentoids, but the cumbersomeness of this base string would be of the same nature as that of the machine language of a computer as compared with the elegance of a sophisticated programming language for the same computer; the computer would be incapable of functioning however unless the elegant programming language can be trans- lated into the cumbersome machine language. From the given base, the grammar would operate by a succession of simultaneously lexical and syn- tactic re-labellings as aimed at in (45c). For this to happen all that is further necessary is a stratified lexicon in which

(1)   the meanings or conceptual content of items of the first stratum will be represented only in terms of base items,

(2)   the content of items of each stratum after the first will be represented primarily in terms of items from the immediately preceding stratum in conjunction, only to such an extent as is absolutely necessary, with items from any farther-removed, preceding stratum, including the base.

4.6   In passing it may be noted that there are two main sets of con- straints on the form of the proposed grammar and that taken together they are very stringent, although the present outline cannot adequately make

them obvious.   Firstly, the form and content of the base is constrained
by our hypothesis concerning the nature of the relationship between language and other psychological abilities, and at the same time by empirical linguistic phenomena, such as those discussed in sections 2 and 3,
irrespective of what our hypotheses are.   Secondly, because, in order
for the grammar to operate, segments of base-level strings need to
correspond precisely with actual meanings in the lexicon, there are constraints on the form of each lexical entry, the order of entries and the
structure of the lexicon as a whole.   In short, the production of an
actual grammar along the suggested lines would require a far more precise specification of syntactic relationships and lexical meanings than
has probably been undertaken in any language so far.

   4.7 It would seem that the utmost economy of the grammar can be
assured only if the lexicon is structured in the way suggested.   Strings
of base sentoids would be processed syntactically and lexically by being
'passed', again as aimed at in (45c), through the successive strata of
the lexicon.   The nature of each stratum may be summarized in its respective order as follows:

51) Configurations of sentoids (S or S_{not} indicating affirmative
    or negative) would be evaluated so that logical relation-
    ships might become labelled and an incidental reduction in
    the number of sentoids be thereby achieved.   Example of an
    entry:

   S_1 *and* S_2 *and* ... *expect*$[S_2$ *and* $S_{1_{not}}$ $]$

   $\rightarrow S_1$ *although* S_2

52) Strings of base VP's will become re-labelled as higher-order
    stative VP's.
    General result of a pass through this stratum:

   ... V_1 *and* V_1 $(... $*and*$ V_1) \rightarrow ... V_2 (... $*and*$ V_1)$

      $V_2 \rightarrow$ beautiful ... animate, born ... intelligent ...
             break, burn, move ... (stative meanings only)

53) A series of strata, through which 'passing' will
    have general results as follows:

   i) $[NP_1 ...$do-so $[NP_1 ... V]] \rightarrow [NP_1 ...V_1]$

      $V_1 \rightarrow \begin{bmatrix} \textit{arrive, come, go}... \\ \textit{run, walk} ... \end{bmatrix}$

ii) $[NP_1 \ldots do\text{-}so [\ldots N_2 \ldots V]]$

$$\rightarrow \left\{ \begin{array}{l} [NP_1 \ldots V_t \ NP_2 \ldots] \ / \ \text{Topicalization of } NP_1 \\ [NP_2 \ldots be\text{-}V_t \qquad NP_1 \ldots] \ / \ \text{Topicalization of } NP_2 \end{array} \right\}$$

$$Vt \rightarrow \left[\begin{array}{l} \text{hit, push} \ldots \\ \text{eat, smoke} \ldots \\ \text{elect, choose} \ldots \\ \text{hold, keep, put} \ldots \end{array} \right]$$

iii) $[NP_1 \ldots be\text{-}so [NP_2 \ldots be\text{-}V_{possess}]]$
adv.

$$\rightarrow \left\{ \begin{array}{l} [NP_1 \ldots have \ NP_2 \ldots] \ / \ \text{Topicalization of } NP_1 \\ [NP_2 \ldots be\text{-}Prep. \ NP_1 \ldots] \ / \ \text{Topicalization } NP_2 \end{array} \right\}$$

iv) $[NP_1 \ldots V_{sensation} \qquad [NP_1 \ldots be\text{-}V]]$
$\phantom{iv)   [NP_1 \ldots V_{}}$ desideration $ V$

$$\rightarrow \left\{ \begin{array}{l} [NP_1 \ldots \left\{ \begin{array}{l} V_{sensation} \ Adj \\ V_{desideration} \ \text{'to'-Infin.} \end{array} \right\}] \ / \ \begin{array}{l} \text{Topicalization} \\ \text{of first occur-} \\ \text{rence of } NP_1 \end{array} \\[2em] [NP_1 \ldots V_{sensation} \ (that) \ NP_1 \ be\text{-}V] \ / \ \begin{array}{l} \text{Primary} \\ \text{and} \\ \text{secondary} \\ \text{topicaliza-} \\ \text{tion} \\ \text{respectively of} \\ \text{the two occur-} \\ \text{rences of } NP_1 \end{array} \end{array} \right.$$

54) A series of strata, through which 'passing' will result
a labelling of nouns, pronouns (including relatives), and
so on, with general results as follows:

i) $[NP \ (be\text{-})V \ldots and \ (be\text{-})V] \ \rightarrow \left\{ \begin{array}{l} [NC + Plu] \ / \ NP \ldots be\text{-}many \\ [\text{Indef. Article} + Nc] / \ NP \ldots be\text{-}one \\ Nc \end{array} \right\}$

ii) $[(\text{Indef.Art})\text{Nc}_1 \ldots (\text{Indef.Art})\text{Nc}_1] \rightarrow (\text{Indef.Art})\text{Nc}_1 \ldots \begin{Bmatrix} \text{Def.Art Nc}_1 \\ \text{Pronoun} \\ \\ \text{Wh-/Focus on} \\ \text{first Nc}_1 \end{Bmatrix}$

iii) $\text{Nc} \rightarrow \begin{Bmatrix} \text{N}_{\text{an/NP}} \ldots \textit{be-'animate'} \\ \\ \text{N}_{\text{inan}} \end{Bmatrix}$

iv) $\text{N}_{\text{an}} \rightarrow \begin{Bmatrix} \text{N}_{\text{hu/NP}} \ldots \textit{be-so and I be-so} \\ \\ \text{N}_{\text{an}} \end{Bmatrix}$

v) $\begin{Bmatrix} \text{N}_{\text{hu}} \\ \\ \\ \text{N}_{\text{an}} \end{Bmatrix} \rightarrow \begin{Bmatrix} \text{N}_{\text{f/NP}} \ldots \textit{be-so}[\text{NP}_2 \text{ belong] mean } [[\text{NP}_3 \ldots \text{be-'born']be-within]} \\ \qquad\qquad\qquad\qquad\qquad\qquad\qquad\qquad\qquad \text{be-possible} \\ \qquad\text{(i.e., has a characteristic indicating that the} \\ \qquad\text{bearing of offspring is possible)} \\ \\ \text{N}_{\text{m}} \end{Bmatrix}$

4.8   At the end of this fourth series of lexical passes, most sentence forms, including the passive voice, and with all the contingent lexis except abstract nouns and nominalizations, would have been generated.   It is envisaged that further processes dependent on the form of lexical items, as well as some processes involving rearrangements of syntactic components of sentences, would continue to apply in the grammar to produce all possible items of syntax and lexis, but discussion of these is impossible here.   It is hoped, however that the preceding outline is adequate to suggest the general form of the grammar that seems necessary if phenomena of the mind earlier illustrated in the Creole-English continuum are to be accounted for.

4.9   In such accounting within the envisaged grammar differentiation between part-of-speech categories would no longer be the barrier it now is to the specification of content relationships between differently structured sentences.   Apart from the strictly theoretical significance of this, there are important practical implications that are particularly crucial in continuum and similar situations where inferences about the cognitive and intellectual capacities of differently socialized speakers sometimes tend to be made on the basis of syntactic and lexical characteristic.   A whole educational tradition going back to the early 60's (based on the earlier works of Bernstein and works such as those in the USA criticized in Labov [1970]) which makes inferences from social-class differences in lexis and syntax, has grown up in such situations.   In such situations as shown in Craig (1974) for example, procedures of linguistic analysis which permit a principled assessment of the underlying conceptual content of sentences, irrespective of syntactic and lexical variation, are urgently needed.

REFERENCES

Alatis, J. (ed.) 1970. Report of the twentieth annual round table meeting on linguistics and language studies. Washington, D.C., Georgetown University Press.

Bach, E. 1968. Nouns and noun phrases. In: Universals in linguistic theory, ed. by E. Bach and R. T. Harms, pp. 91-122. New York, Holt, Rinehart and Winston, Inc.

Bach, E., and R. T. Harms (eds.) 1968. Universals in linguistic theory. New York, Holt, Rinehart and Winston, Inc.

Bailey, B. 1966. Jamaican creole syntax. Cambridge, Cambridge University Press.

Bedell, G. 1974. The arguments about deep structure. Language 50:423-445.

Bernstein, B. 1961. Social structure, language and learning. Educational Research, 3, U.K.

Bickerton, D. 1973. The structure of polylectal grammars. In: Report of the twenty-third annual round table meeting on linguistics and language studies, ed. by R. W. Shuy, pp. 17-42. Washington, D.C., Georgetown University Press.

Bolinger, D. L. 1965. The atomization of meaning. Language 41:555-573.

Chomsky, N. 1957. Syntactic structures. The Hague, Mouton.

_____. 1965. Aspects of the theory of syntax. Cambridge, Mass., MIT Press.

_____. 1970. Remarks on nominalization. In: Readings in English transformational grammar, ed. by R. Jacobs and P. S. Rosenbaum, pp. 184-221. Waltham, Mass., Ginn and Co.

_____. 1972. Studies on semantics in generative grammar. The Hague, Mouton.

Craig, D. 1974. Developmental and social class differences in language. Caribbean Journal of Education 4(3):5-23. University of the West Indies, Jamaica.

Fillmore, C-J. 1968. The case for case. In: Universals in linguistic theory, ed. by E. Bach and R. T. Harms, pp. 1-88. New York, Holt, Rinehart and Winston, Inc.

Fraser, B. 1973. Optional rules in a grammar. In: Report of the twenty-third annual round table meeting on linguistics and language studies, ed. by R. W. Shuy, pp. 1-15. Washington, D.C., Georgetown University Press.

Hasegawa, K. 1968. The passive construction in English. Language 44:230-243.

Hymes, D. (ed.) 1971 Pidginization and creolization of languages. Cambridge, Cambridge University Press.

Jacobs, R., and P. S. Rosenbaum (eds.) 1970. Readings in English transformational grammar. Waltham, Mass., Ginn and Co.

Katz, J. and J. Fodor. 1963. The structure of a semantic theory. Language 39:170-210.

Labov, W. 1971. The notion of 'system' in creole languages. In: Pidginization and creolization of languages, ed. by D. Hymes, pp. 447-472. Cambridge, Cambridge University Press.

_____. The logic of non-standard English. in: Report of the twentieth annual round table meeting on linguistics and language studies, ed. by J. Alatis, pp. 1-43. Washington, D.C., Georgetown University Press.

_____. 1973. Where do grammars stop? In: Report of the twenty-third annual round table meeting on linguistics and language studies, ed. by R. W. Shuy, pp. 43-88. Washington, D.C., Georgetown University Press.

Lakoff, G. 1970. Irregularity in syntax. New York, Holt, Rinehart and Winston.

Lakoff, G., and J. R. Ross. 1967. Is deep structure necessary? Indiana University, Linguistics Club.

McCawley, J. D. 1968. The role of semantics in grammar. In: Universals in linguistic theory, ed. by E. Bach and R. T. Harms, pp. 124-169. New York, Holt, Rinehart and Winston, Inc.

Ross, J. R. 1969. Auxiliaries as main verbs. Journal of Philosophical Linguistics, Evanston, Illinois.

Schachter, P. 1973. On syntactic categories. Indiana University, Linguistics Club.

Shuy, R. W. (ed.) 1973. Report of the twenty-third annual round table meeting on linguistics and language studies. Washington, D.C., Georgetown University Press.

BAHAMIAN ENGLISH--A NON-CONTINUUM?

Alison Shilling
University of Hawaii
and
College of the Bahamas

1. *Introduction*

In studying the speech of the Bahama Islands, reference must obviously be made to existing studies of probably similar speech communities. Geographically and historically these islands lie between the United States mainland and the English-speaking Caribbean; the current debate about the Creole continuum and its applicability to U.S. Black English (BE) is therefore of relevance to the study of the Bahamian language. Also, if the Bahamas can also be placed linguistically between these two territories, it may well shed some light on this debate.

I feel that two questions in particular should be considered to place Bahamian language in a wider perspective: first, what is the relationship of Black and White speech in this community compared with that in similar communities in the U.S. and Caribbean? Second, through analyses of Black speech in these territories, as well as the Bahamas, can the broad lines of a creole/post-creole continuum be drawn for the area as a whole, and what relationship would this have to the White speech of the area?

2. *Related Studies*

Studies of Black speech in the Caribbean are quite comprehensive[1]; White speech, on the other hand, has hardly been treated (the one exception I know of is Ryan [1973]). The reason for this may well be that there are so few Whites in those countries that it can safely be assumed their linguistic influence is negligible; alternatively, they may be clustered almost exclusively at the top of the social-class 'pyramid', so that their speech is acrolectal and hence is identified with the Jamaican English or other 'Standard' which is the 'target' of the continuum.

Black English in the States has more often been compared to Standard than to conversational speech of similar White communities. Wolfram has made comparisons (1973) for Mississippi, but merely of the verb 'to be'. Labov (1968) compared his Black teenagers' speech with that of White New Yorkers; however, Black speech in New York is usually considered to be a transplanted Southern variety, so that Black and White in the North would be expected to be distinct from each other, with or without Creole origins being postulated for the former.

It is difficult for an outsider to gain a clear picture of the Black/White speech relationships in the Southern U.S. Dillard (1972: 216) states a belief that 'Negro dialect' influenced White, but quotes

mainly lexical items and the 'perfective' use of 'done' in 'done gone'.
McDavid and McDavid (1971), on the other hand, see the similarities as
stemming, not from the influence of an African-derived English upon
neighboring White lects, but from a common origin as dialects of English.
They quote a researcher in Memphis as being:

> extremely skeptical of the possibility that 'Black English'
> has any pecularities other than what might be explained by
> the normal processes of 'Cultural lag'. (p. 39)

Black English, according to this view, would simply be a more conservative variety of the local White dialects; forms differing from Standard
would be older dialect forms conserved through BE's isolation from a
changing Standard.

3.   *Bahamian Background*[2]

Like the Caribbean islands, the Bahamas has a largely Black population; however, the speech of the White minority cannot be ignored. They
form about 15 percent of the population,[3] and, although over-represented
in the middle class, include significant numbers of fishermen, small
farmers and laborers etc. There are largely White settlements on several
small Out Islands; far more live in geographically integrated communities, including the capital, Nassau, where half the population of
200,000 lives. Historically, there were few Whites and far fewer Blacks
(numbering only hundreds), until the U.S. Independence, when Loyalists
came to the Bahamas with their slaves. These latter far outnumbered the
resident Blacks; moreover the plantations established were on Out Islands,
rather than near Nassau. When these plantations largely failed, many
rich Whites withdrew abroad, leaving poor Whites and Blacks to fishing,
subsistence farming and wrecking. The Black population intermingled
and increased steadily, with a sudden spurt during the period 1830-1870
when freed Africans were brought in by British men-o-war who were
blockading the slave trade. Communications between settlements had to
be through reef-bound waters, as also were those with the outside world.
However, there was a surprising amount of intercourse with the south-
eastern U.S., even before the tourist boom of the 1950s.

It seems quite possible that our present Black Bahamian Dialect
(BBD) has its origins in the Black English of the mainland, rather than
being an independent development. The slaves brought by the Loyalists
would be those considered reliable--hence slaves of long standing with an
established language. They came as pre-existing units--family or plantation slaves--rather than arriving piecemeal. Before and after this large
influx slaves were often imported from the mainland rather than direct.
The nineteenth-century newcomers from Africa, on the other hand, would
have learnt the then-existing variety of BBD as a normal second language,
and were unlikely to have affected it greatly.

The origins of the White population were more piecemeal. The Loyalist
Whites formed a far smaller percentage of Bahamian Whites than their
slaves did of the Blacks, and with the failure of the plantations some
left the islands. From the start they intermingled freely with the

descendants of pirates, religious refugees and adventurers who had pre-
ceded them and learnt with them to survive the boom and bust vagaries of
Bahamian history. Whites on the whole had far more contact with the
British colonial administrators and with other colonies than did the
Blacks, though Bahamian slaves were somewhat freer than their counter-
parts in the plantation lands (see Craton [1978]).

4. *The Language Situation*

I think that I can safely assume that social class "pyramids" exist
for both Black and White in the Bahamas; also that, with varying percentages, representatives of nearly all levels of social class now exist
in both races, so that these pyramids could now be viewed as matching
life figure 1a. However, until the 1950s the picture was probably more
like figure 1b.

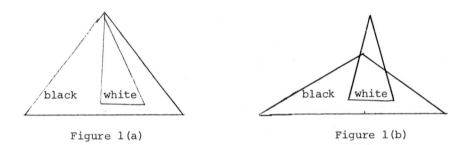

Figure 1(a)   Figure 1(b)

One possible model of a social dialect continuum would also be a pyramid,
that is, with the number of features different from the prestige or "target" language decreasing as one nearer the top. Since both White Bahamian
Dialect (WBD) and Black Bahamian Dialect (BBD) are aiming at the same
target, one would expect them to converge. If they started out as dialects of English from largely similar geographical areas, the language
position should be similar to that of the social classes--broadly speaking that of figure 1b above. BBD would thus have more non-Standard[4]
features, but the WBD variant, if not itself Standard, should be on some
natural track between BBD and Standard. If, however, they "started out"
as Creole and non-Standard dialect respectively, they might well be con-
verging from fundamentally different directions upon the Standard.

There are problems in finding out which process is operating.
First, the amount of mutual influence may have been so great that it is
no longer possible to tell; second, the upwardly mobile Blacks may well
have taken the target to *be* the White form of speech, rather than the
Standard. I will return to these questions after examining a few items
from Bahamian speech.

5. *Syntax*[5]

I have chosen the uses of 'be' and 'do', as they have been covered
quite well in the literature on Afro-American English.

5.1.1. In the BBD basilect there is only the form *is*, with *am* and *are* very seldom appearing and then sometimes inappropriately, as in:

(1) I'm ain' her friend now. (BBD, Nassau, 40m.)

Is appears regularly[6] before noun phrases, intermittently before adjectives and locative expressions and hardly ever in the formation of the present progressive or the 'going to' future tense. Amongst older Black speakers there is a sporadic use of the copula *de* before locatives which is found in other Creoles.

Labov (1969) bases his case for an underlying copula with phonological deletion on several factors. One, the presence in Black English of *am*, clearly does not apply in the case of BBD. For another the position of BBD is less clear; some of the cases where *is* is found before the adjectives are in fact where it is in an "exposed" position (that is, where in Standard English it cannot contract), so that we have variation:

(2) She just want see how bad this nigger. (BBD Nassau. 30m.)
(3) Let me tell you how big it is. (BBD Naussau 20 f.)

Labov (1969) writes his phonological rules to be sensitive to the syntactic environment of the copula, to account for the more widespread deletion before V+*ing* and *gonna* than before NP, so there are obviously strong similarities between BBD and Black English.

5.1.2. White Bahamian speakers use all three forms of the non-past copula. Both WBD and BBD are *r*-less dialects, hence the form *are* is reduced to /ə/ in all weakly-stressed positions, and it is thus difficult to tell in conversation if this residual glide is present. The presence of the auxiliary is made clear, however, before a following vowel by a flap r[ɾ]:

(4) [ðɪᵊɾɛmti] = They are empty. (WBD Spanish Wells 40 f.)

Also, the contracted forms of *is* and *am* are nearly always present; a few WBD speakers, in particular those from racially mixed islands such as Long Island, occasionally lack the copula, and this is similar to the BBD pattern of being less common before NP than elsewhere.

5.1.3. I know of no motivation from English dialects for this syntactic differentiation of *be* environments. It seems most probable that in the Black English and BBD situations we have two stages in decreolisation from the Creole copula situation as outlined in Bailey (1966) and Bickerton (1975). BBD has still basically a syntactic rule for copula insertion before NP but has the beginnings of phonological sensitivity to the "exposed" position of the copula slot. Black English has in the main a phonological rule but it is still syntax-sensitive. The WBD case would thus be possibly further along the same path, though more probably by influence at a decreolised level from BBD than itself developing from a former Creole.

5.2. *be past.* In the past tense, the copula for both BBD and WBD is /wɔz/, often reduced to /(ə)z/, with negative 'wasn't'; 'were' rarely appears in informal style. WBD does not delete 'was'; BBD occasionally does, usually as the second finite verb (or later) in the sentence:

> (5) When she come out the room she crying she say she fall. (BBD, Nassau 28 f.)

> (6) I can't remember what she tell me the boy name. (maybe *is* here) (BBD, Nassau 24 f.)

But in the vast majority of cases *was* appears:

> (7) They was dry up anyway, Chris. (BBD, Nassau 20 f.)

> (8) You and me wasn't on good terms. (BBD, Nassau, 40 m.)

This regular appearance of *was* is similar to Black English (Labov 1979:719), though he implies that *were* is also present in BE.

5.3. *be negative.* For both WBD and BBD *ain'(t)* regularly appears for Standard *be*-present + *not*. Thus we have:

> (9) I ain' go do that. (BBD, Nassau 20 f.)
> (10) She ain' gonna say nothin. (WBD, Spanish Wells 24 f.)
> (11) That ain' no greediness. (BBD, Nassau 20 f.)
> (12) You-all ain' payin no attention. (WBD, Nassau 13 m.)

5.3.1. *ain'* is, of course, the usual non-Standard English negator for *be* and *have*. Its function in BBD seems, however, to be more that of the unmarked negator, taking the place of a Creole *na* still found amongst a very few old speakers. Like other dialects, *ain'* is found negating *gat* or *bin*:

> (13) They ain' gat no petrol... (BBD, Ragged Island 32 f.)

but it is also equivalent to *don't* with stative verbs:

> (14) Maybe you like how she does act...everybody ain' like it you know. (BBD, Ragged Island 78 m.)

and to *didn't* or *hadn't* with all verbs:

> (15) After he see I ain' do it, he walk away. (BBD Cat Island 44 f.)

Few WBD speakers use *ain'* for *don't* or *didn't* though it is as frequent for *be* and *have* +NEG in their speech as in BBD. Use of *ain'* for *didn't* is reported for Black English by Labov (1968); it is a common negator also in Guyanese (see Bickerton [1975]) though its use differs from that in BBD.[7]

5.4. *Existentials.* Here is found the clearest difference between WBD and BBD.

5.4.1. The basic WBD pattern is *it is* (positive), *(i)t ain'* (negative) and *it was(n't)* (past). The dummy *it* is seldom omitted,[8] and the use of *it* rather than *there*, categorical in some Family Island speakers, persists into quite acrolectal speech where most other dialect characteristics have disappeared. Thus we have:

> (16) I's a lot of homes up here but it ain' nothing for them to do. (WBD, Current 45 f.)

> (17) Is it any mangoes? (WBD, Nassau 25 f.)

5.4.2. BBD has several patterns for existential sentences, the most basilectal using *got* or *had*, the mesolectal using *is* with very infrequent use of any dummy subject:

> (18) They got accident up there. You shoulda turn back. (BBD, Nassau 20 f.)

> (19) Only be three live here.... (BBD, Long Island 65 f.)

> (20) Wasn't nothing to do then like today. (BBD, Ragged Island 75 m.)

There are some cases of *it* as dummy subject amongst mesolectal BBD speakers, but they are in the main from settlements near concentrations of all-White speakers. On the whole towards the acrolectal end of the BBD range zero subject is replaced by *there* directly.

5.4.3. Fasold and Wolfrom (1970) and Labov (1968) state that the pattern with dummy *it* is characteristic of Black English. It would be interesting to learn if there are southern U.S. White communities which use it extensively, for in the Bahamas it seems definitely to be a WBD feature which has influenced BBD only marginally.

5.5. *invariant be.* This is the use of *be* for all persons (with *don't be* negative) to signify habitual state.

5.5.1. WBD has this occasionally, substituting for be-present:

> (21) That bes for rent too. (WBD, Current 45 f.)

It is far more frequently found in BBD, with form and meaning the same as in Black English:

> (22) This one gang of fellow up on the roof just be playing. (BBD, Nassau 24 f.)

but more often the form is 'does be', present or past:

> (23) We does be reading play every time. (present) (BBD, Nassau 13 f.)

> (24) She know two people does be sleeping in this bed. (Past) (BBD, Nassau 20 f.)

The auxiliary is frequently reduced to /əz/ or /z/:

> (25) They think they's be actin sharp but they's just be
>   looking tired. (BBD, Nassau 12 f.)

This is evidence to support Rickford's (1974) analysis of the origin of
the 'invariant be' of Black English from this *does be*.[9]

5.5.2. BBD alone also has a form /mʌsi/ or mʌsbi/ which is derived from
the standard 'must be' with extended use. Sometimes the use appears to
be Standard:

> (26) He must be go carry us up there... (BBD, Nassau 20 f.)

but far more often it behaves like an adverb with fixed pre-verbal position:

> (27) They must be had something to do. (BBD, Nassau f.)

It persists well into the acrolect; I had the following exchange in a
classroom with an eighteen-year-old girl:

> (28) Girl (referring to essay): I must be's right.
>   AS: What, you must be *is* right?
>   Girl: No, I must be was right when I wrote it.

5.6. *Do present*.

WBD usually inverts for direct questions, but BBD very seldom; in
this case both will use *do* as support. The form *does* is found in BBD for
the habitual or iterative use mentioned above with *be*. It is found with
both present and past reference, though past is less common.

> (29) Now Chris, what you's do? You's go to the woman or
>   the woman əz come to you? (present) (BBD, Nassau 20 f.)

> (30) How you go tell me she does sleep bad if you ain
>   sleep with her? (past) (BBD, Nassau 20 f.)

5.6.1. *did*: the form *didn't* is found always in WBD and alternating with
ain in BBD as a negator for past action verbs; it is also found in the
affirmative in BBD, seemingly to convey simple past reference or an
irrealis or anterior marker in the basilect:

> (31) The pie cake did taste so good... (BBD, Eleuthera 8 f.)

> (32) They did say in the Bible woman is the root of all
>   evil. (BBD, Nassau 50 m.)

This is not related to the Standard emphatic form--there is no
stress on it, and it does not contrast with anything in context.

5.6.2. *done*: this form is very frequent--once again only in BBD with
few exceptions. It seems to have the completive sense described for

Black English (Fasold and Wolfram 1970) and for Guyanese (Bickerton 1975). We have:

(33)   I done ask forgiveness for that.   (BBD, Nassau 15 f.)

The fact that Standard predicate adjectives are in some ways like surface verbs in BBD is shown by the occurrence of this 'done' before them.

(34)   Mamma say we late now--we done late.   (BBD, Nassau 24 f.)

(35)   Dem dilly done ripe and rotten.   (BBD, Nassau f.)
       (dilly=sapodilla, a fruit)

6.1. *Phonology*

6.1.1.   In phonology there are a few non-Standard characteristics that WBD and BBD share. They are both, as I said, *r*-less dialects; they both simplify word-final consonant clusters by dropping -*t* and -*d*. WBD also reduces /t/ medially and finally after vowel to [ʔ]: e.g., [bɔʔɔl] = *bottle*, [iʔ] = *eat*, [fə'gʰIʔ] = *forget*; this is infrequent in BBD.

6.1.2.   Some features occur in both WBD and BBD but their frequency of occurrence varies. One noticeable, and stigmated, WBD feature is a highly variable /h/; this is absent in some WBD speakers over half the time from words with Standard /h/, and conversely is sometimes found on vowel-initial words. Lexical items are not treated consistently:

(36)   It's a lot of homes...the people what have these
       'homes....some people 'ave...   (WBD, Current 45 g.)

(37)   ...from hend to end.   (WBD, Spanish Wells 65 f.)

Glottal stop is substituted medially:

   [bə'ʔæəməz] = *Bahamas*   [ə'ʔIəʔ] = *ahead*.

Some BBD speakers, particularly older ones, living near the all-White Out Island settlements have this feature, though to a lesser extent than whites.

6.1.3.   Both Black and White speakers are found who use bi-labial [β] for Standard /v/ and /w/. However, it is far more widespread and persistent in BBD than WBD. There may well be some BBD speakers who do not have an underlying /v ∿ w/ distinction, whereas all White speakers I have heard used [β] variably with 'correct' /v/ and /w/. I have not found this mentioned for Black English, save for Gullah (Turner 1949:24). In Jamaican Creole there may well be something similar, as Bailey (1971: 346) has Standard /b/ written for /v/: *biliib* (*believe*). However, /w/ is shown as distinct.

6.2.   There is one difference between BBD and WBD consonants which is, by contrast, sharp and well-defined. BBD, like other Afro-American

English, has [d] and [t] for Standard [θ] and [ð]. WBD nowhere has this, even in most casual style, whereas amongst Blacks consistent use of [θ] and [ð] is not found unless the grammar is almost completely Standard.

6.3. The vowels in both BBD and WBD are variable, and I would not want to postulate differing underlying representations at this stage. However, there are definite phonetic differences.

6.3.1. *BBD vowels* differ from Standard in having the stressed vowels in *same*, *right*, and *down* normally monophthongs: [e], [a], and [a] respectively. (This means that the latter two fall together.) BBD also merges the vowels in *church* and *bird* (Standard [ə:]) with that of *voice* making them both phonetically [θᴵ]. As for some mainland dialects the vowels in *pin* and *pen* are realized as very similar, if not identical, usually a dipthong [ɛə].

6.3.2. *WBD*, on the other hand, does not monophthongise any Standard diphthong. The nuclei in the two diphthongs of *right* and *down* are not [a], as in BBE and Standard, they are [a] and [æ] respectively. The Standard short [ɨ] is diphthongised whenever stressed, but the quality is not lower, but higher, than Standard--almost [iə], falling together with the vowels of *there* and *here* so that we have:

(38)   [βɛlðɛi iəz - ðɛi æv mɔə ɾĩ skiᵘlðiə βi æv iə]

Well, they *is* - they have more in school there
than we have here. (WBD, Current 45 f.)

6.3.3. A less easily measured difference between WBD and BBD is in fact I think possibly more important. It is often difficult to distinguish primary from more weakly-stressed vowels in BBD, since there seems to be more equal stress within words and less reduction of auxiliaries. With WBD it is far easier to identify stresses, with the stressed vowels often diphthongised even where Standard does not have it, and the unstressed vowels greatly reduced. In BBD, when the copula is put in an unstressed position, it is far less often contracted than in WBD.

I have not found clear parallels to these facts in either BE or Creoles, Fasold and Wolfram (1970:59) mention that some Black English words are stressed differently from Standard--they cite *police*, *hotel*, and *July*. In BBD, as elsewhere in the Caribbean, these words are pronounced with equal stress.

7. *The Bahamian Continuum*

From the syntactic features discussed it would not be difficult to place WBD and BBD on the same continuum; one would have to suppose that WBD was too 'near the target' to have the non-Standard *done*, *be*, or *did*. The non-Standard *it is* etc. for *there is* would cause difficulty, since WBD has it but not BBD, but this is only one minor syntactic pattern.

Considering the phonological and phonetic facts as well as the grammatical, it is more difficult to place BBD and WBD on the same continuum. With vowels, the quality of nuclei and monophthongs is far closer to the 'target' in BBD, on the whole, than WBD. The BBD speakers with variable /h/--like those with *it* for existential *there*--seem clearly to have been influenced by a non-Standard form found in WBD and not in mainstream BBD--this does not fit in with a 'more conservative dialect' view of BBD. The [d] and [t] for [θ] and [ð] does not fit this view either, for there is no social class overlapping, but a clear-cut racial distinction.

7.1. The non-Standard features BBD and WBD share, such as the use of *ain'* as preverbal negator, negative-concord and consonant-cluster simplification, are features of many non-Standard English dialects. More important, it seems to me that a continuum, post-Creole or not, must have some systematic educational socio-economic correlates. In the Bahamas, as I said earlier, the social overlap has been considerable for some time, yet non-Standard features found in middle-class Black conversation--as many of these I have mentioned are--are found in neither middle- nor working-class White homes, not even in the more isolated settlements--traditionally the locus of more conservative speech habits.

8. *The Black Language Continuum*

8.1. In contrast to the task of trying to fit together the two types of Bahamian English, it is extremely easy to find similarities between BBD and other Afro-American English. Although the fit is not perfect, the Bahamian features I have examined could place BBD on a continuum with both Black English and Caribbean Creoles.

8.2. In syntax, the use of *done* is found throughout the area, though mentioned less often for BE. *Does* appears in many areas of the Caribbean and in Gullah, whereas *be* alone appears on the U.S. mainland. In the Bahamas the transition postulated by Rickford (1974) of *does be* to *be* can be seen, either fossilized, or changing now. BBD differs from other Caribbean Creoles in not having *a* before nominals, but this would fit with Bickerton's (1975) observation that this is usually replaced directly with *iz* in decreolisation. In BBD *de* before locatives appears to be dropping out without being replaced immediately by *is*, but overall the behavior of the copula in BBD seems to provide a link between Creoles and BE--following the frequency pattern explained in Labov (1969) for BE, though with a substantially higher percentage of zero forms.

The use of *must be* seems again to link BBD with Black English and the Caribbean. A Guyanese form *mosi*, equatable with BBE *must be*, is cited by Bickerton (1973:28):

"shi mosi de bad ..."--she must have been hard up.

mussy is also quoted for BE, and the assimilation into one word makes it appear likely that it occurs as a unit there too.

8.3. In phonology, of course, the [d] and [t] for [θ] and [ð] is the hallmark of BE; it is also found in the Creoles. The lack of variable

/h/ in Black languages seems to confirm this as a White feature. The use of bilabial [β] is similar to Gullah, though I do not think the facts about this, or the vowel-systems, have been fully enough described in Black English; this, and the relative evenness of stress in BBE, might well both be due to a common origin as syllable-timed languages, rather than stress-timed, as with Standard English. The stress in BE may well have 'settled on' the wrong syllable when this language was evolving in stress-timing.

9. *Conclusion*

In discussing the relationship between WBD and BBD one must not neglect the possibility that the two races spoke alike originally and that their present differences result from social separation, which did exist in spite of physical proximity. In other words, there could have been such a wide divergence earlier that there is now no continuity. This would be difficult to disprove; however, unless the similarities between BBD and other Afro-American English are all coincidences, these must have sprung from similar, or common, origins. One would therefore have to postulate that the White Bahamians originally spoke a form of this language also, but are 'taking another path' to the Standard. It seems unnecessary to suppose this, in the face of the relatively rare occurrence of Creole features in their speech.

Finally, it may seem surprising that the upwardly mobile Blacks did not take as their target language the speech of the White Bahamians since these enjoyed until recently far higher status in the community. However, the middle-class Black had much contact with a now largely extinct group of British administrators, etc.; the Black could easily perceive that the White social climber sought to acquire the British accent in preference to his own. The White Out Islands, though economically privileged, did not enjoy high status. The social situation is changing rapidly now, with change to Black government six years ago, and the ever-increasing dependence on the U.S. educationally and economically. It will be interesting to see the effects upon language.

NOTES

1. Consider, amongst others, Bailey (1966) for Jamaican, Bickerton (1975) for Guyanese and Winford (1972) for Trinidadian.

2. I would like to thank Ms. Gail Saunders, Chief Archivist in Nassau, for her help with this section and also for her generously allowing me to copy Dialect tapes. I take responsibility for any distortion caused by summarising.

3. This is based on informal inquiry; there are no statistics on race.

4. I use Standard to refer for convenience both to written Standard English and to spoken British English (R.P.).

5. I base the Bahamian data in my paper upon observation, a few interviews and recorded uniracial conversations.

6. Details of this distribution for different speakers and grammatical
   contexts are found in Shilling (1978), Chapter 2.

7. Further details of this can be found in Shilling (1978), Chapter 3.

8. See Shilling (1978), Chapter 4.

9. The use of *be* alone, the full form *does be* and the contraction *'s be*
   are all common amongst all speakers in BBD, always with the habitual
   reference. This is a clear case of BBD's usefulness in showing
   clearly the link between Black English and Caribbean forms.

REFERENCES

Bailey, B. 1966. Jamaican creole syntax. Cambridge, Cambridge
University Press.

Bailey, B. 1971. Jamaican creole: Can dialect boundaries be defined?
In: Pidginization and creolization of language, ed. by D. Hymes,
pp. 341-348. Cambridge, Cambridge University Press.

Bickerton, D. 1973. The structure of polylectal grammars. In:
Report of the twenty-third annual round table meeting on linguistics
and language studies, ed. by R. W. Shuy, pp. 17-42. Washington,
D.C., Georgetown University Press.

_____. The dynamics of a Creole system. Cambridge, Cambridge
University Press.

Craton, M. 1978. Hobbesian or Panglossian? The William and Mary
Quarterly 35.

Dillard, J. L. 1972. Black English. New York, Random House.

Fasold, R. and W. Wolfram. 1970. Some linguistic features of Negro
dialect. In: Teaching standard English in the Inner City, ed. by
R. Fasold and R. W. Shuy, pp. 41-86. Washington, D.C., Center for
Applied Linguistics.

Labov, W. 1969. Contraction, deletion and inherent variability of
the English copula. Language 45:715-762.

Labov, W., P. Cohen, C. Robbin, and J. Lewis. 1968. A study of the
nonstandard English of Negroes and Puerto Rican speakers in New
York City. Vol. 1. Final Report to the U.S. Office of Education.
Co-operative Research Report No. 3288. New York, Columbia
University.

McDavid, R. I. and V. G. McDavid. 1971. The relationship of the speech of American Negroes to the speech of Whites. In: Black-White speech relationships, ed. by W. Wolfram and N. H. Clarke, pp. 16-40. Washington, D.C., Center for Applied Linguistics.

Rickford, J. 1974. The insights of the mesolect. In: Pidgins and creoles: Current trends and prospects, ed. by D. DeCamp and I. Hancock, pp. 92-117. Washington, D.C., Georgetown University Press.

Ryan, J. S. 1973. Blayk is White on the Bay Islands. Michigan Papers in Linguistics 1:2.

Shilling, A. 1978. Some nonstandard features of Bahamian dialect syntax. Unpublished doctoral dissertation. University of Hawaii.

Turner, L. D. 1949. Africanisms in the Gullah dialect. Chicago, University of Chicago Press.

Winford, D. 1972. A sociolinguistic description of two communities in Trinidad. Unpublished doctoral dissertation. University of York.

Wolfram, W. 1973. Black and White speech relationships in the Deep South--how gray? Paper presented at the Linguistic Society of America Summer Institute, University of Michigan.

SUFFICIENCY CONDITIONS FOR A PRIOR CREOLIZATION
OF BLACK ENGLISH

Robert Berdan
National Center for Bilingual Research,
SWRL Educational Research and Development

*The work on which this paper is based was performed pursuant
to Contract NE-C-00-3-0064 from the National Institute of
Education to SWRL Educational Research and Development.*

The collocation 'prior creolization' used in the title of this paper
is a reflex of a previous use by Southworth (1971) in the title of his
paper for the Mona Conference: 'Detecting prior creolization.' However,
the contents of this paper, like Southworth's paper, will be addressed
primarily to what is more commonly considered the process of pidginization. The condition necessitating this apparent reversal was summarized
quite explictly by Voorhoeve (1971). The process of pidginization is
conceived of as a process of reduction and simplification, while the
process of creolization is conceived of as a process of expansion. All
such processes as simplification and expansion necessarily imply comparison with some known prior language state. As Voorhoeve points out, we
frequently have knowledge of the prior languages from which a pidgin
derives, but lack knowledge of the nature of pidgins from which many of
the contemporary creoles are said to have derived. Thus in many instances
it may be possible to discuss the pidginization, or simplification, processes when it is not possible to discuss the creolization process.

The terminological distinction may in fact be more convincing in
academic discussion than it is in observation of the real world. It is
highly unlikely that processes of reduction and expansion necessarily
occur at mutually exclusive stages in the development of any creole. In
part, any such distinction is an artifact of point of view. Some single
development may add complexity to a pidgin even though it is at the same
time a simplification of a parent language.

Nonetheless, it is the process of simplification that is addressed
in this paper. Simplification is a natural linguistic process, observed
by diachronic linguists for generations. Within the generative tradition, it has come to be conceived of chiefly as simplification of
grammars and their component rules (e.g., Kiparsky 1968, Bach and Harms
1972). Here it can mean a number of different things:

(a) loss of exceptions to a rule

(b) simplification of Structural Description; i.e.,
   rule generalization

(c) simplification of Structural Change

(d) simplification of ordering

(e) rule deletion

There are, of course, other ways that languages may be said to simplify. One may think of languages as becoming easier to learn or easier to understand. It would be preferable if such ease were reflected in simplification of grammars, but the present state of linguistics leaves that relationship somewhat indeterminate.

It is the fact that simplification is a general process of language change, and not unique to the pidginization, that reduces the arguments to be presented here, to sufficiency conditions. It would be much more satisfying to be able to argue on the basis of present form that Black English necessarily did or necessarily did not undergo some earlier stage of pidgin and creolization. A necessity argument, however, would require demonstration that some characteristic of the contemporary language could not have derived from an earlier stage by conventional linguistic change, but could have happened only by undergoing some pidgin stage. That would be very difficult to do, however, given how little is known about the constraints on what is a possible language change.

Sufficiency arguments are less convincing, but not totally without merit. The more mutually contradictory sufficiency arguments that can be made, of course, the less interesting any of them becomes. However, if it is possible to show that some sufficiency argument is substantially more probable than the others, and given the absence of necessity arguments, that highly probable sufficiency argument must be given serious consideration.

Although pidginization and conventional language change share the characteristic of simplification, they differ in one important respect: speed. The spread of language change through a large and discontinuous population is of necessity slow. Pidginization, on the other hand, is rapid--often thought to be accomplished within a single generation. Further, if the nature of the pidgin is determined by the languages involved and the nature of the contact situation, it need not have a unique source. It could arise spontaneously at numerous points. It would not be necessary then to demonstrate the feasibility of transmission of a change from a single source.

Syncretism is, of course, another process involved in pidginization: the importance of elements of one language into the language being acquired. Syncretism is an obvious explanation for many of the features of creoles, but there are also characteristics of creoles that are not to be explained in that way. In particular, it has frequently been noted (e.g., Kay and Sankoff 1974) that although both prior languages in a contact situation may be highly inflected, the resulting pidgin and creole may employ very limited inflectional morphology. This cannot be explained as syncretism, but only as simplification.[1]

Another question must be raised in order to determine if there existed a prior creole stage of Black English. This is the matter of degree: how much divergence from the target language must there be before the result would be called a creole? Is the importation of lexical items sufficient, and if so how many? The question can be repeated substituting each category of linguistic entities from phonetics to semantics.

This paper considers five instances of syntactic simplification. This is not to suggest that these are the only cases of simplification in Black English. Nonetheless, most of these have been frequently discussed, although not from this point of view.

Relative Clause Reduction

Most relative clauses in contemporary standard English can be reduced; a few cannot. Attempts to state the constraints on the relative clause reduction process seem always to necessitate a prose paragraph; they do not yield readily to simply, straightforward, natural rules. Hackenberg (1972) suggests that the constraint is that the noun phrase to be deleted must not have the subject of the embedded sentence. This would account for (1a, b) and for the fact that (2a) is good. It does now however, explain why (2b) is also good, since the underlying subject is deleted.

(1) a. The boy [Sam saw ~~the~~ ~~boy~~] ate the cake.
     b. The boy [~~The~~ ~~boy~~ saw Sam] ate the cake.

(2) a. The boy [~~The~~ ~~boy~~ ~~was~~ seen by Sam] ate the cake.
     b. The boy [Sam was seen by ~~the~~ ~~boy~~] ate the cake.

Nor does that condition explain why both (3a) and (3b) are grammatical.

(3) a. The boy [Sam was looking for ~~the~~ ~~boy~~] ate the cake.
     b. The boy [~~The~~ ~~boy~~ ~~was~~ looking for Sam] ate the cake.

The relevant factor controlling deletion in these cases is not whether the identical noun phrase was surface or deep subject, but whether a subject noun phrase is followed by a finite form of *to be*, either as passive marker, or as tense auxiliary. To allow all of (1) through (3) except (1b) the constraint on relative clause reduction must be some set of disjunct conditions as (4):[2]

(4) Relative clause reduction can occur with identity on any
     noun phrase except the surface subject noun phrase, ex-
     cept that it can occur with any noun phrase if the embedded
     clause contains a finite form of *to be*.

Various devices have been used to make the statement more felicitous. Bever and Langedoen (1972) have an obligatory relative clause reduction rule that operates on all instances in which the finite form of *to be* is initial in the embedded clause. The environment for this rule (their 5d) is established by making formation of relative pronouns optional. However, they then need to establish a condition on the optional relative pronoun formation: 'The [optional pronoun formation] rule is obligatory in most contexts in which the shared noun is the subject of the relative clause and the finite verb of the relative clause is not *be* (1972:35).' Thus relative clause reduction appears to be simplified only by placing what is essentially the same unnatural condition onto the formation of the relative pronoun.

Stockwell et al. (1973:493-499) found it necessary to state the reduction of relative clauses in three separate optional rules: an optional rule of relative *that* deletion, accounting for the sentences of (1, 2):
an optional relative-*be* deletion rule to account for the reduction in
(3); and an additional relative reduction rule to account for such sentences as (5a, b).

(5) a. People owning large houses pay large taxes.   [133]
     b. Anyone having undergone yesterday what he
         underwent deserves a vacation.   [134]

All of this complexity is compelled by the necessity to filter out
garden path sentences like (1b).   It is not just an accident that it is
(1b) that is disallowed in contemporary standard English, and not some
other sentence of the set (1-3).   Of the six sentences only (1b) would
be subject to an alternate surface constituent interpretation comparable
to (6):

(6) *The boy saw Sam [S̸a̸m̸ ate the cake].

Bever and Langendoen (1972) consider the interaction of simplicity of perception strategies with simplicity of grammars.   They suggest that such
structures are not grammatical because of the great likelihood of interpreting a noun phrase followed by a finite verb with which it agrees, as
the subject of that verb.   Discussing the changes that have occurred in
relative clause formation and reduction throughout the history of English,
they argue that sentences such as (1b) have never been allowed:

As far as we can determine from the evidence cited by various
grammarians, such as Abbot, Curme, Jesperson, Mustanoja, Poutsma,
Roberts, Sweet, Visser, and Wilson, at no stage in the history of
English was a relative clause which modifies a nominal preceding
the verb in its own clause allowed to begin with a finite verb.
(Bever and Langendoen, 1972:50).

Deletion of subject relative pronouns have been allowed, when the
relative caluse did not itself modify the subject of the higher sentence.
Bever and Langendoen cite evidence to show that deletion from object position as in (7), was optional in the early Modern English period (c.1550-
1700).

(7) He hit the boy [t̸h̸e̸ b̸o̸y̸ likes Mary].

In what they identify as the next period, 1700-1900, deletion of subject
NPs was possible only in existential sentences (8) and cleft sentences
(9):

(8) There was lots of vulgar people [Ø] live in Grosvenor
     Square [Wilde, cited by Jespersen, p. 145, B & L 43a].

(9) It was haste [Ø] killed the yellow snake.   [Kipling, cited
     by Jespersen, p. 145, B & L 43b].

For contemporary English they find deletion of subject NPs possible only
for interrogative cleft sentences, and then only for some people (10):

    (10) Who is this [∅] opens the door? [Thackery, Poutsma,
          p. 1001, B & L 43c].

    In footnotes, Bever and Langendoen cite two examples from Shakespeare
and from the early twentieth century Irish playwright, John Synge, with
deletion of subject NP in relation clauses modifying sentencial subjects.
'Besides these,' they state, 'we have encountered very few other examples
of this sort in all of English literature ... ' (1972:88, note 11).

    Hackenberg (1972) found numerous examples of reduced relative
clauses with deleted subject NPs in his Appalachian data. Only one of
his example sentences includes an instance of deletion from higher sentence subject. This is with indefinite subject *any*. Such relative
clauses appear to be quite different from others, as pointed out by
Thompson (1971).

    For persons allowing this type of relative clause reduction, the
constraint in (4) must now be complicated to something like (11):

    (11) Relative clause reduction can occur with identity on any
         noun phrase except the surface subject noun phrase, ex-
         cept (1) that it can occur with any noun phrase if the
         embedded clause contains a finite form of *to be*, or (2)
         it can occur with any noun phrase if the identical noun
         phrase in the higher S is not the surface subject of the
         higher S.

This is an extraordinarily complex constraint on a grammatical process.
Bever and Langendoen would argue that its development through time results from the fact that it allows certain compensatory simplification of
perceptual strategies.

    If indeed the process of creolization is one of rule generalization
and rule simplification, Constraint (11) would seem a prime candidate
for extinction. For some speakers of contemporary American Black English,
neither Constraint (11) nor the somewhat less complex Constraint (4) is
needed. Both Subject-Subject and Object-Subject relative clauses can be
reduced, making both (12a) and (12b) grammatical.

    (12) a. The men [t̸h̸e̸ m̸e̸n̸ want the money] are waiting outside.
        b. The police chased the man [t̸h̸e̸ m̸a̸n̸ beat the dog].

    As has been noted, the simplification processes of creolization are
not unique to creole situations. Much of language change which is in-
disputably not creole process involves the loss of complex constraints on
rules. Saying that, however, leaves unanswered the difficult question of
why the simplification of relative clause reduction has occurred in
American Black English, but not in Anglo dialects.

    One reason that other dialects maintain the constraint may be some
perceptual strategy, as suggested by Bever and Langendoen. Black English,

however, possesses another mechanism for providing the perceptual cues
to disambiguate sentences with subject-subject relative reduction.   Smith
(1972) cites the use of the pleonastic pronoun as a device that disambig-
uates reduced relatives.[3]   Thus in sentences from his interviews with
black informants in East Texas, (13a) with the pleonasm is equivalent to
(13b) rather than (13c).

(13) a.   The boy won he a three.
     b.   The boy *who* won did a three.   (= 13a)
     c.   The boy won *who* did a three.   (≠ 13a)

Similarly, in a predicate NP, (14a) is comparable to (14b), not (14c).

(14) a.   My other sister *she* fourteen go to Dogan.
     b.   My other sister is fourteen *who* goes to Dogan.
          (= 14a)
     c.   My other sister *who* is fourteen goes to Dogan.
          (≠ 14a)

The pleonastic pronoun may provide part of the answer.   That is, it
may suggest a reason why Black English has allowed the simplification of
the constraint on relative clause reduction: the dialect contains another
mechanism to simplify the perceptual strategy--the pleonastic pronoun.
The larger question, however, remains unanswered: why have not other
dialects also simplified the constraint?   Black English is not the only
dialect that employs the pleonastic pronoun.

There is, however, another characteristic of Black English that
must be considered.   This is the possibility of deletion of *be*, either
as a tense auxiliary or as a copula.   Sequences which in standard
English must be interpreted as reduced relative clauses, need not have
that interpretation in Black English.   Sentence (15a) can have only the
interpretation (15b) in standard English.   It can also have the quite
different interpretation (15c) in Black English:

(15) a.   The policeman trying to find the man beat the woman.
     b.   [The policeman *who was* trying to find the man] beat
          the woman.
     c.   The policeman *is* trying to find [the man *who* beat
          the woman].

The possibility that the copula and other markers of the finiteness of
the verb phrase can be deleted necessarily alters the perceptual strategies that may be employed.[4]   The lack of case marking also shifts the
set of cues available for interpretation.   What is being suggested here
is that the structure of a proto Black English creole would have been
sufficiently different to alter perceptual strategies.   Such an alteration would remove any motivation for the introduction or maintenace of
the modern English constraints on relative clause reduction.   The result
is a simplification of *Type b*:   rule generalization.

Negation

There are several respects in which contemporary Black English
negation can be considered to be simpler than standard English.   As with

the relative clause reduction, these simplifications can be used to argue
for the possibility of some prior creole stage. Most transformational
treatments of negation would derive (16a, b) from a single source such
as (16c) (e.g., Klima 1964, Stockwell et al. 1973):

> (16) a. John didn't see anyone.
>   b. John saw no one.
>   c. John NEW saw someone.

In (16b) some rule of NEG attraction moves with the element NEG from its
preverbal position and incorporates it into the noun phrase.[5] Movement
rules are frequently considered to be complex rules (e.g., Sanders and
Tai 1972). They can be considered as combinations of the elementary
transformational operations of copying and deletion (cf. Bach 1974:84ff).
In this conceptualization, the derivation of (16b) involves, among many
other things, the copying of the NEG constituent into the object noun
phrase, and the subsequent deletion of the original NEG in the preverbal
position. Sentence (17) which is common to many dialects of English involves only the elementary copying transformation and no deletion:

> (17) John didn't see no one.

Given the prevalence of this negative concord to object noun phrases in
English dialects, there can be no direct argument here for prior creolization of Black English. Rather, it can be observed that, of the possible
models available at the time of possible pidginization, the simpler form
of the rule is found in contemporary Black English.

For speakers of most lects of Black English, sentences of the form
of (17) occur to the exclusion of sentences such as (16a, b). For these
speakers there is no motivation for a rule of *some-any* suppletion (cf.
Stockwell et al. 1973:273).[6] *Any* occurs, but chiefly [-specific] sentences like (18):

> (18) Anybody could tell you that.

There is thus another way in which the use of negative concord allows simplification of the grammar. This is what was discussed initially as Case
(e): deletion of the *some-any* suppletion rule. The effect of this is to
make the grammar conform more closely in syntax to the universal principle for phonology stated by Kay and Sankoff (1974): shallowness of
derivations. Negative pronouns need be subjected to only one stage of
suppletion (e.g., something → nothing) rather than two stages of suppletion (e.g., something → anything → nothing).

There is a third simplification in the process of negation found in
Black English that is less widely distributed in other dialects of
English.[7] In many dialects the process of Neg-Concord is restricted to
clause-mates. In Black English, however, sentences like (19) occur:[8]

> (19) I ain't know [I could do *none* of that] [Labov 1972, #122]

The rule of Neg-Concord operating in most dialects must state that the
variable between the original source of negation and the constituent into
which it is to be copied (the X constituent in Labov's (1972) NEG-Concord)
cannot contain # [
            S

$$(20) \quad W \text{ -- } [Neg] - X - \begin{bmatrix} Indet \\ \\ Verb \end{bmatrix}$$

$$
\begin{array}{cccc}
1 & 2 & 3 & 4 \rightarrow \\
\\
1 & 2 & 3 & 2+4
\end{array}
$$

or some such symbol to exclude tensed clauses. That constraint, however, seems to be relaxed in Black English. The absence of such a constraint may also explain the occurrence of such sentences as (21a, b):

(21) a. It ain't no cat can't get in no coop [Labov 1972, #1]
     b. Wasn't much I couldn't do [Labov 1972, #50]

Removal of this constraint results in simplification of Type (b). That
is, the structural description of a rule has been generalized to apply
to a wider range of strings. In principle, such rule generalizations
are common enough in conventional language change. But this change
results in exactly opposite understandings in different dialects. Labov
raises the question, "What process of change could have produced a sentence which means X in dialect A and not-X in dialect B? And how do
speakers of A and B come to understand each other if this is the case?"
(1972:131). The existence of a prior pidgin would certainly provide a
sufficient condition for the development of such a radical divergence.
The limited nature of communication between Anglos and Blacks at the
time such a pidgin could have developed, and in particular, the limited
expectation for successful communication, could well allow a very simple
grammatical change to create opposite understandings of sentences.

There is another respect in which a grammar with Neg-Concord is
simpler than one with standard English Neg-Attraction. Neg-Concord
allows exclusion of several statements of extrinsic rule ordering that
are needed by Neg-Attraction. For example Neg-Attraction must follow
passive to explain why (22a, b) are grammatical but (22c) is not:

(22) a. Nobody shot any cowboys
     b. No cowboys got shot by anybody.
     c. *Any cowboys got shot by nobody.

With Neg-Concord, however, no such ordering is necessary. Both (23a) and
(23b) are grammatical:

(23) a. Nobody shot no cowboys.
     b. No cowboys got shot by nobody.

Similarly, standard English Neg-Postposing must be ordered after Dative
movement to disallow (24c):

(24) a. He left no money to any of his relatives.
     b. He left none of his relatives any money.
     c. *He left any of relatives no money.

Neg-Concord requires no statement of ordering.

(25) a. He didn't leave none of his relatives no money.
     b. He didn't leave no money to none of his relatives.

Black English thus also evidences simplification of Type d.

There Insertion

Existential sentences seem subject to numerous dialect variations.
Thus along side the current American Standard (26):

(26) There is more food

an inverted (or perhaps uninverted) parallel construction is used in the
English of India (27):

(27) More food is there. (= 26)

For Trinidad, Richards (1970) reports that "The expletive *there* used with
the verb *be* in Standard English is completely lacking in the folk speech
of Trinidad. The forms of this construction have been replaced in folk
speech by the single expression *it have*" (1970:83), as in (28):

(28) *It have* more food.

Paralleling these two constructions in contemporary American Black
English: one with expletive *it* (29a) and another with what seems to be
a non-deictic use of *here go* (29b):

(29) a. It's more food.
     b. Here go more food.

Conventional transformational derivations of existential *there* sentences
(e.g., Burt 1971:22) invert the subject noun phrase and the copula, and
insert the lexical item *there* in initial position. This treatment is
unsatisfactory in several respects. In particular it does not explain
why sentences like (30a, b) are ungrammatical:

(30) a. *There are some men tall.   ← Some men are tall
     b. *There is a man president. ← A man is president

it appears that the predicates that do not allow *there*-insertion are
just those comparable to copular relative clauses that require placement in prenominal position when reduced (31) or do not allow reduction
(32):[9]

(31) a. a man who is tall
     b. a tall man
     c. *a man tall

(32) a. a man who is president
     b. *a president man
     c. *a man president

Another condition on *there* insertion is that the post-copular noun phrase must be indefinite. Sentence (33a) is acceptable but (33b) is not:

(33) a. There was someone who knew what was going on.
      b. *There was the president who knew what was
          going on.

The condition is just the reverse of that found in cleft sentences which allow only definite noun phrases to be placed in the focus position:

(34) a. *It was someone who knew what was going on.
      b.   It was the president who knew what was going on.

A possible way to account for these facts in the grammar would be to derive existential sentences from strings with cleft-like structure, except for the indefinite noun phrase. In other words, underlying (33a) would be something comparable to (34a).

Under this analysis the difference between standard English and Black English existential sentences is not that the one has a *There*-insertion Rule and the other has an *it*-insertion Rule, but that standard English has a rule inserting a semantically empty lexical item, and Black English has no comparable rule. The Black English grammar is simplified by the deletion of a rule that adds little of communicative import, and is thus a likely candidate for exclusion in the development of a pidgin and creole.

As with the constructions already discussed, the existential sentences can be construed only as sufficiency arguments for a prior creolization. Both *it* and *there* have long been used as subjects of existential sentences. Visser (1963:42) cites examples with *it* back as far as the eleventh century and continuing through the time period when Africans would have come into contact with English in the New World. In what appears to be the earliest reference to existential *it* in Black English, Hench (1937) cites it as a relic of the Old English usage. Thus what might be claimed as evidence of creolization, might also be preservation of an early form (cf. Williamson 1969).

Inversion in Questions and Negation

Most generative grammars of English are formulated to include a rule which places the auxiliary to the left of the subject NP in questions and certain constructions with preposed negatives. Stockwell et al. (1973) label this rule Aux-Attraction (1973:287, 612). They described the rule as being obligatory and last cyclic. In contemporary Black English the rule is neither obligatory or last cyclic. Thus all the sentences of (35) and (36) are possible:

(35) a. Can I climb the tree?
      b. I can climb the tree?
      c. Pete asked his friend could he climb the tree?
      d. Pete asked his friend if he could climb the tree?

(36) a. Nobody can't pay the ransom.
    b. Can't nobody pay the ransom.
    c. If nobody can't pay the ransom, they can't get out.
    d. If can't nobody pay the ransom, they can't get out.

There is a sense in which making a rule last-cyclic imposes a formal constraint on the rule: there are certain strings which would otherwise meet its structural description to which it is not allowed to apply. In Black English this constraint is relaxed, both for questions and for emphatic negation.

There are thus four syntactic constructions in which the syntax of Black English can be considered to be simpler than that of contemporary standard English: relative clause reduction, the scope of negative concord, existential sentences, and Auxiliary attraction. There is one other frequently cited divergence in Black English that would appear to be an exception to this pattern: the use of invariant *be*.

Copular Constructions

Black English allows two copular constructions, as has been well documented (e.g., Labov et al. 1968).[10] Their syntactic difference is easily observed; the semantic difference is less apparent. One is identical in form to that used in standard English: it contracts (37a), inverts in questions (37b), and allows contracted negation (37c).

(37) a. John's sick.
    b. Is John sick?
    c. John isn't sick.

The other copula-like construction behaves syntactically like a main verb: questioning and negating with *Do*-Support (38):

(38) a. Do he be sick?
    b. He don't be sick.

It is variously described as having a durative or distributive sense not found in the strictly copular *is*. The semantic distinction, however, seems not to be invariant (cf. Fasold 1969). Its source is variably attributed to semantic distinctions in West African copular systems on the one hand, and to Scots and Irish dialects on the other (Key 1973). In the confusion generated by the lack of historical attestations, two things are clear. The morpheme itself has not been shown to derive from any African language, and a rather comparable use did exist in some English dialects at the relevant time period (Wright 1905:11, 99). But this leaves unanswered the question of why the more complex grammar should be chosen in this instance, if indeed the process involves more than one language. Simplification here has been considered only with respect to the target language. But each of the languages involved ought properly to be considered.

The copular-like constructions of West-African languages are considerably more complex semantically than the English copular system.

Welmers (1973:309) cautions against the "pitfall" of equating any particular construction with the English copula. He isolates four functions
of copular systems in the Niger-Congo languages: identification, description, location and possession. In different languages different members
of this opposition share the same or similar morphology. Schneider (1966)
gives three different forms of copular constructions found in West
African Pidgin English. Bailey (1966) gives two for Jamaican creole.
All of this suggests that the apparent counter-example to the treatment
of Black English differences as simplifications may be no counter-
example at all. It may simply need another point of reference: the
American Black English copular system may be viewed as a simplification
of West African copular systems.

Conclusions

     There are at least four constructions in Black English that can be
viewed as simplifications of standard English grammar: relative clause
reduction, multiple negation, existential sentences and auxiliary inversion. The simplifications are of several types: simplification of
structural descriptions, of structural changes, of ordering constraints,
and deletion of rules. Such facts are consistent with what is known
about the development of pidgins and creoles. That is, the existence of
some prior creole would be sufficient to explain them. However, it is
not necessary to posit such a creole in order to explain these facts.
They could arise independently through normal language change. In some
instances they could derive directly from other dialects. The cases of
multiple negation across sentence boundaries and the relative clause reduction, however, are sufficiently radical and widespread to make natural
change an unlikely source, given the relatively short time span. Necessity arguments for a prior creolization will have to be drawn from
somewhere other than contemporary Black English syntax--from historical
attestations, from knowledge of the contact situation. The distinctive
characteristics of Black English syntax are completely consistent with
a prior creolization, but they do not establish it.

                              NOTES

     [1]It is of course conceivable that the processes of syncretism and
simplification can converge. If so, they would be expected to reinforce
each other.

     [2]For a comparable conjunction of conditions: Relative clause re-
duction can occur under identity of any noun phrase if the embedded S
contains a finite form of *to be* and for other embedded Ss if the identical noun phrase is not the surface subject.

     [3]See Gray (1973) for a discussion of other function of these pro-
nouns.

     [4]*t/d* deletion.

[5]For Stockwell et al. (1973) the rule is the optional case of NEG-Attraction. Labov terms this rule NEG-postposing (1972:191).

[6]*Some-any* suppletion also occurs in standard English in questions. It seems though that at least some speakers of Black English do not employ suppletive *any* in questions. There are no examples of it in the 13,000 word text analyzed by Legum et al. (1971).

[7]Feagin (1979) gives the following sentence from an Anglo teenager, 'We ain't never really had no tornadoes in this area here that I don't remember.'

[8]*Know* is not a verb that allows Neg-Raising so it cannot readily be argued that the NEG has been copied up rather than down.

[9]but see Milsark (1974) for some exceptions.

[10]If 'Zero-copula' is considered to be a separate construction, as by Dillard (1972), then there are three such constructions.

REFERENCES

Bach, Emmon. 1974. Syntactic theory. New York, Holt, Rinehart and Winston.

Bach, Emmon and Robert T. Harms. 1972. How do languages get crazy rules? In: Linguistic change and generative theory, ed. by Robert P. Stockwell and Ronald K. S. Macaulay. Bloomington, Indiana University Press. Pp. 1-21.

Bailey, Beryl Loftman. 1966. Jamaican Creole Syntax: a transformational approach. Cambridge, Cambridge University Press.

Bever, T. G. and D. T. Langendoen. 1972. The interaction of speech perception and grammatical structure in the evolution of language. In: Linguistic change and generative theory, ed. by Robert P. Stockwell and Ronald K. S. Macaulay. Bloomington, Indiana University Press. Pp. 32-95.

Burt, Marina K. 1971. From deep to surface structure. New York, Harper and Row.

Day, Richard. 1972. Patterns of variation in copula and tense in the Hawaiian post Creole continuum. Doctoral dissertation, University of Hawaii. Ann Arbor, University Microfilms.

Dillard, J. L. 1972. Black English, its history and usage in the United States. New York, Random House.

Fasold, Ralph W. 1969. Tense and the form *be* in Black English. Language 45:763-776.

Feagin, Crawford. 1979. Variation and change in Alabama English. Washington, D.C., Georgetown University Press.

Ferguson, Charles A. 1971. Absence of copula and the notion of simplicity. In: Pidginization and creolization of languages, ed. by Dell Hymes. London, Cambridge University Press. Pp. 141-150.

Givón, Talmy. 1979. Prolegomena to any sane creology. In: Readings in creole studies, ed. by I. F. Hancock. Ghent, E. Story-Scientia. Pp. 3-35.

Gray, Wilson. 1973. Appositive pronoun predicatizers in Black English. Paper read at the Second Annual Colloquium on New Ways of Analyzing Variation in English, Washington, D.C.

Gumperz, John J. and Robert Wilson. 1971. Convergence and creoliza- tion. In: Pidginization and creolization of languages, ed. by Dell Hymes. London, Cambridge University Press. Pp. 151-167.

Hackenberg, Robert G. 1972. Appalachian English: a sociolinguistic study. Georgetown University dissertation. Ann Arbor: Univer- sity Microfilm.

Hale, Horatio. 1890. The Oregon trade language or 'Chinook' jargon. London, Whittaker and Co.

Hench, A. L. 1937. A survival of 'it is' = 'there is.' English Studies 19:14.

Hymes, Dell (ed.). 1971. Pidginization and creolization of languages. London, Cambridge University Press.

Kay, Paul and Gillian Sankoff. 1974. A language-universals approach to pidgins and creoles. In: Pidgins and creoles: current trends and prospects, ed. by David DeCamp and Ian F. Hancock. Washington, D.C., Georgetown University Press. Pp. 61-72.

Key, Mary Ritchie. 1973. The history of Black English. Paper read at the conference on the Cognitive and Language Development in the Black Child, St. Louis, Missouri, January 1973.

Kiparsky, Paul. 1968. Linguistic universals and linguistic change. In: Universals in linguistic theory, ed. by Emmon Bach and Robert T. Harms. New York, Holt, Rinehart and Winston. Pp. 170- 202.

Klima, Edward S. 1964. Relatedness between grammatical systems. Language 40:1-20.

Labov, William. 1972. Contraction, deletion, and inherent varia- bility of the English copula. In: Language in the inner city, ed. by William Labov. Philadelphia, University of Pennsylvania Press. Pp. 65-129.

Labov, William, Paul Cohen, Clarence Robins, and John Lewis. 1968. A study of the non-standard English of Negro and Puerto Rican speakers in New York City. Final Report, Cooperative Research Project 3288, 2 vols. Washington, D.C., Office of Education.

Legum, Stanley E., Carol Pfaff, Gene Tinnie, and Michael Nicholas. 1971. The speech of young Black children in Los Angeles. Technical Report TR 33. Los Alamitos, California, SWRL Educational Research and Development.

Milsark, Gary. 1974. Properties, quantification, and *there* insertion. Paper read at the Annual LSA Meeting, New York.

Peet, William, Jr. 1974. Omission of subjective relative pronouns in Hawaiian English restrictive relative clauses. In: Towards tomorrow's linguistics, ed. by Roger W. Shuy and C.-J. N. Bailey. Washington, D.C., Georgetown University Press.

Richards, Henry. 1970. Trinidadian Folk usage and Standard English: a constrastive study. Word 26:79-87.

Sanders, Gerald A. and James H.-Y. Tal. 1972. Immediate dominance and identity deletion. Foundations of Language 8:161-198.

Schneider, Gilbert D. 1966. West African Pidgin-English. Athens, Ohio, Hartford Seminary Foundation.

Smith, Riley B. 1972. Interrelatedness of certain deviant structures in Negro nonstandard dialects. In: Language and cultural diversity in American education, ed. by Roger D. Abrahams and Rudolph C. Troike. Englewood Cliffs, N.J., Prentice-Hall. Pp. 291-294.

Southworth, Franklin C. 1971. Detecting prior creolization: an analysis of the historical origins of Marathi. In: Pidginization and creolization of languages, ed. by Dell Hymes. London, Cambridge University Press. Pp. 255-273.

Stockwell, Robert P. and Ronald K. S. Macaulay (eds.). 1972. Linguistic change and generative theory. Bloomington, Indiana University Press.

Stockwell, Robert P., Paul Schachter, and Barbara Hall Partee. 1973. The major syntactic structures of English. New York, Holt, Rinehart and Winston.

Thompson, Sandra Annear. 1971. The deep structure of relative clauses. In: Studies in linguistic semantics, ed. by Charles J. Fillmore and D. Terence Langendoen. New York, Holt, Rinehart and Winston. Pp. 79-94.

Visser, F. Th. 1963. An historical syntax of the English language. Vol. 1. Leiden, H. J. Brill.

Voorhoeve, Jan. 1971. A note on reduction and expansion in grammar. In: Pidginization and creolization of languages, ed. by Dell Hymes. London, Cambridge University Press. P. 189.

Welmers, Wm. E.   1973.   African language structures.   Berkeley,
      University of California Press.

Whinnom, Keith.   1971.   Linguistic hybridization and the 'special
      case' of pidgins and creoles.   In: Pidginization and creolization
      of languages, ed. by Dell Hymes.   London, Cambridge University
      Press.   Pp. 91-115.

Williamson, Juanita V.   1969.   A note on it is/there is.   Word Study.

Wright, Joseph.   1905.   English dialect dictionary.   London, Oxford.

LEXICALIZATION IN BLACK ENGLISH[1]

Carol W. Pfaff
Freie Universität Berlin

1. INTRODUCTION

Although most scholars now agree that Black English in the United States originated as a creole, underwent decreolization and is now part of a post-creole continuum, there remains disagreement over the extent to which its creole origin is still reflected in its present-day underlying structure. Further, despite general agreement on the existence of certain patterns of sociolinguistic variation in Black English, there is persistent disagreement not only about their implications for the underlying grammar, but also about how they should be described, and even observed.

The present study of variation in Black English[2] provides empirical evidence which illustrates the relationships among models of synchronic and diachronic variation and suggests that lexicalization, a process of restructuring underlying forms, can account for observed synchronic patterns which are unexplained by existing models.

2. MODELS OF SOCIOLINGUISTIC VARIATION

Numerous studies starting with Labov (1966) have demonstrated that sociolinguistic variation is not random "free variation" but is constrained by linguistic and social factors. Models of such constrained variation fall into two classes: variable rule models and implicational wave models. The variable rule model proposed in Labov (1969) generates both interpersonal and intrapersonal variation directly, by means of rules which incorporate social and linguistic constraints on their frequency of application. Thus, for each linguistic feature, a single complex rule accounts for variation in the speech community.[3]

2.1. The variable rule model

Labov's first formulation of variable rules was based on analysis which summed data from members of socially defined groups. This procedure, which is not empirically justified as results of the present study show (cf. section 5), has been criticized by a number of scholars including Bickerton (1973a:19) who argues that:

> ... grammars which contain Labovian variable rules must be based on the behaviour of groups, and that group behaviours can be very misleading with regard to the contents of individual rule systems.

A case in point is the analysis of auxiliary *have*, to be treated further in the present paper (sections 5-6).

Labov et al. (1968:223-225), on the basis of grouping data from adolescent boys, concluded that auxiliary *have* is part of the underlying structure of Black English but is frequently deleted by the same variable rules which account for contraction and deletion of the copula. They attributed the very high frequency of null realization of auxiliary *have* in perfect progressives, such as *he been running*, and in perfectives of copular *be*, such as *he been here*, to the existence of a phonological constraint, claiming that the following *b* in *been* facilitates the operation of the variable rule.

Bickerton (1973a:19) has pointed out the pitfalls inherent in group analysis of infrequently occurring linguistic forms:

> ... in Labov's data, occurrences of *have* seem to be outnumbered by informants, i.e., there must be speakers who, at least while being monitored, never produced *have*. If a speaker, given sufficient opportunity to produce a feature, fails to produce it, it seems not unreasonable to suppose that it forms no part of his grammar. Assuming this would enable us to resolve the contradiction very simply: some BE speakers have *have*, and others do not.

Bickerton's statements make it appear that the issue of group vs. individual analysis of sociolinguistic variation is a crucial distinction between the competing variable rule model and the implicational wave model. However, the Cedergren and Sankoff (1974) formulation of the variable rule model makes it clear that the group vs. individual issue should properly be separated into two independent questions:

1) should data from more than one individual be combined? (is group behavior a better reflection of the grammar of a speech community than the behavior of individual members?) and

2) should single variable rules provide for interpersonal variation?

The Cedergren and Sankoff (1974) modification of the variable rule model treats individual results, thus avoiding some of the problems raised by group analysis, while Rousseau and Sankoff (1978:98-99) suggest that group analysis is legitimate if groups are linguistically rather than socially defined. A solution which is similar in this respect to the Bailey and Bickerton models.

2.2. The implicational wave model

The dynamic or implicational wave model proposed by Bailey (1972) and Bickerton (1971, 1973) regards the grammar as containing sets of categorical rules which generate linguistically defined lects. In this model, which is claimed to directly reflect historical change as well as synchronic variation, interpersonal variation is accounted for in terms of speakers having different rules. Intrapersonal variation is attributed to speakers having lects which are in the process of being "reached" by a spreading rule (Bickerton 1973a:24).

The wave model predicts that implicational relationships will hold between the realizations of linguistic variables. In an early version of this model (DeCamp 1971), it was predicted that all linguistic variables in a speech community would form an implicational scale. In more recent versions, this claim has been modified to predict only that certain closely related linguistic variables will form an implicational scale. Bickerton (1973b) has further suggested that in a creole continuum, lects are characterized by tendencies toward (a) partial selection of target rules of the acrolect, (b) the principle of least effort (minimal change between adjacent lects) and (c) subcategorization of rules by grammatical environments. The analog of such implicational claims in the variable rule model is the assumption that there are hierarchies of constraints on rule application.

As models of linguistic change, both the variable rule model and the implicational wave model focus on the gradual spread of rules and constraints on rules through the speech community. Neither model, however, emphasizes the role of grammatical change brought about through restructuring by children, although it is commonplace in recent generative theory to claim that "basically change comes about through children's restructuring of the grammar (Fromkin and Rodman 1974:220).

3. MODELS OF GRAMMAR RESTRUCTURING

Within generative theory, there are two models of grammar restructuring: the transformational generative (TG) model and the natural generative (NG) model. The TG model focuses on restructuring of rules: rule generalization or restriction, rule addition or loss and rule reordering (King 1969). Underlying lexical representations are regarded as highly resistant to change (Chomsky and Halle 1968:49).

The TG model was adopted by a number of important investigators of Black English in both the creolist and non-creolist camps. Thus, Labov et al. (1968) account for differences between Black and White English in terms of low-level, primarily phonological, rules. The opposing analyses of Black English proposed by creolists such as Stewart and Dillard also adopted the position that differences can be attributed to presence or absence of general, often syntactic or semantic rules. Loflin (1970: 19) provides a formalized partial generative grammar in this vein.

It is apparent from examination of texts or dictionaries of creole languages, however, that one of their most striking characteristics is significant change in form and meaning of words adopted from the source language as demonstrated by Hancock (1977). The NG model as developed by Vennemann and others can incorporate such observations since it provides for restructuring of underlying forms due to rule lexicalization as an integral part of grammar change.

Such lexical restructuring subsequently may contribute to further rule restructuring and rule inversion (Vennemann 1974, Hinnebusch 1974). Discussion of NG restructuring has centered around changes in phonology, but, as I will demonstrate, lexicalization of rules is also an appropriate model for some syntactic features of Black English.

4.   A METHODOLOGICAL NOTE

To investigate the methodological question of whether grouping individuals data is a valid procedure, the group data must be compared with the data from the individuals who make up the group. In order to collect enough data from individuals to allow for the range of intrapersonal variation, it is obviously necessary to obtain multiple instances of linguistic variables from each informant. This poses no problem when high frequency phonological or syntactic variables are the object of investigation, but requires the use of structured elicitation procedures to supplement free conversation data when the issue concerns variables, such as auxiliary *have*, which occur with low frequency in free conversation.[4] Structured techniques also have the advantage of holding linguistic and extra-linguistic environments constant so that hypotheses about implicational relationships among variables or hierarchical relationships among constraints on variable rules can be investigated. In addition, data from each informant are strictly comparable.

The apparent drawback of structured techniques, namely that they elicit relatively formal styles, actually has certain advantages for the study of decreolization.[5] Clearly, overt social pressure to conform, at least in formal situations, to what LePage (1975) has aptly termed the totemized standard language plays a significant part in decreolization.

In the present study, a number of low frequency forms were investigated using elicitation techniques designed to increase their frequency without providing a model of the structures to the informants.[6] In this paper, I will focus on four sets of linguistic variables:

1) 3sg present tense agreement markers on (a) regular verbs such as *walk*, *wave* and *watch*, (b) the irregular verb *have*, both as an auxiliary and as a main verb, and (c) the irregular verb *do* as an auxiliary, both affirmative and negative.

2) perfective aspect marking.

3) possessive marking on nouns and pronouns.

4) the relationship of (3) to the phonological rule of *r*-desulcalization.

The theoretical implications of the results for variables (1) and (2) which pertain to tense/aspect marking will be examined first.

5.   GROUP VS. INDIVIDUAL ANALYSIS

Turning first to the question of how well summing data for individuals reflect the grammar of the speech community, compare Tables 1 and 2, which report the results of structured elicitation of main verb and auxiliary *have*.

Table 1. Realization of Main Verb and Auxiliary *Have*
(Percent of Each Realization by Income and Ethnic Group)

Group	Main Verb							Auxiliary				
	Std has	Std 's got	Nstd have	Nstd got	Nstd gots	Nstd haves	n	Std has	Std 's	Nstd have	Nstd Ø	n
Low Inc Black	13	0	39	45	2	0	663	5	9	0	86	98
Mid Inc Black	41	0	36	24	0	0	323	1	19	2	78	111
Low Inc White	79	2	0	7	12	0	58	-	-	-	-	3
Mid Inc White	88	0	1	4	7	0	282	5	95	0	0	21

Table 2. Realization of Main Verb and Auxiliary *Have* by Individual Informants

MAIN AUX VERB	categorically standard		variable			categorically nonstandard	
	has/-s	has/have	has/got	has/have/got	have	have/got	got
Low-Income							
Cat Std has/-s	0	0	0	0	0	0	0
Var -s/∅	0	2	0	0	2	1	0
Cat Nst ∅	0	3	0	3	2	2	2
No Instances	0	9	1	5	1	9	8
Total	0	14	1	8	5	12	10
Middle-Income							
Cat Std has/-s	1	0	0	0	0	0	0
Var -s/∅	1	1	0	0	0	0	2
Cat Nst ∅	2	1	0	1	6	3	1
No Instances	3	4	0	0	2	2	1
Total	7	6	0	1	8	5	4

Table 1, the group results, shows that, with the exception of middle-income White children's realization of auxiliary *have*, which is categorically standard, all groups appear to be variable for both main verb and auxiliary *have*. The middle-income groups appear to have considerably higher proportions of standard realizations. These results are quite consistent with the results of other studies of Black and White English in the United States.

Table 2, however, which reports the individual results for the Black informants, reveals that rather than inherent variability, many informants of both income groups produce categorically standard or nonstandard realizations. This pattern is quite different from that which emerges from the group analysis and supports Bickerton's claim cited above that group analysis is not an adequate reflection of individual behavior.

6.   IMPLICATIONAL RELATIONSHIPS

Turning now to the empirical verification of the claim that linguistic variables form an implicational scale, consider the data for three sets of variables: (1) auxiliary and main verb *have*, (2) affirmative and negative auxiliary *do*, and (3) regular and irregular verb agreement marking.

6.1.   Auxiliary vs. Main Verb *Have*

The first pair of variables do not form a strict implicational continuum.   Table 2 shows that the realization of the perfect auxiliary does not have any consistent relationship to the realization of the main verb: both standard and nonstandard realizations of the auxiliary occur in the speech of informants who use each of the possible realizations of the main verb.

Before accepting this lack of scaling as crucial counter-evidence to the implicational model, however, recall that any failure of linguistic variables to form an implicational scale is covered by the claim that only closely related variables will scale.   It may well be that, despite their lexical identity, main verb *have* and auxiliary *have* are not closely related enough to form an implicational continuum.   This is reasonable since not only do these forms have radically different syntactic functions, but their typical nonstandard realizations also differ.   The typical nonstandard realization of auxiliary *have* is null, while that of the main verb is a full form (*have* or *got*) unmarked for agreement.   Nonetheless, to avoid circularity, it is essential for proponents of the implicational wave model to provide an independent definition of the notion "closely related variables."

6.2.   Affirmative vs. Negative Auxiliary *Do*

In the second case, the results do conform to the predictions of the implicational wave model.   For agreement marking on the regular verb *do* used as an auxiliary, we are dealing with variables which differ only in negativity.   The present study confirms previous findings (Fasold 1972, Labov et al. 1968) that the negative *doesn't* vs. *don't* is realized as nonstandard more frequently than the affirmative *does* vs. *do*. The expected implicational or hierarchical pattern holds both for groups (see Table 3) and for all but two individuals (see Table 4).

Table 3.   Percent Nonstandard Realization of Agreement on Irregular and Regular Verbs by Income Group

	Main Verb Have	Auxiliary Do	Auxiliary Don't	Regular Main Verb
Low Inc Black	87% (n=663)	85% (n=123)	93% (n=202)	63% (n=582)
Mid Inc Black	59% (n=323)	76% (n=79)	76% (n=131)	58% (n=352)

Table 4.   Lects of Agreement of Irregular Verbs (*have, do, do+not*) and Regular Verbs

	Low-Income	Middle-Income
A: Categorically Nonstandard	4	2
B: Categorically Standard	0	1
C: Irregular Verbs more Standard than Regular	0	4
D: Irregular Verbs less Standard than Regular	23	9
E: Mixed: Some Irregular Verbs more, some less Standard than Regular	19	15
F: All Variable	3	0

6.3.   Regular vs. Irregular Verbs

In the case of agreement marking of regular vs. irregular verbs,[7] we again find a considerable difference in the results of group vs. individual analysis.

From the group data in Table 3, it appears that regular vs. irregular verbs do form an implicational scale: nonstandard realization of irregular verbs occurs with the same or greater frequency than regular verbs. However, the individual results shown in Table 4 give a vastly different picture. Thirty-two different patterns of variation are found. These fall into six general classes:

(A) regular and irregular verbs categorically nonstandard
(B) regular and irregular verbs categorically standard
(C) irregular verbs more standard than regular verbs
(D) irregular verbs less standard than regular verbs
(E) mixed (some irregular verbs more standard than regular
  verbs, others less standard than regular verbs)
(F) regular and irregular verbs all variable

Lects in classes A, B, D and F fit the implicational scale which describes the group behavior, but nearly half the informants (37 of 80) have lects in classes C or E, which contradict this hypothesis.

Implicational asymmetries within related variables may be correlated with social factors as Bickerton (1973b) notes. In a study similar to the present one, but using grouped results, Berdan (1973b:12) found two different patterns of variation significantly correlated with social status. For the group of informants from a low-income school, the proportion of nonstandard realization of irregular verbs was higher than for regular verbs, while for the group from a middle-income school, the situation was reversed.

The data in the present study do not entirely confirm the pattern found by Berdan. Even the group data fail to show the predicted implicational crossover or reordering of constraints on agreement marking, and closer inspection of the individual lects accounts for this failure. Although lects of classes B and C, which have relatively standard realization of agreement on irregular verbs, are confined to middle-income informants, lects in classes A and D, with relatively nonstandard realization of agreement on irregular verbs, are by no means confined to low-income informants.

Furthermore, nearly half the lects (classes E and F) fit neither proposed ordering but show that irregular verbs do not form a class opposed to regular verbs. Within the category of irregular verbs, strict implicational patterns do not hold between the realization of *have* and *do*. The group data show nonagreement of main verb *have* at about the same level as auxiliary affirmative *do*, and somewhat lower than negative *do*. The individual results show that half the lects, spoken by 64 informants, fit this implicational pattern with *have* unmarked for agreement with the same or lower frequency than *do*, but that half the lects, spoken by 16 informants, reverse the pattern, showing nonagreement of *have* more frequently than nonagreement of either or both affirmative or negative *do*. Such non-implications cannot satisfactorily be explained by rule orderings or constraints.

7. LEXICALIZATION

The alternative hypothesis, heretofore obscured by the focus of attention on group data and by the assumption of a TG as opposed to an NG model
of language change, is that individuals' grammars have different underlying lexical representations for the items in question. From a historical point of view, lexicalization occurs when a variable rule becomes
categorical for some lexical items for some informants. Underlying
lexical representations are subsequently changed in the course of language
acquisition, in which children restructure the grammar in accordance with
the primary linguistic data to which they are exposed. Synchronically,
lexicalization shows up in cases, such as 3sg agreement marking discussed
above, where realization of particular lexical items differs either categorically or variably from the realization of other lexical items which
are members of the same natural class. The result is that strict implicational or hierarchical relationships among related variables do not
hold.[8]

8. FURTHER EVIDENCE OF LEXICALIZATION: *I'M*

A second example of lexicalization emerges as a result of examination
of copula deletion in Black English. Labov (1972a:98) formulated the rule
as follows:

$$ \text{ə} \; \rightarrow \; \emptyset \; / \; \text{<+Pro>} \;\; \#\# \; \underset{+T}{\underline{\hspace{2cm}}} \;\; C^1_0 \;\; \#\# \; \text{<+Vb>} $$
$$ * \; \text{<+nas>} $$

The above rule accounts for the categorical preservation of the contracted
copula with the 1sg pronoun (*I'm*) with an invariant phonological constraint,
*<+nas>. This device works simply because no other tense-incorporating form
to which this rule applies has a nasal as its final segment.

There is evidence, however, that categorical preservation of the nasal
in *I'm* should be attributed not to a categorical phonological constraint,
but to lexicalized restructuring of the form. Torrey (1972) reports the
hypercorrect forms *I'm is* and *I'm am* in responses of second grade black
(but not white) children to challenges such as "you're not David!" (when
he was). Labov, who cites these forms (1972a:50) himself suggests that
these children do not segment *I'm* into a sequence of personal pronoun
plus copula, but regard it as an allomorph of *I* in equational sentences,
i.e., they lexically reanalyze the form.

9. FURTHER EVIDENCE OF LEXICALIZATION: POSSESSIVE MARKING

A third case of lexicalization is found in the sociolinguistic variation between the realizations of possessive pronouns *you* vs. *your* and *they*
vs. *their* in Black English. In their discussion in 1968, Labov et al.
claimed that the nonstandard forms *you* and *they* were the output of a
general phonological process, now called r-desulcalization, which could
be shown to operate rather generally to yield r-less forms of *car*, *cart*
and even *Carol* and *Paris*.[9] Dillard (1972:57), on the other hand, argued
that lack of possessive marking is a general syntactic characteristic of

the basilect for nouns as well as pronouns, which also yields forms such as *me book* and *the man hat*.[10]

The storytelling task in the present study elicited multiple occurrences of possessive pronouns, possessive nouns and several words with post-vocalic *r* such as *bear*, *chair*, *stair*, and *there*, which are exact rhymes of the 3pl possessive pronoun *their*. As noted in Legum et al. (1971:42) and in Pfaff (1973:192-193), the varieties of Black English spoken by Los Angeles children are overwhelmingly *r*-ful, but even so, the results of the present study were quite striking. The only instances of *r*-less forms were in the 3pl possessive pronoun (19 of 34 potential instances) and in the 3pl subject pronoun plus the contraction of *be* (*they* for *they're*) (9 of 21 potential instances). Thus it is clear that, for these children, *they* as a possessive pronoun or as a realization of they're is in no way connected with the phonological rule which desulcalizes *r*.

Nor do instances of *they* as 3pl possessive pronouns in the present study appear to be due to a syntactic lack of possessive marking in general. The possessive pronouns *my*, *his* and *her* invariably had standard realizations by speakers who use nonstandard *they* as well as by those with standard *their*. Further, while approximately 50% of the possessive nouns were not inflectionally marked with *-s* (98 of 200 potential instances), such lack of inflectional possessive marking is not implicationally related to the use of *they* for *their*. Thus, for these Los Angeles speakers, they must simply be an alternative underlying lexical representation, the result of lexicalization of general phonological and/or syntactic rules which may still operate productively in other varieties of Black English.[11]

10. LINGUISTIC AND SOCIAL DETERMINANTS OF LEXICALIZATION

Lexicalization, which is related to but not identical with the concept of lexical diffusion of a linguistic change discussed by Wang (1969) and Chen and Wang (1975), is due in part to linguistic factors such as frequency of occurrence and syntactic function. These linguistic factors, incidentally, have been significant in protecting the irregular verbs from regularization in standard English. However, lexicalization appears to be even more strongly influenced by social factors than by structural factors. Labov (1972b:248) noted that singling out particular lexical items is characteristic of linguistic variables which become stereotypes. Thus, he attributed unsystematic variability in non-vernacular styles, i.e., failure to scale implicationally, to conscious correction to the standard realization of stereotyped variables.

The same social process also applies in reverse: association of the nonstandard realizations of stereotyped markers with counterculture values leads to increase of their frequency in vernacular speech. Mitchell-Kernan (1972:209) noted that among black teenagers in Oakland, California, some features of Black English are associated with liberation and separatism of the Black community while other features are stigmatized within the community as "country" or "southern." This situation, she suggests, will lead to the development of new structural distinctions between Black and White English. The present data suggest further that different patterns of agreement are developing as markers of "bad" Black English as opposed to "standard Black English."

11. CONCLUSIONS

On the basis of the above data, it appears that a strict TG model which assumes identical underlying lexical representations in all dialects cannot be maintained. As a result, models of sociolinguistic variation must be broadened to allow for variation in the lexicon as well as in low-level rules. One consequence of lexicalization is that performance is not a direct reflection of competence; identical phonetic performances can be the output of quite different underlying grammatical forms and rules. Because of the range of potential differences in individual speakers' grammars, data from free vernacular conversation must be supplemented by more structured contexts which can elicit linguistic forms and contexts which are crucial for deciding among alternative grammars.

Lexical differences seem to be idiosyncratically distributed among individual members of a social group, although such idiosyncracies are probably conditioned by individuals' attitudes, self-concept, projected self-image and other social factors.[12] In particular lexicalizaton is associated with the existence of linguistic stereotypes. In the case of Black English, at least two (partially conflicting) social forces interact with linguistic factors to increase lexicalization of stereotyped variables: (1) pressure for continued decreolization toward standard English and (2) the positive social value of nonstandard forms as markers of in-group ethnic pride.

NOTES

[1]A somewhat different version of this paper under the title "The process of decreolization in Black English" was originially presented at the Conference.

[2]Data cited are from a structured study (Pfaff 1973) of 81 Black and 30 white low and middle income first grade children in Los Angeles and from a study (Legum et al. 1971) of free conversation of kindergarten, first, second and third grade children. I wish to express my appreciation to William Bright for discussion of versions of this paper.

[3]The variable rule formulation is particularly well suited to account for hearers competent in understanding members of the speech community who speak different varieties of their language. This issue is not addressed in the present paper, which focuses on grammars as models of speakers' production competence.

[4]The fact that some linguistic variables occur with lower frequency in the speech of some social groups is itself an interesting phenomenon. Apparently different social groups have different "favorite" syntactic structures which are used in equivalent communicative situations. In the present study, for example, Black and White first grade children's versions of the Three Bears story yielded evidence that the perfect progressive was less frequently chosen by Black than by White children. Black children tended to use simple past or past progressive forms more frequently. The

choice of alternative syntactic structures appears to be related to an individual's use of standard or nonstandard forms of perfect progressive as well. These issues are treated in further detail in Pfaff (1976).

[5]It is somewhat surprising that Labov (1972a:208) claims that because non-vernacular styles may show irregular phonological and grammatical patterns with a great deal of hypercorrection, they are less valid indicators of linguistic change than working-class vernacular. As Burling (1975:507) points out, Labov's position on the uniformity of working-class vernacular is neither supported by empirical evidence nor consistent with Labov's earlier work (1964, reprinted in 1972a:122-42) in which he demonstrated that hypercorrection in non-vernacular styles by the lower middle-class is one of the major factors in linguistic change.

[6]The elicitation techniques, described in detail in Pfaff (1973) included production tasks, consisting of a series of questions and answers about a set of pictures. The form of the question, together with the content of the picture, highly determined the linguistic structure of the response, but did not contain a model of it. For example, *have* as a main verb was elicited by showing the informant pictures of two familiar items which differed only in the number of some attribute--e.g., bugs with one and three spots. Interviewer's questions of the form, "What's the difference between this bug and that bug?" elicited two instances of main verb *have* (or some other verb indicating possession) for each item, as in (a):

(a) This bug has/have one spot and this bug has/have three spots.
Auxiliary *do*, both affirmative and negative, was elicited by pairs in which one member lacked some inalienable part possessed by the other, e.g., houses with and without windows. Items of this type elicited responses like (b):

(b) This house doesn't/don't have windows and this one does/do.
Regular main verbs were elicited by pictures of people engaged in some recognizable occupation. The interviewer would say, e.g., "This is a dogcatcher. What does he do?" The response had the form (c):

(c) He catches/catch dogs.
In a story telling task, informants were asked to tell the story of Goldilocks and the Three Bears, cued by a set of pictures. This familiar story contains multiple opportunities for the occurrence of perfects, potentially containing auxiliary *have* in statements such as (d):

(d) Someone has/'s/have/∅ been sleeping in my bed.
and possessive nouns and pronouns.

[7]It is reasonable to consider that morphological regularity would be a significant conditioning factor for 3sg agreement marking as it is for past tense marking. Fasold (1972:123-124) disconfirmed the hypothesis that agreement marking of irregular verbs would be more standard than for regular verbs, the pattern found to hold for past tense marking. Instead, he found that certain irregular verbs were more frequently unmarked.

[8]Fasold (1973) has identified diachronic developments of rules which can result in frequency patterns which do not fit strict implicational

schemata. He particularly cites rule stagnation, in which "rules become arrested at the variable stage," as the factor responsible for social markers which are not significant as implicational indicators of linguistic change. This analysis may be appropriate for the speech community as a whole, but, from the point of view of the individual's acquisition of social markers, rule acceleration and/or rule inhibition applied to specific lexical items--i.e., lexicalization--may provide a more appropriate explanation.

[9]Labov (1972a:38-39) expresses a different view, claiming that forms such as *they book* and *you book* have recently been reinterpreted as related to *r*-desulcalization by BEV speakers. However, he gives no supporting evidence that these forms are subject to the same pattern of variable constraints as affect clear cases of phonological *r*-desulcalization or that hypercorrect *r*-ful forms occasionally occur for non-possessive pronouns. Thus it appears that the reinterpretation is not to be attributed to BEV speakers, but simply to Labov's recent rejection of his former analysis of the pronominal forms as the output of a phonological rule.

[10]Dillard's claim that basilect Black English forms are especially common in the speech of some young Black children is discussed in Pfaff (1973:151-159).

[11]The status of *they* for *they're* is different. Six of the seven informants who produced *they* for *they're* also consistently lacked 3sg present tense forms of *be*, both as a copula and as an auxiliary. Thus the forms such as *they going* may be attributed to the operation of a general rule which deletes *be*. See Pfaff (1973:189-191) for further discussion.

[12]These effects are not unique to Black English. Recent work in sociolinguistics which focuses on social psychological correlates of linguistic variation has begun to demonstrate the interrelationships. The effects are particularly clear in cases of recent extensive social change such as is found in the large-scale migration of foreign workers to Western European countries. The Heidelberger Forschungsprojekt Pidgin Deutsch 1975, for example, demonstrates the relationship between workers' intention to immigrate permanently on their patterns of acquisition of German. Gótowos (1979) analyses sociolinguistic behavior of Greek children as a reflection of their parents' strongly ethno-centric attitudes.

Work on attitudes toward nonstandard British dialects also demonstrates the linguistic effects of counter-cultural norms. In a study of persuasiveness of arguments presented in RP and nonstandard dialects, Giles found "nonstandard communicators rated low on expertness but high in trustworthiness" (Giles & Powesland 1975:95). Portz (1978) discusses the acquisition of nonstandard variants by children and adolescents as a phenomena of youth culture which represents awareness of the connotations of nonstandard accents and their positive value as a symbol of counter-culture norms.

REFERENCES

Bailey, C-J. 1972. The patterning of language variation. In: Varieties of present-day American English, ed. by R. W. Bailey and J. L. Robinson, pp. 156-186. New York, Macmillan.

Bailey, C-J. and R. Shuy (eds.) 1973. New ways of analyzing variation in English. Washington, D.C., Georgetown University Press.

Bailey, R. W. and J. L. Robinson. 1972. Varieties of present-day American English. New York, Macmillan.

Berdan, R. 1973a. Probability and variable rules: a formal interpretation. Paper presented at Ann Arbor, Michigan, Linguistic Society of America, Summer Meeting.

Berdan, R. 1973b. The necessity of variable rules. Paper presented at NWAVE-2, Washington, D.C.

Bickerton, D. 1971. Inherent variability and variable rules. Foundations of Language 7:457-492.

Bickerton, D. 1973a. Quantitative versus dynamic paradigms. In: New ways of analyzing variation in English, ed. by C-J. Bailey and R. Shuy, pp. 23-43. Washington, D.C., Georgetown University Press.

Bickerton, D. 1973b. On the nature of a creole continuum. Language 49:640-649.

Burling, R. 1975. Review of W. Labov, *Language in the inner city*. Language 51:505-509.

Cazden, C., V. Johns and D. Hymes (eds.). 1972. Functions of language in the classroom. New York, Teachers College Press.

Cedergren, H. and D. Sankóff. 1974. Variable rules: performance as a statistical reflection of competence. Language 50:333-355.

Chen, M. Y. and W. S-Y Wang. 1975. Sound change: actuation and implementation. Language 51:255-281.

Chomsky, N. and M. Halle. 1968. The sound pattern of English. New York, Harper and Row.

DeCamp, D. 1971. Toward a generative analysis of a post-creole continuum. In: Pidginization and creolization of language, ed. by D. Hymes, pp. 349-370. Cambridge, Cambridge University Press.

Dillard, J. 1972. Black English: Its history and usage in the United States. New York, Random House.

Fasold, R. 1972. Tense marking in Black English. Washington, D.C., Center for Applied Linguistics.

Fasold, R. 1973. The concept of 'earlier-later': more or less
    correct. In: New ways of analyzing variation in English, ed. by
    C-J. Bailey and R. Shuy, pp. 183-197. Washington, D.C., Georgetown
    University Press.

Fromkin, V. and R. Rodman. 1974. An introduction to language. New
    York, Holt, Rinehart and Winston.

Giles, H. and P. F. Powesland. 1975. Speech style and social evaluation.
    New York, Academic Press.

Gótowos, A. 1979. Sprache und Interaktion Griechischer Kinder in der
    Bundesrepublik Deutschland bzw Berlin (West). Unpublished doctoral
    dissertation, Freie Universität Berlin.

Hancock, I. R. 1977. Lexical expansion within a closed system. In:
    Sociocultural dimensions of language change, ed. by B. Blount and
    M. Sanches, pp. 161-171. New York, Academic Press.

Heidelberger Forschungsprojekt Pidgin-Deutsch. 1975. Sprache und
    Kommunikation Ausländischer Arbeiter. Analysen, Berichte,
    Materialien. Kronberg/Ts, Scriptor Verlag.

Hinnebusch, T. J. 1974. Rule inversion and restructuring in Kamba.
    Studies in African Linguistics, Supplement 5:149-168.

King, R. 1969. Historical linguistics and generative grammar.
    Englewood Cliffs, New Jersey, Prentice-Hall.

Labov, W. 1966. The social stratification of English in New York
    City. Washington, D.C., Center for Applied Linguistics.

Labov, W. 1969. Contraction, deletion and inherent variability of
    the English copula. Language 45:715-762.

Labov, W. 1972a. Language in the inner city: Studies in the Black
    English vernacular. (Conduct and Communication No. 3)
    Philadelphia, University of Pennsylvania Press.

Labov, W. 1972b. Sociolinguistic patterns. (Conduct and Communication
    No. 4) Philadelphia, University of Pennsylvania Press.

Labov, W., P. Cohen, C. Robins and J. Lewis. 1968. A study of the
    non-standard English of Negro and Puerto Rican speakers in New
    York City. Columbia University Cooperative Research Project
    No. 3288.

LePage, R. B. 1975. Processes of pidginization and creolization.
    Paper presented at the International Conference on Pidgins and
    Creoles, Honolulu, Hawaii.

Legum, S., C. Pfaff, G. Tinnie and M. Nicholas. 1971. The speech of young Black children in Los Angeles. Technical Report No. 33. Inglewood, California, Southwest Regional Laboratory for Educational Research and Development.

Loflin, M. 1970. On the structure of the verb in a dialect of American Negro English. Linguistics 59:14-28.

Mitchell-Kernan, C. 1972. On the status of Black English for native speakers: an assessment of attitude and values. In: Functions of language in the classroom, ed. by C. Cazden, et al., pp. 195-210. New York, Teachers College Press.

Pfaff, C. W. 1971. Historical and structural aspects of sociolinguistic variation: the copula in Black English. Technical Report No. 37. Inglewood, California, Southwest Regional Laboratory for Educational Research and Development.

Pfaff, C. W. 1973. A sociolinguistic study of Black children in Los Angeles. Unpublished Ph.D. dissertation, U.C.L.A.

Pfaff, C. W. 1976. Hypercorrection and grammar change. Language in Society 5:105-107.

Portz, R. 1978. Acquisition and development of language variation and language attitudes in British school children and adolescents. Paper presented at the World Congress of Sociology, Sociolinguistics Program, Uppsala, Sweden.

Rousseau, P. and D. Sankoff. 1978. A solution to the problem of grouping speakers. In: Linguistic variation: models and methods, ed. by D. Sankoff, pp. 97-117. New York, Academic Press.

Shuy, R. and C-J. Bailey. 1974. Toward tomorrow's linguistics. Washington, D.C., Georgetown University Press.

Torrey, J. 1972. The language of black children in the early grades. New London, Conn., Department of Psychology, Connecticut College.

Vennemann, T. 1974. Phonological concreteness in natural generative grammar. In: Toward tomorrow's linguistics, ed. by R. Shuy and C-J. Bailey, pp. 202-219. Washington, D.C., Georgetown University Press.

Wang, W. S-Y. 1969. Competing changes as a cause of residue. Language 45:9-25.

APPENDIX

LIST OF PAPERS PRESENTED

Alleyne, Mervyn, C. Diachronic vs. Synchronic Rules in the Interpretation of Decreolized Forms.

Anderson, Lloyd. Knots in the Creole Net: Clues for Causal Explanations of Language Change, with Particular Reference to Derek Bickerton's Work on Guyanese Creole.

Baron, Naomi S. Trade Jargons and Pidgins. A Functionalist Approach. [published in Journal of Creole Studies, Vol. 1(1), 1977, pp. 5-28]

Bell, Herman. Pidgin Arabic and the Language Survey of the Sudan.

*Berdan, Robert. Sufficiency Conditions for a Prior Creolization of Black English.

*Bickerton, Derek. Creolization, Linguistic Universals, Natural Semantax and the Brain.

Camden, W. G. Parallels in Structure of Lexicon and Syntax Between New Hebrides Bislama and the South Santo Language as Spoken at Tangoa. [published in Papers in Pidgin and Creole Linguistics No. 2. Pacific Linguistics Series A, No. 57. The Australian National University, Canberra, 1979, pp. 51-117]

Cassidy, Frederic G. The Position of Gullah Alongside Caribbean (Especially Jamaican) Creoles.

Clyne, Michael. German and English Working Pidgins. [published in Papers in Pidgin and Creole Linguistics No. 2. Pacific Linguistics Series A, No. 57. The Australian National University, Canberra, 1979, pp. 135-150]

*Cooper, Vincent O. On the Notion of Decreolization and St. Kitts Creole Personal Pronouns.

*Craig, Dennis R. A Creole English Continuum and the Structure of Language.

DeCamp, David. Polysemy and Communication Networks in a Creole Speech Community.

Dennis, Jamie and Jerrie Scott. Creole Formation and Reorganization.

Domingue, Nicole Z. Another English Creole: Middle English. [published in Journal of Creole Studies, Vol. 1(1), 1977, pp. 89-100]

Durbin, Mridula Adenwala. Generality in Pidgins and Creoles.

---

*published in this volume.

Dyen, Isidore.   Creolization in Genetic Theory.

Ferraz, Luiz.   The Origin and Development of Four Creoles in the
      Gulf of Guinea.

Gebhard, Jerry G.   Variation in Thai Adaptation of English Language
      Features.   [published in Papers in Pidgin and Creole Linguistics
      No. 2.   Pacific Linguistics Series A, No. 57.   The Australian
      National University, Canberra, 1979, pp. 201-216]

Gilbert, Glenn G. and Marija Orlovic.   Pidgin German Spoken by
      Foreign Workers in West Germany.

Hancock, Ian F.   Lexical Expansion within a Closed System.

Heine, Bernd.   Some Generalizations on African-Based Pidgins.

Hull, Alexander.   On the Origin and Chronology of the French-Based
      Creoles.

Huttar, George L.   Some Kwa-Like Features of Djuka Syntax.

Jeroslow, Helen McKinney.   Creole Characteristics in Rural Brazilian
      Speech.

Johnson, Samuel V.   Chinook Jargon Variations: Towards the Compleat
      Chinooker.

Kalmar, Ivan.   Language Simplification: Parallels Between Pidginiza-
      tion and Language Learning.

Klein, Sheldon and V. Rozencvejg.   A Computer Model for the Ontogeny of
      Pidgin and Creole Languages.

Koefoed, Geert.   A Note on Pidgins, Creoles and Greenberg's Universals.
      [published in Utrecht Working Papers in Linguistics, Vol. 1, 1976,
      pp. 11-22]

Lattey, Elsa.   Beyond Variable Rules.   [published in Papers in Pidgin
      and Creole Linguistics No. 2. Pacific Linguistics Series A, No. 57.
      The Australian National University, Canberra, 1979, pp. 21-36]

Le Page, R. B.   Processes of Pidginization and Creolization.

Leap, William L.   "To Be" in Isletan English: A Study of Accountability.

Liem, Nguyen Dang.   Cases and Verbs in Pidgin French in Vietnam (Tay
      Boi).   [published in Papers in Pidgin and Creole Linguistics No. 2.
      Pacific Linguistics Series A, No. 57.   The Australian National
      University, Canberra, 1979, pp. 217-246]

Milon, John R.   The Acquisition of Hawaiian Creoles by a Native Speaker
      of Japanese: A Comparison of Development Stages with a Mature
      System.

Molony, Carol H.   Recent Relexification Processes in Philippine Creole Spanish.

Moorghen, Pierre-Marie J.   Analyse Des Marqueurs Pre-Verbaux Des Creoles de l'ocean Indien.

Mühlhäusler, Peter.   The Functional Possibilities of Lexical Bases in New Guinea Pidgin.   [published in Papers in Pidgin and Creole Linguistics No. 1. Pacific Linguistics Series A, No. 54.   The Australian National University, Canberra, 1978, pp. 121-173]

Muysken, Pieter.   Creolized Features of the Quechua of the Lowlands of Ecuador (LEQ).

Naro, Anthony J.   The Origin of Pidgin Portuguese.   [published in Language 54(2), 1978, pp. 314-347]

Neff, Karen J.   From Lexicon to Syntax: The Case of *Go* in Hawaiian Creole.

Nhial, Abdon Agaw Jok.   Ki-nubi and Juba Arabic: The Relationship Between a Creole and a Pidgin of the Arabic Language.   [published in Sudanese Studies in Linguistics and Folklore.   University of Khartoum, 1975]

Orjala, Paul R.   Interacting Variation Systems in Haitian Creole.

Papen, Robert A.   'Nana k nana, nana k napa' (Some Have It, Some Don't) (Reunion Creole) or the Strange Case of -e Deletion Verbs in Indian Ocean Creoles.

Partmann, Gayle.   A Case of Partial Pidginization: Vehicular Dioula in Ivory Coast.

Peet, William, Jr.   The Nominative Shift in Hawaiian Creole Prominal-ization.   [published in Papers in Pidgin and Creole Linguistics No. 2.   Pacific Linguistics Series A, No. 57.   The Australian National University, Canberra, 1979, pp. 151-161]

Perlman, Alan M.   Towards a Theory of Code-Switching.

*Pfaff, Carol W.   The Process of Decreolization in Black English.

Polomé, Edgar, C.   Swahili Pidgins.

*Rickford, John.   How Does Doz Disappear?

Riego de Dios, Maria Isabelita.   The Cotabato Chabacano (CCh) Verb.   [published in Papers in Pidgin and Creole Linguistics No. 2.   Pacific Linguistics Series A, No. 57.   The Australian National University, Canbera, 1979, pp. 275-290]

*published in this volume

*Roberts, P. A.   The Adequacy of Certain Linguistic Theories for
      Showing Important Relationships in a Creole Language.

Robson, Barbara.   On the Differences Between Creoles and other Natural
      Languages.

Samarin, William J.   Historical, Ephemeral and Inevitable Verbal
      Categories.

Sankoff, Gillian.   The Origins of Syntax in Discourse: Some Evidence
      from Tok Pisin. [published as Sankoff, Gillian and Penelope
      Brown. 1976. The origins of syntax in discourse: A case study
      of Tok Pisin relatives. Language 52(3):631-666]

*Shilling, Alison.   Bahamian English: A Non-Continuum?

Sreedhar, M. V.   Standardization of Naga Pidgin.   [published in
      Journal of Creole Studies, Vol. 1, No. 1, 1977, pp. 157-170]

Stewart, William A.   On Determining the Affinities of Pidgin and
      Creole Languages.

Theban, Laurentiu.   From Creolized Syntax to Universal Semantics.
      [published in Revue Roumaine de Linguistique 20, 1975, pp. 207-224]

Thomason, Sarah G. and Terrence Kaufman.   Toward an Adequate Definition
      of Creolization.

Todd, Loreto.   Dialect or Creole: The Case for the 'Creoloid'.

T'sou, Benjamin K.   The Language of Swonal's (Speakers without a
      Native Language):   A Study on Accelerated Creolization.

Tzeutschler, Harald S.   Why Do Auxiliaries Emerge?

Valdman, Albert.   A Pidgin Origin for Creole French Dialects?:
      Evidence from Ivory Coast Vernacular French.

Vaughn-Cooke, Anna Fay and Mary Hope Lee.   On Inventories and Syllable
      Structures.

Voorhoeve, Jan.   Serial Verbs in Creole.

*Washabaugh, William.   From Preposition to Complementizer in Caribbean
      English Creole

*Winford, Donald.   The Creole Situation in the Context of Sociolinguistic
      Studies.

Woodward, James and Harry Markowicz.   Some Handy New Ideas on Pidgins
      and Creoles: Pidgin Sign Languages.

----

*published in this volume

Woolford, Ellen B. Variation and Change in the i 'Predicate Marker'
of New Guinea Tok Pisin. [published in Papers in Pidgin and
Creole Linguistics No. 2. Pacific Linguistics Series A, No. 57.
The Australian National University, Canberra, 1979, pp. 37-49]

Wurm, S. A. Descriptive and Prescriptive Grammar in New Guinea
Pidgin. [published in Papers in Pidgin and Creole Linguistics
No. 1. Pacific Linguistics Series A, No. 54. The Australian
National University, Canberra, 1978, pp. 175-184]